Programming in Lua

Programming in Lua
Second Edition

Roberto Ierusalimschy

PUC-Rio, Brazil

Lua.org

Rio de Janeiro

Programming in Lua, Second Edition
by Roberto Ierusalimschy

ISBN 85-903798-2-5

The author can be contacted at roberto@lua.org.

Book cover and illustrations by Dimaquina. Lua logo design by Alexandre Nako. Typesetting by the author using LaTeX.

CIP – Biblioteca do Departamento de Informática, PUC-Rio

	Ierusalimschy, Roberto
I22	Programming in Lua / Roberto Ierusalimschy. – 2nd ed. – Rio de Janeiro, 2006.
	xviii, 308 p. : 25 cm.
	Includes index.
	ISBN 85-903798-2-5
	1. Lua (Programming language). I. Title.
	005.133 – dc20

to Ida, Noemi, and Ana Lucia

Contents

Preface

When Waldemar, Luiz, and I started the development of Lua, back in 1993, we could hardly imagine that it would spread as it did. Started as an in-house language for two specific projects, currently Lua is widely used in all areas that can benefit from a simple, extensible, portable, and efficient scripting language, such as embedded systems, mobile devices, web servers, and, of course, games.

We designed Lua, from the beginning, to be integrated with software written in C and other conventional languages. This integration brings many benefits. Lua is a tiny and simple language, partly because it does not try to do what C is already good for, such as sheer performance, low-level operations, and interface with third-party software. Lua relies on C for these tasks. What Lua does offer is what C is not good for: a good distance from the hardware, dynamic structures, no redundancies, ease of testing and debugging. For this, Lua has a safe environment, automatic memory management, and good facilities for handling strings and other kinds of data with dynamic size.

A great part of the power of Lua comes from its libraries. This is not by chance. After all, one of the main strengths of Lua is its extensibility. Many features contribute to this strength. Dynamic typing allows a great degree of polymorphism. Automatic memory management simplifies interfaces, because there is no need to decide who is responsible for allocating and deallocating memory, or how to handle overflows. Higher-order functions and anonymous functions allow a high degree of parameterization, making functions more versatile.

More than an extensible language, Lua is also a *glue language*. Lua supports a component-based approach to software development, where we create an application by gluing together existing high-level components. These components are written in a compiled, statically typed language, such as C or C++; Lua is the glue that we use to compose and connect these components. Usually, the components (or objects) represent more concrete, low-level concepts (such as widgets and data structures) that are not subject to many changes during program development, and that take the bulk of the CPU time of the final program. Lua gives the final shape of the application, which will probably change a lot during the life cycle of the product. However, unlike other glue technologies, Lua is a full-fledged language as well. Therefore, we can use Lua not only to glue components, but also to adapt and reshape them, and to create whole new components.

Of course, Lua is not the only scripting language around. There are other languages that you can use for more or less the same purposes. But Lua offers a set of features that makes it your best choice for many tasks and gives it a unique profile:

Extensibility: Lua's extensibility is so remarkable that many people regard Lua not as a language, but as a kit for building domain-specific languages. Lua has been designed from scratch to be extended, both through Lua code and through external C code. As a proof of concept, Lua implements most of its own basic functionality through external libraries. It is really easy to interface Lua with C/C++, and Lua has been used integrated with several other languages as well, such as Fortran, Java, Smalltalk, Ada, C#, and even with other scripting languages, such as Perl and Ruby.

Simplicity: Lua is a simple and small language. It has few (but powerful) concepts. This simplicity makes Lua easy to learn and contributes to its small size. Its complete distribution (source code, manual, plus binaries for some platforms) fits comfortably in a floppy disk.

Efficiency: Lua has a quite efficient implementation. Independent benchmarks show Lua as one of the fastest languages in the realm of scripting (interpreted) languages.

Portability: When we talk about portability, we are not talking about running Lua both on Windows and on Unix platforms. We are talking about running Lua on all platforms we have ever heard about: PlayStation, XBox, Mac OS-9 and OS X, BeOS, QUALCOMM Brew, MS-DOS, IBM mainframes, RISC OS, Symbian OS, PalmOS, ARM processors, Rabbit processors, plus of course all flavors of Unix and Windows. The source code for each of these platforms is virtually the same. Lua does not use conditional compilation to adapt its code to different machines; instead, it sticks to the standard ANSI (ISO) C. This way, you do not usually need to adapt it to a new environment: if you have an ANSI C compiler, you just have to compile Lua, out of the box.

Audience

Lua users typically fall into three broad groups: those that use Lua already embedded in an application program, those that use Lua stand alone, and those that use Lua and C together.

Many people use Lua embedded in an application program, such as CGILua (for building dynamic Web pages) or a game. These applications use the Lua–C API to register new functions, to create new types, and to change the behavior of some language operations, configuring Lua for their specific domains. Frequently, the users of such applications do not even know that Lua is an independent language adapted for a particular domain; for instance, CGILua users tend to think of Lua as a language specifically designed for the Web; players of a specific game may regard Lua as a language exclusive to that game.

Lua is useful also as a stand-alone language, not only for text-processing and one-shot little programs, but increasingly for medium-to-large projects, too. For such uses, the main functionality of Lua comes from libraries. The standard libraries offer pattern matching and other functions for string handling. (We may regard the stand-alone language as the embedding of Lua into the domain of string and text-file manipulation.) As Lua improves its support for libraries, there has been a proliferation of external packages. The Kepler project (http://www.keplerproject.org), for instance, is a Web development platform for Lua that offers packages for page generation, database access, LDAP, XML, and SOAP. The *LuaForge* site (http://www.luaforge.net) offers a focal point for many Lua packages.

Finally, there are those programmers that work on the other side of the bench, writing applications that use Lua as a C library. Those people will program more in C than in Lua, although they need a good understanding of Lua to create interfaces that are simple, easy to use, and well integrated with the language.

This book has much to offer to all these people. The first part covers the language itself, showing how we can explore all its potential. We focus on different language constructs and use numerous examples to show how to use them for practical tasks. Some chapters in this part cover basic concepts, such as control structures, but there are also advanced topics, such as iterators and coroutines.

The second part is entirely devoted to tables, the sole data structure in Lua. Its chapters discuss data structures, persistence, packages, and object-oriented programming. There we will unveil the real power of the language.

The third part presents the standard libraries. This part is particularly useful for those that use Lua as a stand-alone language, although many other applications also incorporate all or part of the standard libraries. This part devotes one chapter to each standard library: the mathematical library, the table library, the string library, the I/O library, the operating system library, and the debug library.

Finally, the last part of the book covers the API between Lua and C, for those that use C to get the full power of Lua. This part necessarily has a flavor quite different from the rest of the book. There we will be programming in C, not in Lua; therefore, we will be wearing a different hat. For some readers, the discussion of the C API may be of marginal interest; for others, it may be the most relevant part of this book.

About the Second Edition

This book is an updated and expanded version of the first edition of *Programming in Lua* (also known as the *PiL book*). Although the book structure is virtually the same, this new edition has substantial new material.

First, I have updated the whole book to Lua 5.1. Of particular relevance is the chapter about modules and packages, which was mostly rewritten. I also rewrote several examples to show how to benefit from the new features offered by Lua 5.1. Nevertheless, I clearly marked features absent from Lua 5.0, so you can use the book for that version too.

Second, there are several new examples. These examples cover graph representation, tab expansion and compression, an implementation for tuples, and more.

Third, there are two complete new chapters. One is about how to use multiple states and multiple threads from C; it includes a nice example of how to implement a multi-process facility for Lua. The other is about memory management and how to interact with memory allocation and garbage collection.

After the release of the first edition of *Programming in Lua*, several publishers contacted us showing interest in a second edition. In the end, however, we decided to self publish this second edition, as we did with the first one. Despite the limited marketing, this avenue brings several benefits: we have total control over the book contents, we have freedom to choose when to release another edition, we can ensure that the book does not go out of print, and we keep the full rights to offer the book in other forms.

Other Resources

The reference manual is a must for anyone who wants to really learn a language. This book does not replace the Lua reference manual. Quite the opposite, they complement each other. The manual only describes Lua. It shows neither examples nor a rationale for the constructs of the language. On the other hand, it describes the whole language; this book skips over seldom-used dark corners of Lua. Moreover, the manual is the authoritative document about Lua. Wherever this book disagrees with the manual, trust the manual. To get the manual and more information about Lua, visit the Lua site at http://www.lua.org.

You can also find useful information at the Lua users site, kept by the community of users at http://lua-users.org. Among other resources, it offers a tutorial, a list of third-party packages and documentation, and an archive of the official Lua mailing list. You should check also the book's web page:

    http://www.inf.puc-rio.br/~roberto/pil2/

There you can find updated errata, code for some of the examples presented in the book, and some extra material.

This book describes Lua 5.1, although most of its contents also apply to Lua 5.0. The few differences between Lua 5.1 and Lua 5.0 are clearly marked in the text. If you are using a more recent version, check the corresponding manual for occasional differences between versions. If you are using a version older than 5.0, this is a good time to upgrade.

A Few Typographical Conventions

The book encloses "literal strings" between double quotes and single characters, like 'a', between single quotes. Strings that are used as patterns are also
enclosed between single quotes, like '[%w_]*'. The book uses a typewriter font
both for little chunks of code and for identifiers. Larger chunks of code are
shown in display style:

```
-- program "Hello World"
print("Hello World")          --> Hello World
```

The notation --> shows the output of a statement or, occasionally, the result of
an expression:

```
print(10)      --> 10
13 + 3         --> 16
```

Because a double hyphen (--) starts a comment in Lua, there is no problem
if you include these annotations in your programs. Finally, the book uses the
notation <--> to indicate that something is equivalent to something else:

```
this     <-->     that
```

That is, it makes no difference to Lua whether you write this or that.

Acknowledgments

This book would be impossible without the help of several friends and institu-
tions. As always, Luiz Henrique de Figueiredo and Waldemar Celes, Lua co-
developers, offered all kinds of help.

Gavin Wraith, André Carregal, Asko Kauppi, Brett Kapilik, John D. Rams-
dell, and Edwin Moragas reviewed drafts of this book and provided invaluable
suggestions.

Lightning Source, Inc. proved a reliable and efficient option for printing and
distributing the book. Without them, the option of self-publishing the book
would probably not be an option.

Antonio Pedro, from Dimaquina, patiently endured my shifting opinions and
produced the right cover design.

Norman Ramsey kindly provided useful insights about the best way to publish this book.

I also would like to thank PUC-Rio and CNPq for their continuous support
to my work.

Finally, I must express my deep gratitude to Noemi Rodriguez, for illumining
my life.

Part I
The Language

1

Getting Started

To keep with the tradition, our first program in Lua just prints "Hello World":

```
print("Hello World")
```

If you are using the stand-alone Lua interpreter, all you have to do to run your first program is to call the interpreter — usually named lua — with the name of the text file that contains your program. If you write the above program in a file hello.lua, the following command should run it:

```
% lua hello.lua
```

As a more complex example, the next program defines a function to compute the factorial of a given number, then asks the user for a number and prints its factorial:

```
-- defines a factorial function
function fact (n)
  if n == 0 then
    return 1
  else
    return n * fact(n-1)
  end
end

print("enter a number:")
a = io.read("*number")        -- read a number
print(fact(a))
```

If you are using Lua embedded in an application, such as CGILua or IUPLua, you may need to refer to the application manual (or to a "local guru") to learn how to run your programs. Nevertheless, Lua is still the same language; most things that we will see here are valid regardless of how you are using Lua. I recommend that you start your study of Lua by using the stand-alone interpreter (lua) to run your first examples and experiments.

1.1   Chunks

Each piece of code that Lua executes, such as a file or a single line in interactive mode, is called a *chunk*. A chunk is simply a sequence of commands (or statements).

Lua needs no separator between consecutive statements, but you can use a semicolon if you wish. My personal convention is to use semicolons only to separate two or more statements written in the same line. Line breaks play no role in Lua's syntax; for instance, the following four chunks are all valid and equivalent:

```
a = 1
b = a*2

a = 1;
b = a*2;

a = 1; b = a*2

a = 1  b = a*2    -- ugly, but valid
```

A chunk may be as simple as a single statement, such as in the "Hello World" example, or it may be composed of a mix of statements and function definitions (which are actually assignments, as we will see later), such as the factorial example. A chunk may be as large as you wish. Because Lua is used also as a data-description language, chunks with several megabytes are not uncommon. The Lua interpreter has no problems at all with large chunks.

Instead of writing your program to a file, you may run the stand-alone interpreter in interactive mode. If you call lua without any arguments, you will get its prompt:

```
Lua 5.1  Copyright (C) 1994-2006 Lua.org, PUC-Rio
>
```

Thereafter, each command that you type (such as print "Hello World") executes immediately after you enter it. To exit the interactive mode and the interpreter, just type the end-of-file control character (ctrl-D in Unix, ctrl-Z in DOS/Windows), or call the exit function, from the Operating System library — you have to type os.exit().

In interactive mode, Lua usually interprets each line that you type as a complete chunk. However, if it detects that the line does not form a complete chunk, it waits for more input, until it has a complete chunk. This way you can enter a multi-line definition, such as the `factorial` function, directly in interactive mode. However, it is usually more convenient to put such definitions in a file, and then call Lua to run this file.

You may use the `-i` option to instruct Lua to start an interactive session after running the given chunk. A command line like

```
% lua -i prog
```

will run the chunk in file `prog` and then prompt you for interaction. This is especially useful for debugging and manual testing. At the end of this chapter we will see other options for the stand-alone interpreter.

Another way to run chunks is with the `dofile` function, which immediately executes a file. For instance, suppose you have a file `lib1.lua` with the following code:

```
function norm (x, y)
  return (x^2 + y^2)^0.5
end

function twice (x)
  return 2*x
end
```

Then, in interactive mode, you can type

```
> dofile("lib1.lua")      -- load your library
> n = norm(3.4, 1.0)
> print(twice(n))         --> 7.0880180586677
```

The `dofile` function is useful also when you are testing a piece of code. You may work with two windows: one is a text editor with your program (in a file `prog.lua`, say) and the other is a console running Lua in interactive mode. After saving a modification in your program, you execute `dofile("prog.lua")` in the Lua console to load the new code; then you can exercise the new code, calling its functions and printing the results.

1.2 Some Lexical Conventions

Identifiers in Lua can be any string of letters, digits, and underscores, not beginning with a digit; for instance

```
i       j       i10     _ij
aSomewhatLongName    _INPUT
```

You should avoid identifiers starting with an underscore followed by one or more upper-case letters (e.g., `_VERSION`); they are reserved for special uses in Lua. Usually, I reserve the identifier `_` (a single underscore) for dummy variables.

In Lua, the concept of what a letter is dependents on the locale. With a proper locale, you can use variable names such as índice or ação. However, such names will make your program unsuitable to run in systems that do not support that locale.

The following words are reserved; we cannot use them as identifiers:

```
and        break      do         else       elseif
end        false      for        function   if
in         local      nil        not        or
repeat     return     then       true       until
while
```

Lua is case-sensitive: **and** is a reserved word, but And and AND are two other different identifiers.

A comment starts anywhere with a double hyphen (--) and runs until the end of the line. Lua also offers block comments, which start with --[[and run until the next]].[1] A common trick, when we want to comment out a piece of code, is to enclose the code between --[[and --]], like here:

```
--[[
print(10)            -- no action (comment)
--]]
```

To reactivate the code, we add a single hyphen to the first line:

```
---[[
print(10)            --> 10
--]]
```

In the first example, the -- in the last line is still inside the block comment. In the second example, the sequence ---[[starts an ordinary, single-line comment, instead of a block comment. So, the first and the last lines become independent comments. In this case, the print is outside comments.

1.3   Global Variables

Global variables do not need declarations. You simply assign a value to a global variable to create it. It is not an error to access a non-initialized variable; you just get the special value **nil** as the result:

```
print(b)   --> nil
b = 10
print(b)   --> 10
```

Usually, you do not need to delete global variables; if your variable is going to have a short life, you should use a local variable. But, if you need to delete a global variable, just assign **nil** to it:

```
b = nil
print(b)   --> nil
```

After this assignment, Lua behaves as if the variable had never been used. In other words, a global variable is *existent* if (and only if) it has a non-nil value.

---

[1]Actually, block comments can be more complex than that, as we will see in Section 2.4.

1.4   The Stand-Alone Interpreter

The stand-alone interpreter (also called `lua.c` due to its source file, or simply `lua` due to its executable) is a small program that allows the direct use of Lua. This section presents its main options.

When the interpreter loads a file, it ignores its first line if this line starts with a number sign ('#'). This feature allows the use of Lua as a script interpreter in Unix systems. If you start your script with something like

```
#!/usr/local/bin/lua
```

(assuming that the stand-alone interpreter is located at `/usr/local/bin`), or

```
#!/usr/bin/env lua
```

then you can call the script directly, without explicitly calling the Lua interpreter.

The usage of `lua` is

```
lua [options] [script [args]]
```

Everything is optional. As we have seen already, when we call `lua` without arguments the interpreter enters in interactive mode.

The `-e` option allows us to enter code directly into the command line, like here:

```
% lua -e "print(math.sin(12))"   --> -0.53657291800043
```

(Unix needs the double quotes to stop the shell from interpreting the parentheses.)

The `-l` option loads a library. As we saw previously, `-i` enters interactive mode after running the other arguments. So, for instance, the call

```
% lua -i -l a -e "x = 10"
```

will load the a library, then execute the assignment `x=10`, and finally present a prompt for interaction.

Whenever the global variable `_PROMPT` is defined, `lua` uses its value as the prompt when interacting. So, you can change the prompt with a call like this:

```
% lua -i -e "_PROMPT=' lua> '"
 lua>
```

We are assuming that "%" is the shell's prompt. In the example, the outer quotes stop the shell from interpreting the inner quotes, which are interpreted by Lua. More exactly, Lua receives the following command to run:

```
_PROMPT=' lua> '
```

This assigns the string " lua> " to the global variable `_PROMPT`.

In interactive mode, you can print the value of any expression by writing a line that starts with an equal sign followed by the expression:

```
> = math.sin(3)              --> 0.14112000805987
> a = 30
> = a                        --> 30
```

This feature helps to use Lua as a calculator.

Before running its arguments, lua looks for an environment variable named LUA_INIT. If there is such a variable and its content is @*filename*, then lua runs the given file. If LUA_INIT is defined but does not start with '@', then lua assumes that it contains Lua code and runs it. LUA_INIT gives us great power when configuring the stand-alone interpreter, because we have the full power of Lua in the configuration. We can pre-load packages, change the prompt and the path, define our own functions, rename or delete functions, and so on.

A script can retrieve its arguments in the global variable arg. In a call like

```
% lua script a b c
```

lua creates the table arg with all the command-line arguments, before running the script. The script name goes into index 0; its first argument ("a" in the example), goes to index 1, and so on. Preceding options go to negative indices, as they appear before the script. For instance, in the call

```
% lua -e "sin=math.sin" script a b
```

lua collects the arguments as follows:

```
arg[-3] = "lua"
arg[-2] = "-e"
arg[-1] = "sin=math.sin"
arg[0] = "script"
arg[1] = "a"
arg[2] = "b"
```

More often than not, the script uses only the positive indices (arg[1] and arg[2], in the example).

In Lua 5.1, a script can also retrieve its arguments through the vararg syntax. In the main body of a script, the expression ... (three dots) results in the arguments to the script. We will discuss the vararg syntax in Section 5.2.

2

Types and Values

Lua is a dynamically typed language. There are no type definitions in the language; each value carries its own type.

There are eight basic types in Lua: *nil*, *boolean*, *number*, *string*, *userdata*, *function*, *thread*, and *table*. The type function gives the type name of a given value:

```
print(type("Hello world"))   --> string
print(type(10.4*3))          --> number
print(type(print))           --> function
print(type(type))            --> function
print(type(true))            --> boolean
print(type(nil))             --> nil
print(type(type(X)))         --> string
```

The last line will result in "string" no matter the value of X, because the result of type is always a string.

Variables have no predefined types; any variable may contain values of any type:

```
print(type(a))    --> nil    ('a' is not initialized)
a = 10
print(type(a))    --> number
a = "a string!!"
print(type(a))    --> string
a = print         -- yes, this is valid!
a(type(a))        --> function
```

Notice the last two lines: functions are first-class values in Lua; so, we can manipulate them like any other value. (More about this facility in Chapter 6.)

Usually, when you use a single variable for different types, the result is messy code. However, sometimes the judicious use of this facility is helpful, for instance in the use of **nil** to differentiate a normal return value from an abnormal condition.

2.1 Nil

Nil is a type with a single value, **nil**, whose main property is to be different from any other value. As we have seen, a global variable has a **nil** value by default, before its first assignment, and you can assign **nil** to a global variable to delete it. Lua uses **nil** as a kind of non-value, to represent the absence of a useful value.

2.2 Booleans

The boolean type has two values, **false** and **true**, which represent the traditional boolean values. However, booleans do not hold a monopoly of condition values: in Lua, any value may represent a condition. Conditionals (such as the ones in control structures) consider both **false** and **nil** as false and anything else as true. Beware that, unlike some other scripting languages, Lua considers both zero and the empty string as true in conditional tests.

2.3 Numbers

The number type represents real (double-precision floating-point) numbers. Lua has no integer type, as it does not need it. There is a widespread misconception about floating-point arithmetic errors; some people fear that even a simple increment can go weird with floating-point numbers. The fact is that, when you use a double to represent an integer, there is no rounding error at all (unless the number is greater than 10^{14}). Specifically, a Lua number can represent any 32-bit integer without rounding problems. Moreover, most modern CPUs do floating-point arithmetic as fast as (or even faster than) integer arithmetic.

Nevertheless, it is easy to compile Lua so that it uses another type for numbers, such as longs or single-precision floats. This is particularly useful for platforms without hardware support for floating point. See file `luaconf.h` in the distribution for detailed instructions.

We can write numeric constants with an optional decimal part, plus an optional decimal exponent. Examples of valid numeric constants are:

```
4      0.4      4.57e-3      0.3e12      5e+20
```

2.4 Strings

Strings in Lua have the usual meaning: a sequence of characters. Lua is eight-bit clean and its strings may contain characters with any numeric code, including embedded zeros. This means that you can store any binary data into a string.

Strings in Lua are immutable values. You cannot change a character inside a string, as you may in C; instead, you create a new string with the desired modifications, as in the next example:

```
a = "one string"
b = string.gsub(a, "one", "another")   -- change string parts
print(a)        --> one string
print(b)        --> another string
```

Strings in Lua are subject to automatic memory management, like all other Lua objects (tables, functions, etc.). This means that you do not have to worry about allocation and deallocation of strings; Lua handles this for you. A string may contain a single letter or an entire book. Lua handles long strings quite efficiently. Programs that manipulate strings with 100K or 1M characters are not unusual in Lua.

We can delimit literal strings by matching single or double quotes:

```
a = "a line"
b = 'another line'
```

As a matter of style, you should use always the same kind of quotes (single or double) in a program, unless the string itself has quotes; then you use the other quote, or escape these quotes with backslashes. Strings in Lua can contain the following C-like escape sequences:

\a	bell
\b	back space
\f	form feed
\n	newline
\r	carriage return
\t	horizontal tab
\v	vertical tab
\\	backslash
\"	double quote
\'	single quote

The following examples illustrate their use:

```
> print("one line\nnext line\n\"in quotes\", 'in quotes'")
one line
next line
"in quotes", 'in quotes'

> print('a backslash inside quotes: \'\\\'')
a backslash inside quotes: '\'
```

```
> print("a simpler way: '\\'")
a simpler way: '\'
```

We can specify a character in a string also by its numeric value through the escape sequence \ddd, where *ddd* is a sequence of up to three *decimal* digits. As a somewhat complex example, the two literals "alo\n123\"" and '\97lo\10\04923"' have the same value, in a system using ASCII: 97 is the ASCII code for 'a', 10 is the code for newline, and 49 is the code for the digit '1'. (In this example we must write 49 with three digits, as \049, because it is followed by another digit; otherwise Lua would read the number as 492.)

We can delimit literal strings also by matching double square brackets, as we do with long comments. Literals in this bracketed form may run for several lines and do not interpret escape sequences. Moreover, this form ignores the first character of the string when this character is a newline. This form is especially convenient for writing strings that contain program pieces, as in the following example:

```
page = [[
<html>
<head>
<title>An HTML Page</title>
</head>
<body>
 <a href="http://www.lua.org">Lua</a>
</body>
</html>
]]

write(page)
```

Sometimes, you may want to enclose a piece of code containing something like a=b[c[i]] (notice the]] in this code). Or you may need to enclose some code that already has some code commented out. To handle such cases, you can add any number of equal signs between the two open brackets, as in [===[.[2] After this change, the literal string ends only at the next closing brackets with the same number of equal signs in between (]===], in our example). Pairs of brackets with a different number of equal signs are simply ignored. By choosing an appropriate number of signs, you can enclose any literal string without having to add escapes into it.

This same facility is valid for comments, too. For instance, if you start a long comment with --[=[, it extends until the next]=]. This facility allows you easily to comment out a piece of code that contains parts already commented out.

Lua provides automatic conversions between numbers and strings at run time. Any numeric operation applied to a string tries to convert the string to a number:

---

[2]This facility is new in Lua 5.1.

```
print("10" + 1)            --> 11
print("10 + 1")            --> 10 + 1
print("-5.3e-10"*"2")      --> -1.06e-09
print("hello" + 1)         -- ERROR (cannot convert "hello")
```

Lua applies such coercions not only in arithmetic operators, but also in other places that expect a number.

Conversely, whenever Lua finds a number where it expects a string, it converts the number to a string:

```
print(10 .. 20)            --> 1020
```

(The .. is the string concatenation operator in Lua. When you write it right after a numeral, you must separate them with a space; otherwise, Lua thinks that the first dot is a decimal point.)

Today we are not sure that these automatic coercions were a good idea in the design of Lua. As a rule, it is better not to count on them. They are handy in a few places, but add complexity to the language and sometimes to programs that use them. After all, strings and numbers are different things, despite these conversions. A comparison like 10=="10" is false, because 10 is a number and "10" is a string. If you need to convert a string to a number explicitly, you can use the function tonumber, which returns **nil** if the string does not denote a proper number:

```
line = io.read()      -- read a line
n = tonumber(line)    -- try to convert it to a number
if n == nil then
  error(line .. " is not a valid number")
else
  print(n*2)
end
```

To convert a number to a string, you can call the function tostring, or concatenate the number with the empty string:

```
print(tostring(10) == "10")    --> true
print(10 .. "" == "10")        --> true
```

Such conversions are always valid.

In Lua 5.1, you can get the length of a string using the prefix operator '#' (called the *length operator*):

```
a = "hello"
print(#a)              --> 5
print(#"good\0bye")    --> 8
```

2.5 Tables

The table type implements associative arrays. An associative array is an array that can be indexed not only with numbers, but also with strings or any other value of the language, except **nil**. Moreover, tables have no fixed size; you can add as many elements as you want to a table dynamically. Tables are the main (in fact, the only) data structuring mechanism in Lua, and a powerful one. We use tables to represent ordinary arrays, symbol tables, sets, records, queues, and other data structures, in a simple, uniform, and efficient way. Lua uses tables to represent modules, packages, and objects as well. When we write io.read, we mean "the read function from the io module". For Lua, this means "index the table io using the string "read" as the key".

Tables in Lua are neither values nor variables; they are *objects*. If you are familiar with arrays in Java or Scheme, then you have a fair idea of what I mean. You may think of a table as a dynamically allocated object; your program manipulates only references (or pointers) to them. There are no hidden copies or creation of new tables behind the scenes. Moreover, you do not have to declare a table in Lua; in fact, there is no way to declare one. You create tables by means of a *constructor expression*, which in its simplest form is written as {}:

```
a = {}              -- create a table and store its reference in 'a'
k = "x"
a[k] = 10           -- new entry, with key="x" and value=10
a[20] = "great"     -- new entry, with key=20 and value="great"
print(a["x"])       --> 10
k = 20
print(a[k])         --> "great"
a["x"] = a["x"] + 1    -- increments entry "x"
print(a["x"])       --> 11
```

A table is always anonymous. There is no fixed relationship between a variable that holds a table and the table itself:

```
a = {}
a["x"] = 10
b = a               -- 'b' refers to the same table as 'a'
print(b["x"])       --> 10
b["x"] = 20
print(a["x"])       --> 20
a = nil             -- only 'b' still refers to the table
b = nil             -- no references left to the table
```

When a program has no references to a table left, Lua's garbage collector will eventually delete the table and reuse its memory.

Each table may store values with different types of indices, and it grows as needed to accommodate new entries:

```
a = {}      -- empty table
-- create 1000 new entries
for i=1,1000 do a[i] = i*2 end
print(a[9])     --> 18
a["x"] = 10
print(a["x"])   --> 10
print(a["y"])   --> nil
```

Notice the last line: like global variables, table fields evaluate to **nil** when they are not initialized. Also like global variables, you can assign **nil** to a table field to delete it. This is not a coincidence: Lua stores global variables in ordinary tables. We will discuss this subject further in Chapter 14.

To represent records, you use the field name as an index. Lua supports this representation by providing a.name as syntactic sugar for a["name"]. So, we could write the last lines of the previous example in a cleaner manner as follows:

```
a.x = 10                    -- same as a["x"] = 10
print(a.x)                  -- same as print(a["x"])
print(a.y)                  -- same as print(a["y"])
```

For Lua, the two forms are equivalent and can be intermixed freely; for a human reader, each form may signal a different intention. The dot notation clearly shows that we are using the table as a record, where we have some set of fixed, pre-defined keys. The string notation gives the idea that the table may have any string as a key, and that for some reason we are manipulating that specific key.

A common mistake for beginners is to confuse a.x with a[x]. The first form represents a["x"], that is, a table indexed by the string "x". The second form is a table indexed by the value of the variable x. See the difference:

```
a = {}
x = "y"
a[x] = 10                   -- put 10 in field "y"
print(a[x])    --> 10       -- value of field "y"
print(a.x)     --> nil      -- value of field "x" (undefined)
print(a.y)     --> 10       -- value of field "y"
```

To represent a conventional array or a list, you simply use a table with integer keys. There is neither a way nor a need to declare a size; you just initialize the elements you need:

```
-- read 10 lines storing them in a table
a = {}
for i=1,10 do
  a[i] = io.read()
end
```

Since you can index a table with any value, you can start the indices of an array with any number that pleases you. However, it is customary in Lua to start arrays with 1 (and not with 0, as in C) and several facilities stick to this convention.

In Lua 5.1, the length operator '#' returns the last index (or the size) of an array or list.[3] For instance, you could print the lines read in the last example with the following code:

---

[3]Lua 5.0 did not support the length operator. You can get a somewhat similar result with the function table.getn.

```
-- print the lines
for i=1, #a do
  print(a[i])
end
```

The length operator provides several common Lua idioms:

```
print(a[#a])              -- prints the last value of list 'a'
a[#a] = nil               -- removes this last value
a[#a+1] = v               -- appends 'v' to the end of the list
```

As an example, the following code shows an alternative way to read the first 10 lines of a file:

```
a = {}
for i=1,10 do
  a[#a+1] = io.read()
end
```

Because an array is actually a table, the concept of its "size" can be somewhat fuzzy. For instance, what should be the size of the following array?

```
a = {}
a[10000] = 1
```

Remember that any non-initialized index results in **nil**; Lua uses this value as a sentinel to find the end of the array. When the array has *holes*—nil elements inside it—the length operator may assume any of these nil elements as the end marker. Of course, this unpredictability is hardly what you want. Therefore, you should avoid using the length operator on arrays that may contain holes. Most arrays cannot contain holes (e.g., in our previous example a file line cannot be **nil**) and, therefore, most of the time the use of the length operator is safe. If you really need to handle arrays with holes up to their last index, you can use the function table.maxn,[4] which returns the largest numerical positive index of a table:

```
a = {}
a[10000] = 1
print(table.maxn(a))           --> 10000
```

Because we can index a table with any type, when indexing a table we have the same subtleties that arise in equality. Although we can index a table both with the number 0 and with the string "0", these two values are different (according to equality) and therefore denote different entries in a table. Similarly, the strings "+1", "01", and "1" all denote different entries. When in doubt about the actual types of your indices, use an explicit conversion to be sure:

---

[4]This function is new in Lua 5.1.

```
i = 10; j = "10"; k = "+10"
a = {}
a[i] = "one value"
a[j] = "another value"
a[k] = "yet another value"
print(a[j])              --> another value
print(a[k])              --> yet another value
print(a[tonumber(j)])   --> one value
print(a[tonumber(k)])   --> one value
```

You can introduce subtle bugs in your program if you do not pay attention to this point.

2.6 Functions

Functions are first-class values in Lua. This means that functions can be stored in variables, passed as arguments to other functions, and returned as results. Such facilities give great flexibility to the language: a program may redefine a function to add new functionality, or simply erase a function to create a secure environment when running a piece of untrusted code (such as code received through a network). Moreover, Lua offers good support for functional programming, including nested functions with proper lexical scoping; just wait until Chapter 6. Finally, first-class functions play a key role in Lua's object-oriented facilities, as we will see in Chapter 16.

Lua can call functions written in Lua and functions written in C. All the standard libraries in Lua are written in C. They comprise functions for string manipulation, table manipulation, I/O, access to basic operating system facilities, mathematical functions, and debugging. Application programs may define other functions in C.

We will discuss Lua functions in Chapter 5 and C functions in Chapter 26.

2.7 Userdata and Threads

The userdata type allows arbitrary C data to be stored in Lua variables. It has no predefined operations in Lua, except assignment and equality test. Userdata are used to represent new types created by an application program or a library written in C; for instance, the standard I/O library uses them to represent files. We will discuss more about userdata later, when we get to the C API.

We will explain the thread type in Chapter 9, where we discuss coroutines.

3

Expressions

Expressions denote values. Expressions in Lua include the numeric constants and string literals, variables, unary and binary operations, and function calls. Expressions include also the unconventional function definitions and table constructors.

3.1 Arithmetic Operators

Lua supports the usual arithmetic operators: the binary '+' (addition), '-' (subtraction), '*' (multiplication), '/' (division), '^' (exponentiation), '%' (modulo),[5] and the unary '-' (negation). All of them operate on real numbers. For instance, x^0.5 computes the square root of x, while x^(-1/3) computes the inverse of its cubic root.

The modulo operator is defined by the following rule:

```
a % b == a - floor(a/b)*b
```

For integer arguments, it has the usual meaning, with the result always having the same sign as the second argument. For real arguments, it has some extra uses. For instance, x%1 is the fractional part of x, and so x-x%1 is its integer part. Similarly, x-x%0.01 is x with exactly two decimal digits:

```
x = math.pi
print(x - x%0.01)        --> 3.14
```

---

[5]The modulo operation is new in Lua 5.1.

As another example of the use of the modulo operator, suppose you want to check whether a vehicle turning a given angle will start to backtrack. If the angle is given in degrees, you can use the following formula:

```lua
local tolerance = 10
function isturnback (angle)
  angle = angle % 360
  return (math.abs(angle - 180) < tolerance)
end
```

This definition works even for negative angles:

```lua
print(isturnback(-180))        --> true
```

If we want to work with radians instead of degrees, we simply change the constants in our function:

```lua
local tolerance = 0.17
function isturnback (angle)
  angle = angle % (2*math.pi)
  return (math.abs(angle - math.pi) < tolerance)
end
```

The operation `angle % (2*math.pi)` is all we need to normalize any angle to a value in the interval $[0, 2\pi)$.

3.2 Relational Operators

Lua provides the following relational operators:

```
<   >   <=  >=  ==   ~=
```

All these operators always result in **true** or **false**.

The operator `==` tests for equality; the operator `~=` is the negation of equality. We can apply both operators to any two values. If the values have different types, Lua considers them not equal. Otherwise, Lua compares them according to their types. Specifically, **nil** is equal only to itself.

Lua compares tables, userdata, and functions by reference, that is, two such values are considered equal only if they are the very same object. For instance, after the code

```lua
a = {}; a.x = 1; a.y = 0
b = {}; b.x = 1; b.y = 0
c = a
```

you have that `a==c` but `a~=b`.

We can apply the order operators only to two numbers or to two strings. Lua compares strings in alphabetical order, which follows the locale set for Lua. For instance, with the European Latin-1 locale, we have `"acai"<"açaí"<"acorde"`. Values other than numbers and strings can be compared only for equality (and inequality).

When comparing values with different types, you must be careful: remember that "0" is different from 0. Moreover, 2<15 is obviously true, but "2"<"15" is false (alphabetical order). To avoid inconsistent results, Lua raises an error when you mix strings and numbers in an order comparison, such as 2<"15".

3.3 Logical Operators

The logical operators are **and**, **or**, and **not**. Like control structures, all logical operators consider both **false** and **nil** as false, and anything else as true. The operator **and** returns its first argument if it is false; otherwise, it returns its second argument. The operator **or** returns its first argument if it is not false; otherwise, it returns its second argument:

```
print(4 and 5)          --> 5
print(nil and 13)       --> nil
print(false and 13)     --> false
print(4 or 5)           --> 4
print(false or 5)       --> 5
```

Both **and** and **or** use short-cut evaluation, that is, they evaluate their second operand only when necessary. Short-cut evaluation ensures that expressions like (type(v)=="table" and v.tag=="h1") do not cause run-time errors. (Lua will not try to evaluate v.tag when v is not a table.)

A useful Lua idiom is x=x or v, which is equivalent to

```
if not x then x = v end
```

That is, it sets x to a default value v when x is not set (provided that x is not set to **false**).

Another useful idiom is (a and b) or c (or simply a and b or c, because **and** has a higher precedence than **or**), which is equivalent to the C expression a?b:c, provided that b is not false. For instance, we can select the maximum of two numbers x and y with a statement like

```
max = (x > y) and x or y
```

When x>y, the first expression of the **and** is true, so the **and** results in its second expression (x), which is always true (because it is a number), and then the **or** expression results in the value of its first expression, x. When x>y is false, the **and** expression is false and so the **or** results in its second expression, which is y.

The operator **not** always returns **true** or **false**:

```
print(not nil)       --> true
print(not false)     --> true
print(not 0)         --> false
print(not not nil)   --> false
```

3.4   Concatenation

Lua denotes the string concatenation operator by .. (two dots). If any of its operands is a number, Lua converts this number to a string:

```
print("Hello " .. "World")   --> Hello World
print(0 .. 1)                --> 01
```

Remember that strings in Lua are immutable values. The concatenation operator always creates a new string, without any modification to its operands:

```
a = "Hello"
print(a .. " World")   --> Hello World
print(a)               --> Hello
```

3.5   Precedence

Operator precedence in Lua follows the table below, from the higher to the lower priority:

```
          ^
not  #     - (unary)
*    /     %
+    -
..
<    >    <=   >=   ~=   ==
and
or
```

All binary operators are left associative, except for '^' (exponentiation) and '..' (concatenation), which are right associative. Therefore, the following expressions on the left are equivalent to those on the right:

```
a+i < b/2+1          <-->      (a+i) < ((b/2)+1)
5+x^2*8              <-->      5+((x^2)*8)
a < y and y <= z     <-->      (a < y) and (y <= z)
-x^2                 <-->      -(x^2)
x^y^z                <-->      x^(y^z)
```

When in doubt, always use explicit parentheses. It is easier than looking it up in the manual, and you will probably have the same doubt when you read the code again.

3.6   Table Constructors

Constructors are expressions that create and initialize tables. They are a distinctive feature of Lua and one of its most useful and versatile mechanisms.

The simplest constructor is the empty constructor, {}, which creates an empty table; we have seen it before. Constructors also initialize arrays (called also *sequences* or *lists*). For instance, the statement

```
days = {"Sunday", "Monday", "Tuesday", "Wednesday",
          "Thursday", "Friday", "Saturday"}
```

will initialize days[1] with the string "Sunday" (the first element of the constructor has index 1, not 0), days[2] with "Monday", and so on:

```
print(days[4])   --> Wednesday
```

Lua also offers a special syntax to initialize a table record-like, as in the next example:

```
a = {x=10, y=20}
```

This previous line is equivalent to these commands:

```
a = {}; a.x=10; a.y=20
```

No matter what constructor we use to create a table, we can always add fields to and remove fields from the result:

```
w = {x=0, y=0, label="console"}
x = {math.sin(0), math.sin(1), math.sin(2)}
w[1] = "another field"    -- add key 1 to table 'w'
x.f = w                   -- add key "f" to table 'x'
print(w["x"])             --> 0
print(w[1])               --> another field
print(x.f[1])             --> another field
w.x = nil                 -- remove field "x"
```

That is, *all tables are created equal*; constructors affect only their initialization.

Every time Lua evaluates a constructor, it creates and initializes a new table. So, we can use tables to implement linked lists:

```
list = nil
for line in io.lines() do
  list = {next=list, value=line}
end
```

This code reads lines from the standard input and stores them in a linked list, in reverse order. Each node in the list is a table with two fields: value, with the line contents, and next, with a reference to the next node. The following code traverses the list and prints its contents:

```
local l = list
while l do
  print(l.value)
  l = l.next
end
```

(Because we implemented our list as a stack, the lines will be printed in reverse order.) Although instructive, we seldom use the above implementation in real Lua programs; lists are better implemented as arrays, as we will see in Chapter 11.

We can mix record-style and list-style initializations in the same constructor:

```
polyline = {color="blue", thickness=2, npoints=4,
              {x=0,   y=0},
              {x=-10, y=0},
              {x=-10, y=1},
              {x=0,   y=1}
            }
```

The above example also illustrates how we can nest constructors to represent more complex data structures. Each of the elements polyline[i] is a table representing a record:

```
print(polyline[2].x)      --> -10
print(polyline[4].y)      --> 1
```

Those two constructor forms have their limitations. For instance, you cannot initialize fields with negative indices, nor with string indices that are not proper identifiers. For such needs, there is another, more general, format. In this format, we explicitly write the index to be initialized as an expression, between square brackets:

```
opnames = {["+"] = "add", ["-"] = "sub",
           ["*"] = "mul", ["/"] = "div"}

i = 20; s = "-"
a = {[i+0] = s, [i+1] = s..s, [i+2] = s..s..s}

print(opnames[s])      --> sub
print(a[22])           --> ---
```

This syntax is more cumbersome, but more flexible too: both the list-style and the record-style forms are special cases of this more general syntax. The constructor {x=0, y=0} is equivalent to {["x"]=0, ["y"]=0}, and the constructor {"r", "g", "b"} is equivalent to {[1]="r", [2]="g", [3]="b"}.

For those that really want their arrays starting at 0, it is not too difficult to write the following:

```
days = {[0]="Sunday", "Monday", "Tuesday", "Wednesday",
        "Thursday", "Friday", "Saturday"}
```

Now, the first value, "Sunday", is at index 0. This zero does not affect the other fields; "Monday" naturally goes to index 1, because it is the first list value in the constructor; the other values follow it. Despite this facility, I do not recommend the use of arrays starting at 0 in Lua. Most built-in functions assume that arrays start at index 1, and therefore they will not handle such arrays correctly.

You can always put a comma after the last entry. These trailing commas are optional, but are always valid:

```
a = {[1]="red", [2]="green", [3]="blue",}
```

With such flexibility, programs that generate Lua tables do not need to handle the last element as a special case.

Finally, you can always use a semicolon instead of a comma in a constructor. I usually reserve semicolons to delimit different sections in a constructor, for instance to separate its list part from its record part:

```
{x=10, y=45; "one", "two", "three"}
```

4

Statements

Lua supports an almost conventional set of statements, similar to those in C or Pascal. The conventional statements include assignment, control structures, and procedure calls. Lua also supports some not so conventional statements, such as multiple assignments and local variable declarations.

4.1 Assignment

Assignment is the basic means of changing the value of a variable or a table field:

```
a = "hello" .. "world"
t.n = t.n + 1
```

Lua allows *multiple assignment*, where a list of values is assigned to a list of variables in one step. Both lists have their elements separated by commas. For instance, in the assignment

```
a, b = 10, 2*x
```

the variable a gets the value 10 and b gets 2*x.

In a multiple assignment, Lua first evaluates all values and only then executes the assignments. Therefore, we can use a multiple assignment to swap two values, as in

```
x, y = y, x                 -- swap 'x' for 'y'
a[i], a[j] = a[j], a[i]     -- swap 'a[i]' for 'a[j]'
```

Lua always adjusts the number of values to the number of variables: when the list of values is shorter than the list of variables, the extra variables receive **nil** as their values; when the list of values is longer, the extra values are silently discarded:

```
a, b, c = 0, 1
print(a, b, c)          --> 0    1    nil
a, b = a+1, b+1, b+2    -- value of b+2 is ignored
print(a, b)             --> 1    2
a, b, c = 0
print(a, b, c)          --> 0    nil    nil
```

The last assignment in the above example shows a common mistake. To initialize a set of variables, you must provide a value for each one:

```
a, b, c = 0, 0, 0
print(a, b, c)          --> 0    0    0
```

Actually, most of the previous examples are somewhat artificial. I seldom use multiple assignment simply to write several unrelated assignments in one line. A multiple assignment is not faster than its equivalent single assignments. But often we really need multiple assignment. We already saw an example, to swap two values. A more frequent use is to collect multiple returns from function calls. As we will discuss in detail in Section 5.1, a function call can return multiple values. In such cases, a single expression can supply the values for several variables. For instance, in the assignment a, b=f() the call to f returns two results: a gets the first and b gets the second.

4.2   Local Variables and Blocks

Besides global variables, Lua supports local variables. We create local variables with the **local** statement:

```
j = 10          -- global variable
local i = 1     -- local variable
```

Unlike global variables, local variables have their scope limited to the block where they are declared. A *block* is the body of a control structure, the body of a function, or a chunk (the file or string where the variable is declared):

```
x = 10
local i = 1          -- local to the chunk

while i <= x do
  local x = i*2      -- local to the while body
  print(x)           --> 2, 4, 6, 8, ...
  i = i + 1
end
```

```
if i > 20 then
  local x           -- local to the "then" body
  x = 20
  print(x + 2)      -- (would print 22 if test succeeded)
else
  print(x)          --> 10  (the global one)
end

print(x)            --> 10  (the global one)
```

Beware that this example will not work as expected if you enter it in interactive mode. In interactive mode, each line is a chunk by itself (unless it is not a complete command). As soon as you enter the second line of the example (local i=1), Lua runs it and starts a new chunk in the next line. By then, the **local** declaration is already out of scope. To solve this problem, we can delimit the whole block explicitly, bracketing it with the keywords **do–end**. Once you enter the **do**, the command completes only at the corresponding **end**, so Lua does not execute each line by itself.

These **do** blocks are useful also when you need finer control over the scope of some local variables:

```
do
  local a2 = 2*a
  local d = (b^2 - 4*a*c)^(1/2)
  x1 = (-b + d)/a2
  x2 = (-b - d)/a2
end             -- scope of 'a2' and 'd' ends here
print(x1, x2)
```

It is good programming style to use local variables whenever possible. Local variables help you avoid cluttering the global environment with unnecessary names. Moreover, the access to local variables is faster than to global ones. Finally, a local variable usually vanishes as soon as its scope ends, allowing its value to be freed by the garbage collector.

Lua handles local-variable declarations as statements. As such, you can write local declarations anywhere you can write a statement. The scope of the declared variables begins after the declaration and goes until the end of the block. Each declaration may include an initial assignment, which works the same way as a conventional assignment: extra values are thrown away; extra variables get **nil**. If a declaration has no initial assignment, it initializes all its variables with **nil**:

```
local a, b = 1, 10
if a < b then
  print(a)    --> 1
  local a     -- '= nil' is implicit
  print(a)    --> nil
end           -- ends the block started at 'then'
print(a, b)   --> 1    10
```

A common idiom in Lua is

```
local foo = foo
```

This code creates a local variable, foo, and initializes it with the value of the global variable foo. (The local foo becomes visible only *after* its declaration.) This idiom is useful when the chunk needs to preserve the original value of foo even if later some other function changes the value of the global foo; it also speeds up the access to foo.

Because many languages force you to declare all local variables at the beginning of a block (or a procedure), some people think it is a bad practice to use declarations in the middle of a block. Quite the opposite: by declaring a variable only when you need it, you seldom need to declare it without an initial value (and therefore you seldom forget to initialize it). Moreover, you shorten the scope of the variable, which increases readability.

4.3   Control Structures

Lua provides a small and conventional set of control structures, with **if** for conditional execution and **while**, **repeat**, and **for** for iteration. All control structures have an explicit terminator: **end** terminates **if**, **for** and **while** structures; and **until** terminates **repeat** structures.

The condition expression of a control structure may result in any value. Lua treats as true all values different from **false** and **nil**. (In particular, Lua treats both that 0 and the empty string as true.)

if then else

An **if** statement tests its condition and executes its *then-part* or its *else-part* accordingly. The else-part is optional.

```
if a < 0 then a = 0 end

if a < b then return a else return b end

if line > MAXLINES then
  showpage()
  line = 0
end
```

To write nested **if**s you can use **elseif**. It is similar to an **else** followed by an **if**, but it avoids the need for multiple **end**s:

```
if op == "+" then
  r = a + b
elseif op == "-" then
  r = a - b
elseif op == "*" then
  r = a*b
elseif op == "/" then
  r = a/b
else
  error("invalid operation")
end
```

Because Lua has no switch statement, such chains are common.

while

As usual, Lua first tests the **while** condition; if the condition is false, then the loop ends; otherwise, Lua executes the body of the loop and repeats the process.

```
local i = 1
while a[i] do
  print(a[i])
  i = i + 1
end
```

repeat

As the name implies, a **repeat–until** statement repeats its body until its condition is true. The test is done after the body, so the body is always executed at least once.

```
-- print the first non-empty input line
repeat
  line = os.read()
until line ~= ""
print(line)
```

Unlike in most other languages, in Lua the scope of a local variable declared inside the loop includes the condition:[6]

```
local sqr = x/2
repeat
  sqr = (sqr + x/sqr)/2
  local error = math.abs(sqr^2 - x)
until error < x/10000        -- 'error' still visible here
```

---

[6]This facility is new in Lua 5.1.

Numeric for

The **for** statement has two variants: the *numeric* **for** and the *generic* **for**.

A numeric **for** has the following syntax:

```
for var=exp1,exp2,exp3 do
  <something>
end
```

This loop will execute *something* for each value of var from exp1 to exp2, using exp3 as the *step* to increment var. This third expression is optional; when absent, Lua assumes 1 as the step value. As typical examples of such loops, we have

```
for i=1,f(x) do print(i) end

for i=10,1,-1 do print(i) end
```

If you want a loop without an upper limit, you can use the constant math.huge:

```
for i=1,math.huge do
  if (0.3*i^3 - 20*i^2 - 500 >= 0) then
    print(i)
    break
  end
end
```

The **for** loop has some subtleties that you should learn in order to make good use of it. First, all three expressions are evaluated once, before the loop starts. For instance, in our previous example, f(x) is called only once. Second, the control variable is a local variable automatically declared by the **for** statement and is visible only inside the loop. A typical mistake is to assume that the variable still exists after the loop ends:

```
for i=1,10 do print(i) end
max = i        -- probably wrong! 'i' here is global
```

If you need the value of the control variable after the loop (usually when you break the loop), you must save its value into another variable:

```
-- find a value in a list
local found = nil
for i=1,#a do
  if a[i] < 0 then
    found = i        -- save value of 'i'
    break
  end
end
print(found)
```

Third, you should never change the value of the control variable: the effect of such changes is unpredictable. If you want to end a **for** loop before its normal termination, use **break** (as we did in the previous example).

Generic for

The generic **for** loop traverses all values returned by an iterator function:

```
-- print all values of array 'a'
for i,v in ipairs(a) do print(v) end
```

The basic Lua library provides ipairs, a handy iterator function to traverse an array. For each step in that loop, i gets an index, while v gets the value associated with this index. A similar example shows how we traverse all keys of a table:

```
-- print all keys of table 't'
for k in pairs(t) do print(k) end
```

Despite its apparent simplicity, the generic **for** is powerful. With proper iterators, we can traverse almost anything in a readable fashion. The standard libraries provide several iterators, which allow us to iterate over the lines of a file (io.lines), the pairs of a table (pairs), the entries of an array (ipairs), the words of a string (string.gmatch), and so on. Of course, we can write our own iterators. Although the use of the generic **for** is easy, the task of writing iterator functions has its subtleties. We will cover this topic later, in Chapter 7.

The generic loop shares two properties with the numeric loop: the loop variables are local to the loop body and you should never assign any value to them.

Let us see a more concrete example of the use of a generic **for**. Suppose you have a table with the names of the days of the week:

```
days = {"Sunday", "Monday", "Tuesday", "Wednesday",
        "Thursday", "Friday", "Saturday"}
```

Now you want to translate a name into its position in the week. You can search the table, looking for the given name. Frequently, however, a more efficient approach in Lua is to build a *reverse table*, say revDays, that has the names as indices and the numbers as values. This table would look like this:

```
revDays = {["Sunday"] = 1,   ["Monday"] = 2,
           ["Tuesday"] = 3,   ["Wednesday"] = 4,
           ["Thursday"] = 5, ["Friday"] = 6,
           ["Saturday"] = 7}
```

Then, all you have to do to find the order of a name is to index this reverse table:

```
x = "Tuesday"
print(revDays[x])     --> 3
```

Of course, we do not need to declare the reverse table manually. We can build it automatically from the original one:

```
revDays = {}
for k,v in pairs(days) do
  revDays[v] = k
end
```

The loop will do the assignment for each element of days, with the variable k getting the key (1, 2, ...) and v the value ("Sunday", "Monday", ...).

4.4   break and return

The **break** and **return** statements allow us to jump out of a block.

We use the **break** statement to finish a loop. This statement breaks the inner loop (**for**, **repeat**, or **while**) that contains it; it cannot be used outside a loop. After the break, the program continues running from the point immediately after the broken loop.

A **return** statement returns occasional results from a function or simply finishes a function. There is an implicit return at the end of any function, so you do not need to use one if your function ends naturally, without returning any value.

For syntactic reasons, a **break** or **return** can appear only as the last statement of a block; in other words, as the last statement in your chunk or just before an **end**, an **else**, or an **until**. For instance, in the next example, **break** is the last statement of the **then** block.

```
local i = 1
while a[i] do
  if a[i] == v then break end
  i = i + 1
end
```

Usually, these are the places where we use these statements, because any other statement following them would be unreachable. Sometimes, however, it may be useful to write a **return** or a **break** in the middle of a block; for instance, you may be debugging a function and want to avoid its execution. In such cases, you can use an explicit **do** block around the statement:

```
function foo ()
  return                  --<< SYNTAX ERROR
  -- 'return' is the last statement in the next block
  do return end        -- OK
  <other statements>
end
```

5

Functions

Functions are the main mechanism for abstraction of statements and expressions in Lua. Functions can both carry out a specific task (what is sometimes called *procedure* or *subroutine* in other languages) or compute and return values. In the first case, we use a function call as a statement; in the second case, we use it as an expression:

```
print(8*9, 9/8)
a = math.sin(3) + math.cos(10)
print(os.date())
```

In both cases, we write a list of arguments enclosed in parentheses. If the function call has no arguments, we still must write an empty list () to indicate the call. There is a special case to this rule: if the function has one single argument and that argument is either a literal string or a table constructor, then the parentheses are optional:

```
print "Hello World"      <-->      print("Hello World")
dofile 'a.lua'           <-->      dofile ('a.lua')
print [[a multi-line     <-->      print([[a multi-line
 message]]                          message]])
f{x=10, y=20}            <-->      f({x=10, y=20})
type{}                   <-->      type({})
```

Lua also offers a special syntax for object-oriented calls, the colon operator. An expression like o:foo(x) is just another way to write o.foo(o, x), that is, to call o.foo adding o as a first extra argument. In Chapter 16, we will discuss such calls (and object-oriented programming) in more detail.

A Lua program can use functions defined both in Lua and in C (or in any other language used by the host application). For instance, all functions from the standard Lua library are written in C. But this fact has no relevance to Lua programmers: when calling a function, there is no difference between functions defined in Lua and functions defined in C.

As we have seen in other examples, a function definition has a conventional syntax, like here:

```
function add (a)
  local sum = 0
  for i,v in ipairs(a) do
    sum = sum + v
  end
  return sum
end
```

In this syntax, a function definition has a *name* (add, in the previous example), a list of *parameters*, and a *body*, which is a list of statements.

Parameters work exactly as local variables, initialized with the values of the arguments passed in the function call. You can call a function with a number of arguments different from its number of parameters. Lua adjusts the number of arguments to the number of parameters, as it does in a multiple assignment: extra arguments are thrown away; extra parameters get **nil**. For instance, if we have a function like

```
function f(a, b) return a or b end
```

we will have the following mapping from arguments to parameters:

```
CALL                PARAMETERS

f(3)                a=3, b=nil
f(3, 4)             a=3, b=4
f(3, 4, 5)          a=3, b=4    (5 is discarded)
```

Although this behavior can lead to programming errors (easily spotted at run time), it is also useful, especially for default arguments. For instance, consider the following function, to increment a global counter:

```
function incCount (n)
  n = n or 1
  count = count + n
end
```

This function has 1 as its default argument; that is, the call incCount(), without arguments, increments count by one. When you call incCount(), Lua first initializes n with **nil**; the or results in its second operand and, as a result, Lua assigns a default 1 to n.

5.1 Multiple Results

An unconventional, but quite convenient feature of Lua is that functions may return multiple results. Several predefined functions in Lua return multiple values. An example is the `string.find` function, which locates a pattern in a string. This function returns two indices when it finds the pattern: the index of the character where the pattern match starts and the one where it ends. A multiple assignment allows the program to get both results:

```
s, e = string.find("hello Lua users", "Lua")
print(s, e)    --> 7      9
```

Functions written in Lua also can return multiple results, by listing them all after the **return** keyword. For instance, a function to find the maximum element in an array can return both the maximum value and its location:

```
function maximum (a)
  local mi = 1              -- index of the maximum value
  local m = a[mi]           -- maximum value
  for i,val in ipairs(a) do
    if val > m then
      mi = i; m = val
    end
  end
  return m, mi
end

print(maximum({8,10,23,12,5}))      --> 23    3
```

Lua always adjusts the number of results from a function to the circumstances of the call. When we call a function as a statement, Lua discards all results from the function. When we use a call as an expression, Lua keeps only the first result. We get all results only when the call is the last (or the only) expression in a list of expressions. These lists appear in four constructions in Lua: multiple assignments, arguments to function calls, table constructors, and **return** statements. To illustrate all these cases, we will assume the following definitions for the next examples:

```
function foo0 () end                -- returns no results
function foo1 () return "a" end     -- returns 1 result
function foo2 () return "a","b" end -- returns 2 results
```

In a multiple assignment, a function call as the last (or only) expression produces as many results as needed to match the variables:

```
x,y = foo2()        -- x="a", y="b"
x = foo2()          -- x="a", "b" is discarded
x,y,z = 10,foo2()   -- x=10, y="a", z="b"
```

If a function has no results, or not as many results as we need, Lua produces **nil**s for the missing values:

```
x,y = foo0()        -- x=nil, y=nil
x,y = foo1()        -- x="a", y=nil
x,y,z = foo2()      -- x="a", y="b", z=nil
```

A function call that is not the last element in the list always produces exactly one result:

```
x,y = foo2(), 20        -- x="a", y=20
x,y = foo0(), 20, 30  -- x=nil, y=20, 30 is discarded
```

When a function call is the last (or the only) argument to another call, all results from the first call go as arguments. We have seen examples of this construction already, with `print`:

```
print(foo0())           -->
print(foo1())           --> a
print(foo2())           --> a    b
print(foo2(), 1)        --> a    1
print(foo2() .. "x")    --> ax              (see next)
```

When the call to `foo2` appears inside an expression, Lua adjusts the number of results to one; so, in the last line, only the "a" is used in the concatenation.

The `print` function may receive a variable number of arguments. If we write `f(g())` and `f` has a fixed number of arguments, Lua adjusts the number of results of `g` to the number of parameters of `f`, as we saw previously.

A constructor collects all results from a call, without any adjustments:

```
t = {foo0()}            -- t = {}  (an empty table)
t = {foo1()}            -- t = {"a"}
t = {foo2()}            -- t = {"a", "b"}
```

As always, this behavior happens only when the call is the last in the list; calls in any other position produce exactly one result:

```
t = {foo0(), foo2(), 4}    -- t[1] = nil, t[2] = "a", t[3] = 4
```

Finally, a statement like `return f()` returns all values returned by `f`:

```
function foo (i)
  if i == 0 then return foo0()
  elseif i == 1 then return foo1()
  elseif i == 2 then return foo2()
  end
end

print(foo(1))      --> a
print(foo(2))      --> a  b
print(foo(0))      -- (no results)
print(foo(3))      -- (no results)
```

You can force a call to return exactly one result by enclosing it in an extra pair of parentheses:

```
print((foo0()))         --> nil
print((foo1()))         --> a
print((foo2()))         --> a
```

Beware that a **return** statement does not need parentheses around the returned value; any pair of parentheses placed there counts as an extra pair. So, a statement like return(f(x)) always returns one single value, no matter how many values f returns. Maybe this is what you want, maybe not.

A special function with multiple returns is unpack. It receives an array and returns as results all elements from the array, starting from index 1:

```
print(unpack{10,20,30})    --> 10    20    30
a,b = unpack{10,20,30}     -- a=10, b=20, 30 is discarded
```

An important use for unpack is in a *generic call* mechanism. A generic call mechanism allows you to call any function, with any arguments, dynamically. In ANSI C, for instance, there is no way to code a generic call. You can declare a function that receives a variable number of arguments (with stdarg.h) and you can call a variable function, using pointers to functions. However, you cannot call a function with a variable number of arguments: each call you write in C has a fixed number of arguments, and each argument has a fixed type. In Lua, if you want to call a variable function f with variable arguments in an array a, you simply write this:

```
f(unpack(a))
```

The call to unpack returns all values in a, which become the arguments to f. For instance, if we execute

```
f = string.find
a = {"hello", "ll"}
```

then the call f(unpack(a)) returns 3 and 4, the same results as returned by the static call string.find("hello", "ll").

Although the predefined unpack function is written in C, we could write it also in Lua, using recursion:

```
function unpack (t, i)
  i = i or 1
  if t[i] then
    return t[i], unpack(t, i + 1)
  end
end
```

The first time we call it, with a single argument, i gets 1. Then the function returns t[1] followed by all results from unpack(t,2), which in turn returns t[2] followed by all results from unpack(t,3), and so on, until the last non-nil element.

5.2 Variable Number of Arguments

Some functions in Lua receive a variable number of arguments. For instance, we have already called print with one, two, and more arguments. Although

print is defined in C, we can define functions that accept a variable number of
arguments in Lua, too.

As a simple example, the following function returns the summation of all its
arguments:

```
function add (...)
  local s = 0
  for i, v in ipairs{...} do
    s = s + v
  end
  return s
end

print(add(3, 4, 10, 25, 12))    --> 54
```

The three dots (...) in the parameter list indicate that the function accepts a
variable number of arguments. When this function is called, all its arguments
are collected internally; we call these collected arguments the *varargs* (*variable
arguments*) of the function. A function can access its varargs using again the
three dots, now as an expression. In our example, the expression {...} results
in an array with all collected arguments. The function then traverses the array
to add its elements.

The expression ... behaves like a multiple return function returning all
varargs of the current function. For instance, the command

```
local a, b = ...
```

creates two local variables with the values of the first two optional arguments
(or **nil** if there are no such arguments). Actually, we can emulate the usual
parameter-passing mechanism of Lua translating

```
function foo (a, b, c)
```

to

```
function foo (...)
  local a, b, c = ...
```

Those who like Perl's parameter-passing mechanism may enjoy this second form.

A function like the following one

```
function id (...) return ... end
```

simply returns all arguments in its call: it is a multi-value identity function.
The next function behaves exactly like another function foo, except that before
the call it prints a message with its arguments:

```
function foo1 (...)
  print("calling foo:", ...)
  return foo(...)
end
```

This is a useful trick for tracing calls to a specific function.

Let us see another useful example. Lua provides separate functions for formatting text (`string.format`) and for writing text (`io.write`). It is straightforward to combine both functions into a single one:

```
function fwrite (fmt, ...)
  return io.write(string.format(fmt, ...))
end
```

Notice the presence of a fixed parameter `fmt` before the dots. Vararg functions may have any number of fixed parameters before the vararg part. Lua assigns the first arguments to these parameters and only the extra arguments (if any) go to the varargs. Below we show some examples of calls and the corresponding parameter values:

```
CALL                        PARAMETERS

fwrite()                    fmt = nil, no varargs
fwrite("a")                 fmt = "a", no varargs
fwrite("%d%d", 4, 5)        fmt = "%d%d", varargs = 4 and 5
```

To iterate over its variable arguments, a function may use the expression `{...}` to collect them all in a table, as we did in our definition of add. In the rare occasions when the vararg list may contain valid **nil**s, we can use the select function. A call to `select` has always one fixed argument, the *selector*, plus a variable number of extra arguments. If the selector is a number n, select returns its n-th extra argument; otherwise, the selector should be the string `"#"`, so that `select` returns the total number of extra arguments. The following loop shows how we can use `select` to iterate over all vararg parameters of a function:

```
for i=1, select('#', ...) do
  local arg = select(i, ...)      -- get i-th parameter
  <loop body>
end
```

Specifically, the call `select("#", ...)` returns the exact number of extra parameters, including **nil**s.

Lua 5.0 had a different mechanism for variable number of arguments. The syntax for declaring a vararg function was the same, with three dots as the last parameter. However, Lua 5.0 did not have the ... expression. Instead, a vararg function had a hidden local variable, called `arg`, that received a table with the varargs. This table also got an n field with the total number of extra arguments. We can simulate this old behavior as follows:

```
function foo (a, b, ...)
  local arg = {...};  arg.n = select("#", ...)
  <function body>
end
```

The drawback of the old mechanism is that it creates a new table each time the program calls a vararg function. With the new mechanism, we can create a table to collect varargs only when needed.

5.3 Named Arguments

The parameter passing mechanism in Lua is *positional*: when we call a function, arguments match parameters by their positions. The first argument gives the value to the first parameter, and so on. Sometimes, however, it is useful to specify the arguments by name. To illustrate this point, let us consider the function os.rename (from the os library), which renames a file. Quite often, we forget which name comes first, the new or the old; therefore, we may want to redefine this function to receive two named arguments:

```
-- invalid code
rename(old="temp.lua", new="temp1.lua")
```

Lua has no direct support for this syntax, but we can have the same final effect, with a small syntax change. The idea here is to pack all arguments into a table and use this table as the only argument to the function. The special syntax that Lua provides for function calls, with just one table constructor as argument, helps the trick:

```
rename{old="temp.lua", new="temp1.lua"}
```

Accordingly, we define rename with only one parameter and get the actual arguments from this parameter:

```
function rename (arg)
   return os.rename(arg.old, arg.new)
end
```

This style of parameter passing is especially helpful when the function has many parameters, and most of them are optional. For instance, a function that creates a new window in a GUI library may have dozens of arguments, most of them optional, which are best specified by names:

```
w = Window{ x=0, y=0, width=300, height=200,
            title = "Lua", background="blue",
            border = true
          }
```

The Window function then has the freedom to check for mandatory arguments, add default values, and the like. Assuming a primitive _Window function that actually creates the new window (and that needs all arguments in a proper order), we could define Window as in Listing 5.1.

Listing 5.1. A function with named optional parameters:

```
function Window (options)
  -- check mandatory options
  if type(options.title) ~= "string" then
    error("no title")
  elseif type(options.width) ~= "number" then
    error("no width")
  elseif type(options.height) ~= "number" then
    error("no height")
  end

  -- everything else is optional
  _Window(options.title,
          options.x or 0,      -- default value
          options.y or 0,      -- default value
          options.width, options.height,
          options.background or "white",   -- default
          options.border       -- default is false (nil)
          )
end
```

6

More About Functions

Functions in Lua are first-class values with proper lexical scoping.

What does it mean for functions to be "first-class values"? It means that, in Lua, a function is a value with the same rights as conventional values like numbers and strings. Functions can be stored in variables (both global and local) and in tables, can be passed as arguments, and can be returned by other functions.

What does it mean for functions to have "lexical scoping"? It means that functions can access variables of their enclosing functions. (It also means that Lua properly contains the lambda calculus.) As we will see in this chapter, this apparently innocuous property brings great power to the language, because it allows us to apply in Lua many powerful programming techniques from the functional-language world. Even if you have no interest at all in functional programming, it is worth learning a little about how to explore these techniques, because they can make your programs smaller and simpler.

A somewhat confusing notion in Lua is that functions, like all other values, are anonymous; they do not have names. When we talk about a function name, such as print, we are actually talking about a variable that holds that function. Like any other variable holding any other value, we can manipulate such variables in many ways. The following example, although a little silly, shows the point:

```
a = {p = print}
a.p("Hello World")      --> Hello World
print = math.sin        -- 'print' now refers to the sine function
a.p(print(1))           --> 0.841470
sin = a.p               -- 'sin' now refers to the print function
sin(10, 20)             --> 10      20
```

(Later we will see more useful applications for this facility.)

If functions are values, are there expressions that create functions? Yes. In fact, the usual way to write a function in Lua, such as

```
function foo (x)  return 2*x  end
```

is just an instance of what we call *syntactic sugar*; in other words, it is simply a pretty way to write the following code:

```
foo = function (x)  return 2*x  end
```

So, a function definition is in fact a statement (an assignment, more specifically) that creates a value of type "function" and assigns it to a variable. We can see the expression function (x) *body* end as a function constructor, just as {} is a table constructor. We call the result of such function constructors an *anonymous function*. Although we often assign functions to global variables, giving them something like a name, there are several occasions when functions remain anonymous. Let us see some examples.

The table library provides a function table.sort, which receives a table and sorts its elements. Such a function must allow unlimited variations in the sort order: ascending or descending, numeric or alphabetical, tables sorted by a key, and so on. Instead of trying to provide all kinds of options, sort provides a single optional parameter, which is the *order function*: a function that receives two elements and returns whether the first must come before the second in the sorted list. For instance, suppose we have a table of records like this:

```
network = {
  {name = "grauna",  IP = "210.26.30.34"},
  {name = "arraial", IP = "210.26.30.23"},
  {name = "lua",     IP = "210.26.23.12"},
  {name = "derain",  IP = "210.26.23.20"},
}
```

If we want to sort the table by the field name, in reverse alphabetical order, we just write this:

```
table.sort(network, function (a,b) return (a.name > b.name) end)
```

See how handy the anonymous function is in this statement.

A function that gets another function as an argument, such as sort, is what we call a *higher-order function*. Higher-order functions are a powerful programming mechanism, and the use of anonymous functions to create their function arguments is a great source of flexibility. But remember that higher-order functions have no special rights; they are a direct consequence of the ability of Lua to handle functions as first-class values.

To further illustrate the use of higher-order functions, we will write a naive implementation of a common higher-order function, the derivative. In an informal definition, the derivative of a function f in a point x is the value of $(f(x + d) - f(x))/d$ when d becomes infinitesimally small. We can compute an approximation of the derivative as follows:

```
function derivative (f, delta)
  delta = delta or 1e-4
  return function (x)
           return (f(x + delta) - f(x))/delta
         end
end
```

Given a function f, the call derivative(f) returns (an approximation of) its derivative, which is another function:

```
c = derivative(math.sin)
print(math.cos(10), c(10))
  -->   -0.83907152907645   -0.83904432662041
```

Because functions are first-class values in Lua, we can store them not only in global variables, but also in local variables and in table fields. As we will see later, the use of functions in table fields is a key ingredient for some advanced uses of Lua, such as modules and object-oriented programming.

6.1 Closures

When a function is written enclosed in another function, it has full access to local variables from the enclosing function; this feature is called *lexical scoping*. Although this visibility rule may sound obvious, it is not. Lexical scoping, plus first-class functions, is a powerful concept in a programming language, but few languages support it.

Let us start with a simple example. Suppose you have a list of student names and a table that associates names to grades; you want to sort the list of names according to their grades (higher grades first). You can do this task as follows:

```
names = {"Peter", "Paul", "Mary"}
grades = {Mary = 10, Paul = 7, Peter = 8}
table.sort(names, function (n1, n2)
  return grades[n1] > grades[n2]      -- compare the grades
end)
```

Now, suppose you want to create a function to do this task:

```
function sortbygrade (names, grades)
  table.sort(names, function (n1, n2)
    return grades[n1] > grades[n2]      -- compare the grades
  end)
end
```

The interesting point in the example is that the anonymous function given to sort accesses the parameter grades, which is local to the enclosing function sortbygrade. Inside this anonymous function, grades is neither a global variable nor a local variable, but what we call a *non-local variable*. (For historical reasons, non-local variables are also called *upvalues* in Lua.)

Why is this point so interesting? Because functions are first-class values. Consider the following code:

```
function newCounter ()
  local i = 0
  return function ()          -- anonymous function
           i = i + 1
           return i
         end
end

c1 = newCounter()
print(c1())  --> 1
print(c1())  --> 2
```

In this code, the anonymous function refers to a non-local variable, i, to keep its counter. However, by the time we call the anonymous function, i is already out of scope, because the function that created this variable (newCounter) has returned. Nevertheless, Lua handles this situation correctly, using the concept of *closure*. Simply put, a closure is a function plus all it needs to access non-local variables correctly. If we call newCounter again, it will create a new local variable i, so we will get a new closure, acting over this new variable:

```
c2 = newCounter()
print(c2())  --> 1
print(c1())  --> 3
print(c2())  --> 2
```

So, c1 and c2 are different closures over the same function, and each acts upon an independent instantiation of the local variable i.

Technically speaking, what is a value in Lua is the closure, not the function. The function itself is just a prototype for closures. Nevertheless, we will continue to use the term "function" to refer to a closure whenever there is no possibility of confusion.

Closures provide a valuable tool in many contexts. As we have seen, they are useful as arguments to higher-order functions such as sort. Closures are valuable for functions that build other functions too, like our newCounter example; this mechanism allows Lua programs to incorporate sophisticated programming techniques from the functional world. Closures are useful for *callback* functions, too. A typical example here occurs when you create buttons in a conventional GUI toolkit. Each button has a callback function to be called when the user presses the button; you want different buttons to do slightly different things when pressed. For instance, a digital calculator needs ten similar buttons, one for each digit. You can create each of them with a function like this:

```
function digitButton (digit)
  return Button{ label = tostring(digit),
                 action = function ()
                            add_to_display(digit)
                          end
               }
end
```

In this example, we assume that Button is a toolkit function that creates new buttons; label is the button label; and action is the callback closure to be called when the button is pressed. The callback can be called a long time after digitButton did its task and after the local variable digit went out of scope, but it can still access this variable.

Closures are valuable also in a quite different context. Because functions are stored in regular variables, we can easily redefine functions in Lua, even predefined functions. This facility is one of the reasons why Lua is so flexible. Frequently, when you redefine a function you need the original function in the new implementation. For instance, suppose you want to redefine the function sin to operate in degrees instead of radians. This new function must convert its argument and then call the original sin function to do the real work. Your code could look like this:

```
oldSin = math.sin
math.sin = function (x)
  return oldSin(x*math.pi/180)
end
```

A cleaner way to do this redefinition is as follows:

```
do
  local oldSin = math.sin
  local k = math.pi/180
  math.sin = function (x)
    return oldSin(x*k)
  end
end
```

Now, we keep the old version in a private variable; the only way to access it is through the new version.

You can use this same technique to create secure environments, also called *sandboxes*. Secure environments are essential when running untrusted code, such as code received through the Internet by a server. For instance, to restrict the files a program can access, we can redefine the io.open function using closures:

```
do
  local oldOpen = io.open
  local access_OK = function (filename, mode)
    <check access>
  end
  io.open = function (filename, mode)
    if access_OK(filename, mode) then
      return oldOpen(filename, mode)
    else
      return nil, "access denied"
    end
  end
end
```

What makes this example nice is that, after this redefinition, there is no way for the program to call the unrestricted `open` function except through the new, restricted version. It keeps the insecure version as a private variable in a closure, inaccessible from the outside. With this technique, you can build Lua sandboxes in Lua itself, with the usual benefits: simplicity and flexibility. Instead of a one-size-fits-all solution, Lua offers you a meta-mechanism, so that you can tailor your environment for your specific security needs.

6.2   Non-Global Functions

An obvious consequence of first-class functions is that we can store functions not only in global variables, but also in table fields and in local variables.

We have already seen several examples of functions in table fields: most Lua libraries use this mechanism (e.g., `io.read`, `math.sin`). To create such functions in Lua, we only have to put together the regular syntax for functions and for tables:

```
Lib = {}
Lib.foo = function (x,y) return x + y end
Lib.goo = function (x,y) return x - y end
```

Of course, we can also use constructors:

```
Lib = {
  foo = function (x,y) return x + y end,
  goo = function (x,y) return x - y end
}
```

Moreover, Lua offers yet another syntax to define such functions:

```
Lib = {}
function Lib.foo (x,y) return x + y end
function Lib.goo (x,y) return x - y end
```

When we store a function into a local variable, we get a *local function*, that is, a function that is restricted to a given scope. Such definitions are particularly useful for packages: because Lua handles each chunk as a function, a chunk may declare local functions, which are visible only inside the chunk. Lexical scoping ensures that other functions in the package can use these local functions:

```
local f = function (<params>)
  <body>
end

local g = function (<params>)
  <some code>
  f()                -- 'f' is visible here
  <some code>
end
```

Lua supports such uses of local functions with a syntactic sugar for them:

```
local function f (<params>)
  <body>
end
```

A subtle point arises in the definition of recursive local functions. The naive approach does not work here:

```
local fact = function (n)
  if n == 0 then return 1
  else return n*fact(n-1)    -- buggy
  end
end
```

When Lua compiles the call `fact(n-1)` in the function body, the local `fact` is not yet defined. Therefore, this expression calls a global `fact`, not the local one. To solve this problem, we must first define the local variable and then define the function:

```
local fact
fact = function (n)
  if n == 0 then return 1
  else return n*fact(n-1)
  end
end
```

Now the `fact` inside the function refers to the local variable. Its value when the function is defined does not matter; by the time the function executes, `fact` already has the right value.

When Lua expands its syntactic sugar for local functions, it does not use the naive definition. Instead, a definition like

```
local function foo (<params>)  <body>  end
```

expands to

```
local foo
foo = function (<params>)  <body>  end
```

So, we can use this syntax for recursive functions without worrying:

```
local function fact (n)
  if n == 0 then return 1
  else return n*fact(n-1)
  end
end
```

Of course, this trick does not work if you have indirect recursive functions. In such cases, you must use the equivalent of an explicit forward declaration:

```
local f, g    -- 'forward' declarations
```

```
function g ()
  <some code>  f()  <some code>
end

function f ()
  <some code>  g()  <some code>
end
```

Beware not to write `local function f` in the last definition. Otherwise, Lua would create a fresh local variable `f`, leaving the original `f` (the one that `g` is bound to) undefined.

6.3   Proper Tail Calls

Another interesting feature of functions in Lua is that Lua does tail-call elimination. (This means that Lua is *properly tail recursive*, although the concept does not involve recursion directly.)

A *tail call* is a goto dressed as a call. A tail call happens when a function calls another as its last action, so it has nothing else to do. For instance, in the following code, the call to g is a tail call:

```
function f (x)  return g(x)  end
```

After `f` calls `g`, it has nothing else to do. In such situations, the program does not need to return to the calling function when the called function ends. Therefore, after the tail call, the program does not need to keep any information about the calling function in the stack. When g returns, control can return directly to the point where f was called. Some language implementations, such as the Lua interpreter, take advantage of this fact and actually do not use any extra stack space when doing a tail call. We say that these implementations do *tail-call elimination*.

Because tail calls use no stack space, there is no limit on the number of nested tail calls that a program can make. For instance, we can call the following function passing any number as argument; it will never overflow the stack:

```
function foo (n)
  if n > 0 then return foo(n - 1) end
end
```

A subtle point when we assume tail-call elimination is what is a tail call. Some apparently obvious candidates fail the criterion that the calling function has nothing else to do after the call. For instance, in the following code, the call to g is not a tail call:

```
function f (x)  g(x)  end
```

The problem in this example is that, after calling g, f still has to discard occasional results from g before returning. Similarly, all the following calls fail the criterion:

```
return g(x) + 1       -- must do the addition
return x or g(x)      -- must adjust to 1 result
return (g(x))         -- must adjust to 1 result
```

In Lua, only a call with the form return*func*(*args*) is a tail call. However, both *func* and its arguments can be complex expressions, because Lua evaluates them before the call. For instance, the next call is a tail call:

```
return x[i].foo(x[j] + a*b, i + j)
```

As I said earlier, a tail call is a goto. As such, a quite useful application of tail calls in Lua is for programming state machines. Such applications can represent each state by a function; to change state is to go to (or to call) a specific function. As an example, let us consider a simple maze game. The maze has several rooms, each with up to four doors: north, south, east, and west. At each step, the user enters a movement direction. If there is a door in this direction, the user goes to the corresponding room; otherwise, the program prints a warning. The goal is to go from an initial room to a final room.

This game is a typical state machine, where the current room is the state. We can implement this maze with one function for each room. We use tail calls to move from one room to another. Listing 6.1 shows how we could write a small maze with four rooms.

We start the game with a call to the initial room:

```
room1()
```

Without tail-call elimination, each user move would create a new stack level. After some number of moves, there would be a stack overflow. With tail-call elimination, there is no limit to the number of moves that a user can make, because each move actually performs a goto to another function, not a conventional call.

For this simple game, you may find that a data-driven program, where you describe the rooms and movements with tables, is a better design. However, if the game has several special situations in each room, then this state-machine design is quite appropriate.

Listing 6.1. A maze game:

```
function room1 ()
  local move = io.read()
  if move == "south" then return room3()
  elseif move == "east" then return room2()
  else
    print("invalid move")
    return room1()   -- stay in the same room
  end
end

function room2 ()
  local move = io.read()
  if move == "south" then return room4()
  elseif move == "west" then return room1()
  else
    print("invalid move")
    return room2()
  end
end

function room3 ()
  local move = io.read()
  if move == "north" then return room1()
  elseif move == "east" then return room4()
  else
    print("invalid move")
    return room3()
  end
end

function room4 ()
  print("congratulations!")
end
```

7

Iterators and the Generic for

In this chapter, we cover how to write iterators for the generic **for**. Starting with simple iterators, we will learn how to use all the power of the generic **for** to write simpler and more efficient iterators.

7.1   Iterators and Closures

An *iterator* is any construction that allows you to iterate over the elements of a collection. In Lua, we typically represent iterators by functions: each time we call the function, it returns the "next" element from the collection.

Every iterator needs to keep some state between successive calls, so that it knows where it is and how to proceed from there. Closures provide an excellent mechanism for this task. Remember that a closure is a function that accesses one or more local variables from its enclosing environment. These variables keep their values across successive calls to the closure, allowing the closure to remember where it is along a traversal. Of course, to create a new closure we must also create its non-local variables. Therefore, a closure construction typically involves two functions: the closure itself and a *factory*, the function that creates the closure.

As an example, let us write a simple iterator for a list. Unlike ipairs, this iterator does not return the index of each element, only its value:

```
function values (t)
  local i = 0
  return function ()  i = i + 1; return t[i]  end
end
```

In this example, values is the factory. Each time we call this factory, it creates a new closure (the iterator itself). This closure keeps its state in its external variables t and i. Each time we call the iterator, it returns a next value from the list t. After the last element the iterator returns **nil**, which signals the end of the iteration.

We can use this iterator in a **while** loop:

```
t = {10, 20, 30}
iter = values(t)            -- creates the iterator
while true do
  local element = iter()    -- calls the iterator
  if element == nil then break end
  print(element)
end
```

However, it is easier to use the generic **for**. After all, it was designed for this kind of iteration:

```
t = {10, 20, 30}
for element in values(t) do
  print(element)
end
```

The generic **for** does all the bookkeeping for an iteration loop: it keeps the iterator function internally, so we do not need the iter variable; it calls the iterator on each new iteration; and it stops the loop when the iterator returns **nil**. (In the next section we will see that the generic **for** does even more than that.)

As a more advanced example, Listing 7.1 shows an iterator to traverse all the words from the current input file. To do this traversal, we keep two values: the current line (variable line) and where we are on this line (variable pos). With this data, we can always generate the next word. The main part of the iterator function is the call to string.find. This call searches for a word in the current line, starting at the current position. It describes a "word" using the pattern '%w+', which matches one or more alphanumeric characters. If it finds the word, the function updates the current position to the first character after the word and returns this word.[7] Otherwise, the iterator reads a new line and repeats the search. If there are no more lines, it returns **nil** to signal the end of the iteration.

Despite its complexity, the use of allwords is straightforward:

```
for word in allwords() do
  print(word)
end
```

This is a common situation with iterators: they may not be easy to write, but are easy to use. This is not a big problem; more often than not, end users programming in Lua do not define iterators, but just use those provided by the application.

---

[7]The string.sub call extracts a substring from line between the given positions; we will see it in more detail in Section 20.2.

Listing 7.1. Iterator to traverse all words from the input file:

```
function allwords ()
  local line = io.read()   -- current line
  local pos = 1            -- current position in the line
  return function ()       -- iterator function
    while line do          -- repeat while there are lines
      local s, e = string.find(line, "%w+", pos)
      if s then            -- found a word?
        pos = e + 1        -- next position is after this word
        return string.sub(line, s, e)     -- return the word
      else
        line = io.read()   -- word not found; try next line
        pos = 1            -- restart from first position
      end
    end
    return nil             -- no more lines: end of traversal
  end
end
```

7.2   The Semantics of the Generic for

One drawback of those previous iterators is that we need to create a new closure to initialize each new loop. For most situations, this is not a real problem. For instance, in the allwords iterator, the cost of creating one single closure is negligible compared to the cost of reading a whole file. However, in some situations this overhead can be inconvenient. In such cases, we can use the generic **for** itself to keep the iteration state. In this section we will see the facilities that the generic **for** offers to hold state.

We saw that the generic **for** keeps the iterator function internally, during the loop. Actually, it keeps three values: the iterator function, an *invariant state*, and a *control variable*. Let us see the details now.

The syntax for the generic **for** is as follows:

```
for <var-list> in <exp-list> do
  <body>
end
```

Here, *var-list* is a list of one or more variable names, separated by commas, and *exp-list* is a list of one or more expressions, also separated by commas. More often than not, the expression list has only one element, a call to an iterator factory. For instance, in the code

```
for k, v in pairs(t) do  print(k, v)  end
```

the list of variables is k,v and the list of expressions has the single element pairs(t). Often the list of variables has only one variable too, as in the next loop:

```
for line in io.lines() do
  io.write(line, "\n")
end
```

We call the first variable in the list the *control variable*. Its value is never **nil** during the loop, because when it becomes **nil** the loop ends.

The first thing the **for** does is to evaluate the expressions after the **in**. These expressions should result in the three values kept by the **for**: the iterator function, the invariant state, and the initial value for the control variable. Like in a multiple assignment, only the last (or the only) element of the list can result in more than one value; and the number of values is adjusted to three, extra values being discarded or **nil**s added as needed. (When we use simple iterators, the factory returns only the iterator function, so the invariant state and the control variable get **nil**.)

After this initialization step, the **for** calls the iterator function with two arguments: the invariant state and the control variable. (From the standpoint of the **for** construct, the invariant state has no meaning at all. The **for** only passes the state value from the initialization step to the calls to the iterator function.) Then the **for** assigns the values returned by the iterator function to the variables declared by its variable list. If the first value returned (the one assigned to the control variable) is **nil**, the loop terminates. Otherwise, the **for** executes its body and calls the iteration function again, repeating the process.

More precisely, a construction like

```
for var_1, ..., var_n in <explist> do <block> end
```

is equivalent to the following code:

```
do
  local _f, _s, _var = <explist>
  while true do
    local var_1, ... , var_n = _f(_s, _var)
    _var = var_1
    if _var == nil then break end
    <block>
  end
end
```

So, if our iterator function is f, the invariant state is s, and the initial value for the control variable is a_0, the control variable will loop over the values $a_1 = f(s, a_0)$, $a_2 = f(s, a_1)$, and so on, until a_i is **nil**. If the **for** has other variables, they simply get the extra values returned by each call to f.

7.3 Stateless Iterators

As the name implies, a stateless iterator is an iterator that does not keep any state by itself. Therefore, we may use the same stateless iterator in multiple loops, avoiding the cost of creating new closures.

For each iteration, the **for** loop calls its iterator function with two arguments: the invariant state and the control variable. A stateless iterator generates the next element for the iteration using only these two values. A typical example of this kind of iterator is ipairs, which iterates over all elements of an array:

```
a = {"one", "two", "three"}
for i, v in ipairs(a) do
  print(i, v)
end
```

The state of the iteration is the table being traversed (that is the invariant state, which does not change during the loop), plus the current index (the control variable). Both ipairs (the factory) and the iterator are quite simple; we could write them in Lua as follows:

```
local function iter (a, i)
  i = i + 1
  local v = a[i]
  if v then
    return i, v
  end
end

function ipairs (a)
  return iter, a, 0
end
```

When Lua calls ipairs(a) in a **for** loop, it gets three values: the iter function as the iterator, a as the invariant state, and zero as the initial value for the control variable. Then, Lua calls iter(a, 0), which results in 1,a[1] (unless a[1] is already **nil**). In the second iteration, it calls iter(a, 1), which results in 2,a[2], and so on, until the first nil element.

The pairs function, which iterates over all elements of a table, is similar, except that the iterator function is the next function, which is a primitive function in Lua:

```
function pairs (t)
  return next, t, nil
end
```

The call next(t, k), where k is a key of the table t, returns a next key in the table, in an arbitrary order, plus the value associated with this key as a second return value. The call next(t, nil) returns a first pair. When there are no more pairs, next returns **nil**.

Some people prefer to use next directly, without calling pairs:

```
for k, v in next, t do
  <loop body>
end
```

Remember that the expression list of the **for** loop is adjusted to three results, so
Lua gets next, t, and **nil**, which is exactly what it gets when it calls pairs(t).

An iterator to traverse a linked list is another interesting example of a
stateless iterator. (As we already mentioned, linked lists are not frequent in
Lua, but sometimes we need them.)

```
local function getnext (list, node)
  return not node and list or node.next
end

function traverse (list)  return getnext, list, nil  end
```

The trick here is to use the list main node as the invariant state (the second
value returned by traverse) and the current node as the control variable. The
first time the iterator function getnext is called, node will be **nil**, and so the
function will return list as the first node. In subsequent calls node will not be
nil, and so the iterator will return node.next, as expected. As usual, it is trivial
to use the iterator:

```
list = nil
for line in io.lines() do
  list = {val = line, next = list}
end

for node in traverse(list) do
  print(node.val)
end
```

7.4   Iterators with Complex State

Frequently, an iterator needs to keep more state than fits into a single invariant
state and a control variable. The simplest solution is to use closures. An
alternative solution is to pack all it needs into a table and use this table as
the invariant state for the iteration. Using a table, an iterator can keep as much
data as it needs along the loop. Moreover, it can change this data as it goes.
Although the state is always the same table (and therefore invariant), the table
contents change along the loop. Because such iterators have all their data in
the state, they typically ignore the second argument provided by the generic **for**
(the iterator variable).

As an example of this technique, we will rewrite the iterator allwords, which
traverses all the words from the current input file. This time, we will keep its
state using a table with two fields: line and pos.

The function that starts the iteration is simple. It must return the iterator
function and the initial state:

```
local iterator    -- to be defined later

function allwords ()
  local state = {line = io.read(), pos = 1}
  return iterator, state
end
```

The iterator function does the real work:

```
function iterator (state)
  while state.line do        -- repeat while there are lines
    -- search for next word
    local s, e = string.find(state.line, "%w+", state.pos)
    if s then                -- found a word?
      -- update next position (after this word)
      state.pos = e + 1
      return string.sub(state.line, s, e)
    else                     -- word not found
      state.line = io.read() -- try next line...
      state.pos = 1          -- ... from first position
    end
  end
  return nil                 -- no more lines: end loop
end
```

Whenever possible, you should try to write stateless iterators, those that keep all their state in the **for** variables. With them, you do not create new objects when you start a loop. If you cannot fit your iteration into this model, then you should try closures. Besides being more elegant, typically a closure is more efficient than an iterator using tables is: first, it is cheaper to create a closure than a table; second, access to non-local variables is faster than access to table fields. Later we will see yet another way to write iterators, with coroutines. This is the most powerful solution, but a little more expensive.

7.5   True Iterators

The name "iterator" is a little misleading, because our iterators do not iterate: what iterates is the **for** loop. Iterators only provide the successive values for the iteration. Maybe a better name would be "generator", but "iterator" is already well established in other languages, such as Java.

However, there is another way to build iterators wherein iterators actually do the iteration. When we use such iterators, we do not write a loop; instead, we simply call the iterator with an argument that describes what the iterator must do at each iteration. More specifically, the iterator receives as argument a function that it calls inside its loop.

As a concrete example, let us rewrite once more the allwords iterator using this style:

```
function allwords (f)
  for line in io.lines() do
    for word in string.gmatch(line, "%w+") do
      f(word)    -- call the function
    end
  end
end
```

To use this iterator, we must supply the loop body as a function. If we want only to print each word, we simply use `print`:

```
allwords(print)
```

Often, we use an anonymous function as the body. For instance, the next code fragment counts how many times the word "hello" appears in the input file:

```
local count = 0
allwords(function (w)
  if w == "hello" then count = count + 1 end
end)
print(count)
```

The same task, written with the previous iterator style, is not very different:

```
local count = 0
for w in allwords() do
  if w == "hello" then count = count + 1 end
end
print(count)
```

True iterators were popular in older versions of Lua, when the language did not have the **for** statement. How do they compare with generator-style iterators? Both styles have approximately the same overhead: one function call per iteration. On the one hand, it is easier to write the iterator with true iterators (although we can recover this easiness with coroutines). On the other hand, the generator style is more flexible. First, it allows two or more parallel iterations. (For instance, consider the problem of iterating over two files comparing them word by word.) Second, it allows the use of **break** and **return** inside the iterator body. With a true iterator, a **return** returns from the anonymous function, not from the function doing the iteration. Overall, I usually prefer generators.

8

Compilation, Execution, and Errors

Although we refer to Lua as an interpreted language, Lua always precompiles source code to an intermediate form before running it. (This is not a big deal: many interpreted languages do the same.) The presence of a compilation phase may sound out of place in an interpreted language like Lua. However, the distinguishing feature of interpreted languages is not that they are not compiled, but that the compiler is part of the language runtime and that, therefore, it is possible (and easy) to execute code generated on the fly. We may say that the presence of a function like dofile is what allows Lua to be called an interpreted language.

8.1 Compilation

Previously, we introduced dofile as a kind of primitive operation to run chunks of Lua code, but dofile is actually an auxiliary function: loadfile does the hard work. Like dofile, loadfile loads a Lua chunk from a file, but it does not run the chunk. Instead, it only compiles the chunk and returns the compiled chunk as a function. Moreover, unlike dofile, loadfile does not raise errors, but instead returns error codes, so that we can handle the error. We could define dofile as follows:

```
function dofile (filename)
  local f = assert(loadfile(filename))
  return f()
end
```

Note the use of `assert` to raise an error if `loadfile` fails.

For simple tasks, `dofile` is handy, because it does the complete job in one call. However, `loadfile` is more flexible. In case of error, `loadfile` returns **nil** plus the error message, which allows us to handle the error in customized ways. Moreover, if we need to run a file several times, we can call `loadfile` once and call its result several times. This is much cheaper than several calls to `dofile`, because the file is compiled only once.

The `loadstring` function is similar to `loadfile`, except that it reads its chunk from a string, not from a file. For instance, after the code

```
f = loadstring("i = i + 1")
```

`f` will be a function that, when invoked, executes `i=i+1`:

```
i = 0
f(); print(i)    --> 1
f(); print(i)    --> 2
```

The `loadstring` function is powerful; we should use it with care. It is also an expensive function (when compared to some alternatives) and may result in incomprehensible code. Before you use it, make sure that there is no simpler way to solve the problem at hand.

If you want to do a quick-and-dirty `dostring` (i.e., to load and run a chunk), you may call the result from `loadstring` directly:

```
loadstring(s)()
```

However, if there is any syntax error, `loadstring` will return **nil** and the final error message will be something like *"attempt to call a nil value"*. For clearer error messages, use `assert`:

```
assert(loadstring(s))()
```

Usually, it does not make sense to use `loadstring` on a literal string. For instance, the code

```
f = loadstring("i = i + 1")
```

is roughly equivalent to

```
f = function () i = i + 1 end
```

but the second code is much faster, because it is compiled only once, when its enclosing chunk is compiled. In the first code, each call to `loadstring` involves a new compilation.

Because `loadstring` does not compile with lexical scoping, the two codes in the previous example are not equivalent. To see the difference, let us change the example a little:

```
i = 32
local i = 0
f = loadstring("i = i + 1; print(i)")
g = function () i = i + 1; print(i) end
f()                 --> 33
g()                 --> 1
```

The g function manipulates the local i, as expected, but f manipulates a global i, because loadstring always compiles its strings in the global environment.

The most typical use of loadstring is to run external code, that is, pieces of code that come from outside your program. For instance, you may want to plot a function defined by the user; the user enters the function code and then you use loadstring to evaluate it. Note that loadstring expects a chunk, that is, statements. If you want to evaluate an expression, you must prefix it with **return**, so that you get a statement that returns the value of the given expression. See the example:

```
print "enter your expression:"
local l = io.read()
local func = assert(loadstring("return " .. l))
print("the value of your expression is " .. func())
```

Because the function returned by loadstring is a regular function, you can call it several times:

```
print "enter function to be plotted (with variable 'x'):"
local l = io.read()
local f = assert(loadstring("return " .. l))
for i=1,20 do
  x = i    -- global 'x' (to be visible from the chunk)
  print(string.rep("*", f()))
end
```

(The string.rep function replicates a string a given number of times.)

If we go deeper, we find out that the real primitive in Lua is neither loadfile nor loadstring, but load. Instead of reading a chunk from a file, like loadfile, or from a string, like loadstring, load receives a *reader function* that it calls to get its chunk. The reader function returns the chunk in parts; load calls it until it returns **nil**, which signals the chunk's end. We seldom use load; its main use is when the chunk in not in a file (e.g., it is created dynamically or read from another source) and too big to fit comfortably in memory (otherwise we could use loadstring).

Lua treats any independent chunk as the body of an anonymous function with a variable number of arguments. For instance, loadstring("a = 1") returns the equivalent of the following expression:

```
function (...) a = 1 end
```

Like any other function, chunks can declare local variables:

```
f = loadstring("local a = 10; print(a + 20)")
f()             --> 30
```

Using these features, we can rewrite our plot example to avoid the use of a global variable x:

```
print "enter function to be plotted (with variable 'x'):"
local l = io.read()
local f = assert(loadstring("local x = ...; return " .. l))
for i=1,20 do
  print(string.rep("*", f(i)))
end
```

We append the declaration "local x = ..." in the beginning of the chunk to declare x as a local variable. We then call f with an argument i that becomes the value of the vararg expression (...).

The load functions never raise errors. In case of any kind of error, they return **nil** plus an error message:

```
print(loadstring("i i"))
  --> nil     [string "i i"]:1: '=' expected near 'i'
```

Moreover, these functions never have any kind of side effect. They only compile the chunk to an internal representation and return the result, as an anonymous function. A common mistake is to assume that loading a chunk defines functions. In Lua, function definitions are assignments; as such, they are made at runtime, not at compile time. For instance, suppose we have a file foo.lua like this:

```
function foo (x)
  print(x)
end
```

We then run the command

```
f = loadfile("foo.lua")
```

After this command, foo is compiled, but it is not defined yet. To define it, you must run the chunk:

```
print(foo)     --> nil
f()            -- defines 'foo'
foo("ok")      --> ok
```

In a production-quality program that needs to run external code, you should handle any errors reported when loading a chunk. Moreover, if the code cannot be trusted, you may want to run the new chunk in a protected environment, to avoid unpleasant side effects when running the code.

8.2 C Code

Unlike code written in Lua, C code needs to be linked with an application before use. In most popular systems, the easiest way to do this link is with a dynamic linking facility. However, this facility is not part of the ANSI C specification; that is, there is no portable way to implement it.

Normally, Lua does not include any facility that cannot be implemented in ANSI C. However, dynamic linking is different. We can view it as the mother of all other facilities: once we have it, we can dynamically load any other facility that is not in Lua. Therefore, in this particular case, Lua breaks its portability rules and implements a dynamic linking facility for several platforms. The standard implementation offers this support for Windows, Mac OS X, Linux, FreeBSD, Solaris, and some other Unix implementations. It should not be difficult to extend this facility to other platforms; check your distribution. (To check it, run print(package.loadlib("a","b")) from the Lua prompt and see the result. If it complains about a non-existent file, then you have dynamic linking facility. Otherwise, the error message indicates that this facility is not supported or not installed.)

Lua provides all the functionality of dynamic linking in a single function, called package.loadlib. It has two string arguments: the complete path of the library and the name of a function. So, a typical call to it looks like the next fragment:

```
local path = "/usr/local/lib/lua/5.1/socket.so"
local f = package.loadlib(path, "luaopen_socket")
```

The loadlib function loads the given library and links Lua to it. However, it does not call the function. Instead, it returns the C function as a Lua function. If there is any error loading the library or finding the initialization function, loadlib returns **nil** plus an error message.

The loadlib function is a very low level function. We must provide the full path of the library and the correct name for the function (including occasional leading underscores included by the compiler). Usually, we load C libraries using require. This function searches for the library and uses loadlib to load an initialization function for the library. Once called, this initialization function registers in Lua the functions from that library, much as a typical Lua chunk defines other functions. We will discuss require in Section 15.1, and more details about C libraries in Section 26.2.

8.3 Errors

Errare humanum est. Therefore, we must handle errors the best way we can. Because Lua is an extension language, frequently embedded in an application, it cannot simply crash or exit when an error happens. Instead, whenever an error occurs, Lua ends the current chunk and returns to the application.

Any unexpected condition that Lua encounters raises an error. Errors occur when you (that is, your program) try to add values that are not numbers, to call values that are not functions, to index values that are not tables, and so on.[8] You can also explicitly raise an error calling the error function with the error message as an argument. Usually, this function is the appropriate way to handle errors in your code:

```
print "enter a number:"
n = io.read("*number")
if not n then error("invalid input") end
```

Such combination of if not *condition* then error end is so common that Lua has a built-in function just for this job, called assert:

```
print "enter a number:"
n = assert(io.read("*number"), "invalid input")
```

The assert function checks whether its first argument is not false and simply returns this argument; if the argument is false (that is, **false** or **nil**), assert raises an error. Its second argument, the message, is optional. Beware, however, that assert is a regular function. As such, Lua always evaluates its arguments before calling the function. Therefore, if you have something like

```
n = io.read()
assert(tonumber(n), "invalid input: " .. n .. " is not a number")
```

Lua will always do the concatenation, even when n is a number. It may be wiser to use an explicit test in such cases.

When a function finds an unexpected situation (an *exception*), it can assume two basic behaviors: it can return an error code (typically **nil**) or it can raise an error, calling the error function. There are no fixed rules for choosing between these two options, but we can provide a general guideline: an exception that is easily avoided should raise an error; otherwise, it should return an error code.

For instance, let us consider the sin function. How should it behave when called on a table? Suppose it returns an error code. If we need to check for errors, we would have to write something like

```
local res = math.sin(x)
if not res then      -- error?
  <error-handling code>
```

However, we could as easily check this exception *before* calling the function:

```
if not tonumber(x) then      -- x is not a number?
  <error-handling code>
```

Frequently we check neither the argument nor the result of a call to sin; if the argument is not a number, it means probably something wrong in our program. In such situations, to stop the computation and to issue an error message is the simplest and most practical way to handle the exception.

---

[8]You can modify this behavior using *metatables*, as we will see later.

On the other hand, let us consider the io.open function, which opens a file. How should it behave when called to read a file that does not exist? In this case, there is no simple way to check for the exception before calling the function. In many systems, the only way of knowing whether a file exists is trying to open it. Therefore, if io.open cannot open a file because of an external reason (such as "file does not exist" or "permission denied"), it returns **nil**, plus a string with the error message. In this way, you have a chance to handle the situation in an appropriate way, for instance by asking the user for another file name:

```
local file, msg
repeat
  print "enter a file name:"
  local name = io.read()
  if not name then return end   -- no input
  file, msg = io.open(name, "r")
  if not file then print(msg) end
until file
```

If you do not want to handle such situations, but still want to play safe, you simply use assert to guard the operation:

```
file = assert(io.open(name, "r"))
```

This is a typical Lua idiom: if io.open fails, assert will raise an error.

```
file = assert(io.open("no-file", "r"))
  --> stdin:1: no-file: No such file or directory
```

Notice how the error message, which is the second result from io.open, goes as the second argument to assert.

8.4   Error Handling and Exceptions

For many applications, you do not need to do any error handling in Lua; the application program does this handling. All Lua activities start from a call by the application, usually asking Lua to run a chunk. If there is any error, this call returns an error code, so that the application can take appropriate actions. In the case of the stand-alone interpreter, its main loop just prints the error message and continues showing the prompt and running the commands.

If you need to handle errors in Lua, you must use the pcall function (*protected call*) to encapsulate your code.

Suppose you want to run a piece of Lua code and to catch any error raised while running that code. Your first step is to encapsulate that piece of code in a function; let us call it foo:

```
function foo ()
  <some code>
  if unexpected_condition then error() end
  <some code>
  print(a[i])    -- potential error: 'a' may not be a table
  <some code>
end
```

Then, you call foo with pcall:

```
if pcall(foo) then
  -- no errors while running 'foo'
  <regular code>
else
  -- 'foo' raised an error: take appropriate actions
  <error-handling code>
end
```

Of course, you can call pcall with an anonymous function:

```
if pcall(function ()
  <protected code>
end) then
  <regular code>
else
  <error-handling code>
end
```

The pcall function calls its first argument in *protected mode*, so that it catches any errors while the function is running. If there are no errors, pcall returns **true**, plus any values returned by the call. Otherwise, it returns **false**, plus the error message.

Despite its name, the error message does not have to be a string. Any Lua value that you pass to error will be returned by pcall:

```
local status, err = pcall(function () error({code=121}) end)
print(err.code)   --> 121
```

These mechanisms provide all we need to do exception handling in Lua. We *throw* an exception with error and *catch* it with pcall. The error message identifies the kind or error.

8.5   Error Messages and Tracebacks

Although you can use a value of any type as an error message, usually error messages are strings describing what went wrong. When there is an internal error (such as an attempt to index a non-table value), Lua generates the error message; otherwise, the error message is the value passed to the error function. Whenever the message is a string, Lua tries to add some information about the location where the error happened:

```
local status, err = pcall(function () a = "a"+1 end)
print(err)
  --> stdin:1: attempt to perform arithmetic on a string value

local status, err = pcall(function () error("my error") end)
print(err)
  --> stdin:1: my error
```

The location information gives the file name (stdin, in the example) plus the line number (1, in the example).

The error function has an additional second parameter, which gives the *level* where it should report the error; you can use this parameter to blame someone else for the error. For instance, suppose you write a function whose first task is to check whether it was called correctly:

```
function foo (str)
  if type(str) ~= "string" then
    error("string expected")
  end
  <regular code>
end
```

Then, someone calls your function with a wrong argument:

```
foo({x=1})
```

As it is, Lua points its finger to your function — after all, it was foo that called error — and not to the real culprit, the caller. To correct this problem, you inform error that the error you are reporting occurred on level 2 in the calling hierarchy (level 1 is your own function):

```
function foo (str)
  if type(str) ~= "string" then
    error("string expected", 2)
  end
  <regular code>
end
```

Frequently, when an error happens, we want more debug information than only the location where the error occurred. At least, we want a traceback, showing the complete stack of calls leading to the error. When pcall returns its error message, it destroys part of the stack (the part that went from it to the error point). Consequently, if we want a traceback, we must build it before pcall returns. To do this, Lua provides the xpcall function. Besides the function to be called, it receives a second argument, an *error handler function*. In case of error, Lua calls this error handler *before the stack unwinds*, so that it can use the debug library to gather any extra information it wants about the error. Two common error handlers are debug.debug, which gives you a Lua prompt so that you can inspect by yourself what was going on when the error happened; and debug.traceback, which builds an extended error message with a traceback.[9] The latter is the function that the stand-alone interpreter uses to build its error messages. You also can call debug.traceback at any moment to get a traceback of the current execution:

```
print(debug.traceback())
```

---

[9]Later we will see more about these functions, when we discuss the debug library.

9

Coroutines

A *coroutine* is similar to a thread (in the sense of multithreading): it is a line of execution, with its own stack, its own local variables, and its own instruction pointer; but sharing global variables and mostly anything else with other coroutines. The main difference between threads and coroutines is that, conceptually (or literally, in a multiprocessor machine), a program with threads runs several threads concurrently. Coroutines, on the other hand, are collaborative: at any given time, a program with coroutines is running only one of its coroutines, and this running coroutines suspends its execution only when it explicitly requests to be suspended.

Coroutine is a powerful concept. As such, several of its main uses are complex. Do not worry if you do not understand some of the examples in this chapter on your first reading. You can read the rest of the book and come back here later. But please come back; it will be time well spent.

9.1 Coroutine Basics

Lua packs all its coroutine-related functions in the `coroutine` table. The `create` function creates new coroutines. It has a single argument, a function with the code that the coroutine will run. It returns a value of type `thread`, which represents the new coroutine. Quite often, the argument to `create` is an anonymous function, like here:

```
co = coroutine.create(function () print("hi") end)

print(co)    --> thread: 0x8071d98
```

A coroutine can be in one of four different states: suspended, running, dead, and normal. When we create a coroutine, it starts in the suspended state. This means that a coroutine does not run its body automatically when we create it. We can check the state of a coroutine with the `status` function:

```
print(coroutine.status(co))    --> suspended
```

The function `coroutine.resume` (re)starts the execution of a coroutine, changing its state from suspended to running:

```
coroutine.resume(co)    --> hi
```

In this example, when the coroutine body runs it simply prints "hi" and terminates, leaving the coroutine in the dead state, from which it does not return:

```
print(coroutine.status(co))    --> dead
```

Until now, coroutines look like nothing more than a complicated way to call functions. The real power of coroutines stems from the `yield` function, which allows a running coroutine to suspend its own execution so that it can be resumed later. Let us see a simple example:

```
co = coroutine.create(function ()
      for i=1,10 do
        print("co", i)
        coroutine.yield()
      end
    end)
```

Now, when we resume this coroutine, it starts its execution and runs until the first `yield`:

```
coroutine.resume(co)    --> co    1
```

If we check its status, we can see that the coroutine is suspended and therefore can be resumed again:

```
print(coroutine.status(co))    --> suspended
```

From the coroutine's point of view, all activity that happens while it is suspended is happening inside its call to `yield`. When we resume the coroutine, this call to `yield` finally returns and the coroutine continues its execution until the next yield or until its end:

```
coroutine.resume(co)    --> co    2
coroutine.resume(co)    --> co    3
  . . .
coroutine.resume(co)    --> co    10
coroutine.resume(co)     -- prints nothing
```

During the last call to resume, the coroutine body finished the loop and then returned, so the coroutine is dead now. If we try to resume it again, resume returns **false** plus an error message:

```
print(coroutine.resume(co))
    --> false    cannot resume dead coroutine
```

Note that resume runs in protected mode. Therefore, if there is any error inside a coroutine, Lua will not show the error message, but instead will return it to the resume call.

When a coroutine resumes another, it is not suspended; after all, we cannot resume it. However, it is not running either, because the running coroutine is the other one. So, its own status is what we call the *normal* state.

A useful facility in Lua is that a pair resume–yield can exchange data. The first resume, which has no corresponding yield waiting for it, passes its extra arguments as arguments to the coroutine main function:

```
co = coroutine.create(function (a,b,c)
        print("co", a,b,c)
      end)
coroutine.resume(co, 1, 2, 3)     --> co  1  2  3
```

A call to resume returns, after the **true** that signals no errors, any arguments passed to the corresponding yield:

```
co = coroutine.create(function (a,b)
        coroutine.yield(a + b, a - b)
      end)
print(coroutine.resume(co, 20, 10))  --> true  30  10
```

Symmetrically, yield returns any extra arguments passed to the corresponding resume:

```
co = coroutine.create (function ()
        print("co", coroutine.yield())
      end)
coroutine.resume(co)
coroutine.resume(co, 4, 5)     --> co  4  5
```

Finally, when a coroutine ends, any values returned by its main function go to the corresponding resume:

```
co = coroutine.create(function ()
        return 6, 7
      end)
print(coroutine.resume(co))    --> true  6  7
```

We seldom use all these facilities in the same coroutine, but all of them have their uses.

For those that already know something about coroutines, it is important to clarify some concepts before we go on. Lua offers what I call *asymmetric coroutines*. This means that it has a function to suspend the execution of a coroutine and a different function to resume a suspended coroutine. Some other languages offer *symmetric coroutines*, where there is only one function to transfer control from any coroutine to another.

Some people call asymmetric coroutine *semi-coroutines* (being not symmetrical, they are not really *co*). However, other people use the same term *semi-coroutine* to denote a restricted implementation of coroutines, where a coroutine can suspend its execution only when it is not calling any function, that is, when it has no pending calls in its control stack. In other words, only the main body of such semi-coroutines can yield. A *generator* in Python is an example of this meaning of semi-coroutines.

Unlike the difference between symmetric and asymmetric coroutines, the difference between coroutines and generators (as presented in Python) is a deep one; generators are simply not powerful enough to implement several interesting constructions that we can write with full coroutines. Lua offers full, asymmetric coroutines. Those that prefer symmetric coroutines can implement them on top of the asymmetric facilities of Lua. It is an easy task. (Basically, each transfer does a yield followed by a resume.)

9.2   Pipes and Filters

One of the most paradigmatic examples of coroutines is the producer–consumer problem. Let us suppose that we have a function that continually produces values (e.g., reading them from a file) and another function that continually consumes these values (e.g., writing them to another file). Typically, these two functions look like this:

```
function producer ()
  while true do
    local x = io.read()      -- produce new value
    send(x)                  -- send to consumer
  end
end

function consumer ()
  while true do
    local x = receive()           -- receive from producer
    io.write(x, "\n")             -- consume new value
  end
end
```

(In this implementation, both the producer and the consumer run forever. It is easy to change them to stop when there are no more data to handle.) The problem here is how to match send with receive. It is a typical instance of the who-has-the-main-loop problem. Both the producer and the consumer are active, both have their own main loops, and both assume that the other is a callable service. For this particular example, it is easy to change the structure of one of the functions, unrolling its loop and making it a passive agent. However, this change of structure may be far from easy in other real scenarios.

Coroutines provide an ideal tool to match producers and consumers, because a resume–yield pair turns upside-down the typical relationship between caller and callee. When a coroutine calls `yield`, it does not enter into a new function; instead, it returns a pending call (to `resume`). Similarly, a call to `resume` does not start a new function, but returns a call to `yield`. This property is exactly what we need to match a `send` with a `receive` in such a way that each one acts as if it were the master and the other the slave. So, `receive` resumes the producer, so that it can produce a new value; and `send` yields the new value back to the consumer:

```
function receive ()
  local status, value = coroutine.resume(producer)
  return value
end

function send (x)
  coroutine.yield(x)
end
```

Of course, the producer must now be a coroutine:

```
producer = coroutine.create(
  function ()
    while true do
    local x = io.read()      -- produce new value
      send(x)
    end
  end)
```

In this design, the program starts by calling the consumer. When the consumer needs an item, it resumes the producer, which runs until it has an item to give to the consumer, and then stops until the consumer resumes it again. Therefore, we have what we call a *consumer-driven* design.

We can extend this design with filters, which are tasks that sit between the producer and the consumer doing some kind of transformation in the data. A *filter* is a consumer and a producer at the same time, so it resumes a producer to get new values and yields the transformed values to a consumer. As a trivial example, we can add to our previous code a filter that inserts a line number at the beginning of each line. The code is in Listing 9.1. The final bit simply creates the components it needs, connects them, and starts the final consumer:

```
p = producer()
f = filter(p)
consumer(f)
```

Or better yet:

```
consumer(filter(producer()))
```

Listing 9.1. Producer–consumer with filters:

```lua
function receive (prod)
  local status, value = coroutine.resume(prod)
  return value
end

function send (x)
  coroutine.yield(x)
end

function producer ()
  return coroutine.create(function ()
    while true do
      local x = io.read()      -- produce new value
      send(x)
    end
  end)
end

function filter (prod)
  return coroutine.create(function ()
    for line = 1, math.huge do
      local x = receive(prod)    -- get new value
      x = string.format("%5d %s", line, x)
      send(x)          -- send it to consumer
    end
  end)
end

function consumer (prod)
  while true do
    local x = receive(prod)    -- get new value
    io.write(x, "\n")            -- consume new value
  end
end
```

Listing 9.2. Function to generate all permutations of the first n elements of a:

```
function permgen (a, n)
  n = n or #a              -- default for 'n' is size of 'a'
  if n <= 1 then           -- nothing to change?
    printResult(a)
  else
    for i=1,n do
      -- put i-th element as the last one
      a[n], a[i] = a[i], a[n]
      -- generate all permutations of the other elements
      permgen(a, n - 1)
      -- restore i-th element
      a[n], a[i] = a[i], a[n]
    end
  end
end
```

If you thought about Unix pipes after reading the previous example, you are not alone. After all, coroutines are a kind of (non-preemptive) multithreading. While with pipes each task runs in a separate process, with coroutines each task runs in a separate coroutine. Pipes provide a buffer between the writer (producer) and the reader (consumer) so there is some freedom in their relative speeds. This is important in the context of pipes, because the cost of switching between processes is high. With coroutines, the cost of switching between tasks is much smaller (roughly the same as a function call), so the writer and the reader can run hand in hand.

9.3 Coroutines as Iterators

We can see loop iterators as a particular example of the producer–consumer pattern: an iterator produces items to be consumed by the loop body. Therefore, it seems appropriate to use coroutines to write iterators. Indeed, coroutines provide a powerful tool for this task. Again, the key feature is their ability to turn upside-down the relationship between caller and callee. With this feature, we can write iterators without worrying about how to keep state between successive calls to the iterator.

To illustrate this kind of use, let us write an iterator to traverse all permutations of a given array. It is not an easy task to write directly such an iterator, but it is not so difficult to write a recursive function that generates all these permutations. The idea is simple: put each array element in the last position, in turn, and recursively generate all permutations of the remaining elements. The code is in Listing 9.2. To put it to work, we must define an appropriate printResult function and call permgen with proper arguments:

```
function printResult (a)
  for i = 1, #a do
    io.write(a[i], " ")
  end
  io.write("\n")
end

permgen ({1,2,3,4})
  --> 2 3 4 1
  --> 3 2 4 1
  --> 3 4 2 1
    . . .
  --> 2 1 3 4
  --> 1 2 3 4
```

After we have the generator ready, it is an automatic task to convert it to an iterator. First, we change printResult to yield:

```
function permgen (a, n)
  n = n or #a
  if n <= 1 then
    coroutine.yield(a)
  else
    <as before>
```

Then, we define a factory that arranges for the generator to run inside a coroutine, and then create the iterator function. The iterator simply resumes the coroutine to produce the next permutation:

```
function permutations (a)
  local co = coroutine.create(function () permgen(a) end)
  return function ()    -- iterator
    local code, res = coroutine.resume(co)
    return res
  end
end
```

With this machinery in place, it is trivial to iterate over all permutations of an array with a **for** statement:

```
for p in permutations{"a", "b", "c"} do
  printResult(p)
end
  --> b c a
  --> c b a
  --> c a b
  --> a c b
  --> b a c
  --> a b c
```

The `permutations` function uses a common pattern in Lua, which packs a call to resume with its corresponding coroutine inside a function. This pattern is so common that Lua provides a special function for it: `coroutine.wrap`. Like `create`, `wrap` creates a new coroutine. Unlike `create`, `wrap` does not return the coroutine itself; instead, it returns a function that, when called, resumes the coroutine. Unlike the original `resume`, that function does not return an error code as its first result; instead, it raises the error in case of error. Using `wrap`, we can write `permutations` as follows:

```
function permutations (a)
  return coroutine.wrap(function () permgen(a) end)
end
```

Usually, `coroutine.wrap` is simpler to use than `coroutine.create`. It gives us exactly what we need from a coroutine: a function to resume it. However, it is also less flexible. There is no way to check the status of a coroutine created with `wrap`. Moreover, we cannot check for runtime errors.

9.4 Non-Preemptive Multithreading

As we saw earlier, coroutines allow a kind of collaborative multithreading. Each coroutine is equivalent to a thread. A pair yield–resume switches control from one thread to another. However, unlike regular multithreading, coroutines are non preemptive. While a coroutine is running, it cannot be stopped from the outside. It suspends execution only when it explicitly requests so (through a call to `yield`). For several applications this is not a problem, quite the opposite. Programming is much easier in the absence of preemption. You do not need to be paranoid about synchronization bugs, because all synchronization among threads is explicit in the program. You just need to ensure that a coroutine yields only when it is outside a critical region.

However, with non-preemptive multithreading, whenever any thread calls a blocking operation, the whole program blocks until the operation completes. For most applications, this is an unacceptable behavior, which leads many programmers to disregard coroutines as a real alternative to conventional multithreading. As we will see here, this problem has an interesting (and obvious, with hindsight) solution.

Let us assume a typical multithreading situation: we want to download several remote files through HTTP. Of course, to download several remote files, we must know how to download one remote file. In this example, we will use the *LuaSocket* library, developed by Diego Nehab. To download a file, we must open a connection to its site, send a request to the file, receive the file (in blocks), and close the connection. In Lua, we can write this task as follows. First, we load the LuaSocket library:

```
require "socket"
```

Then, we define the host and the file we want to download. In this example, we will download the HTML 3.2 Reference Specification from the World Wide Web Consortium site:

```
host = "www.w3.org"
file = "/TR/REC-html32.html"
```

Then, we open a TCP connection to port 80 (the standard port for HTTP connections) of that site:

```
c = assert(socket.connect(host, 80))
```

This operation returns a connection object, which we use to send the file request:

```
c:send("GET " .. file .. " HTTP/1.0\r\n\r\n")
```

Next, we read the file in blocks of 1 Kbyte, writing each block to the standard output:

```
while true do
  local s, status, partial = c:receive(2^10)
  io.write(s or partial)
  if status == "closed" then break end
end
```

The `receive` function returns either a string with what it read or **nil** in case of error; in the later case it also returns an error code (`status`) and what it read until the error (`partial`). When the host closes the connection we print that remaining input and break the receive loop.

After downloading the file, we close the connection:

```
c:close()
```

Now that we know how to download one file, let us return to the problem of downloading several files. The trivial approach is to download one at a time. However, this sequential approach, where we start reading a file only after finishing the previous one, is too slow. When reading a remote file, a program spends most of its time waiting for data to arrive. More specifically, it spends most of its time blocked in the call to `receive`. So, the program could run much faster if it downloaded all files concurrently. Then, while a connection has no data available, the program can read from another connection. Clearly, coroutines offer a convenient way to structure these simultaneous downloads. We create a new thread for each download task. When a thread has no data available, it yields control to a simple dispatcher, which invokes another thread.

To rewrite the program with coroutines, we first rewrite the previous download code as a function. The result is in Listing 9.3. Because we are not interested in the remote file contents, this function counts and prints the file size, instead of writing the file to the standard output. (With several threads reading several files, the output would intermix all files.) In this new code, we use an

Listing 9.3. Function to download a Web page:

```
function download (host, file)
  local c = assert(socket.connect(host, 80))
  local count = 0    -- counts number of bytes read
  c:send("GET " .. file .. " HTTP/1.0\r\n\r\n")
  while true do
    local s, status, partial = receive(c)
    count = count + #(s or partial)
    if status == "closed" then break end
  end
  c:close()
  print(file, count)
end
```

auxiliary function (`receive`) to receive data from the connection. In the sequential approach, its code would be like this:

```
function receive (connection)
  return connection:receive(2^10)
end
```

For the concurrent implementation, this function must receive data without blocking. Instead, if there is not enough data available, it yields. The new code is like this:

```
function receive (connection)
  connection:settimeout(0)        -- do not block
  local s, status, partial = connection:receive(2^10)
  if status == "timeout" then
    coroutine.yield(connection)
  end
  return s or partial, status
end
```

The call to `settimeout(0)` makes any operation over the connection a non-blocking operation. When the operation status is "`timeout`", it means that the operation returned without completion. In this case, the thread yields. The non-false argument passed to `yield` signals to the dispatcher that the thread is still performing its task. Notice that, even in case of a timeout, the connection returns what it read until the timeout, which is in the `partial` variable.

Listing 9.4 shows the dispatcher plus some auxiliary code. Table `threads` keeps a list of all live threads for the dispatcher. Function `get` ensures that each download runs in an individual thread. The dispatcher itself is mainly a loop that goes through all threads, resuming them one by one. It must also remove from the list the threads that have finished their tasks. It stops the loop when there are no more threads to run.

Listing 9.4. The dispatcher:

```
threads = {}      -- list of all live threads

function get (host, file)
  -- create coroutine
  local co = coroutine.create(function ()
    download(host, file)
  end)
  -- insert it in the list
  table.insert(threads, co)
end

function dispatch ()
  local i = 1
  while true do
    if threads[i] == nil then     -- no more threads?
      if threads[1] == nil then break end    -- list is empty?
      i = 1                       -- restart the loop
    end
    local status, res = coroutine.resume(threads[i])
    if not res then     -- thread finished its task?
      table.remove(threads, i)
    else
      i = i + 1
    end
  end
end
```

Finally, the main program creates the threads it needs and calls the dispatcher. For instance, to download four documents from the W3C site, the main program could be like this:

```
host = "www.w3.org"

get(host, "/TR/html401/html40.txt")
get(host, "/TR/2002/REC-xhtml1-20020801/xhtml1.pdf")
get(host, "/TR/REC-html32.html")
get(host, "/TR/2000/REC-DOM-Level-2-Core-20001113/DOM2-Core.txt")

dispatch()    -- main loop
```

My machine takes six seconds to download these four files using coroutines. With the sequential implementation, it takes more than twice this time (15 seconds).

Despite the speedup, this last implementation is far from optimal. Everything goes fine while at least one thread has something to read. However, when

Listing 9.5. Dispatcher using `select`:

```
function dispatch ()
  local i = 1
  local connections = {}
  while true do
    if threads[i] == nil then    -- no more threads?
      if threads[1] == nil then break end
      i = 1                      -- restart the loop
      connections = {}
    end
    local status, res = coroutine.resume(threads[i])
    if not res then    -- thread finished its task?
      table.remove(threads, i)
    else               -- time out
      i = i + 1
      connections[#connections + 1] = res
      if #connections == #threads then    -- all threads blocked?
        socket.select(connections)
      end
    end
  end
end
```

no thread has data to read, the dispatcher does a busy wait, going from thread to thread only to check that they still have no data. As a result, this coroutine implementation uses almost 30 times more CPU than the sequential solution.

To avoid this behavior, we can use the `select` function from LuaSocket. It allows a program to block while waiting for a status change in a group of sockets. The changes in our implementation are small. We have to change only the dispatcher; the new version is in Listing 9.5. Along the loop, this new dispatcher collects the timed-out connections in table `connections`. Remember that `receive` passes such connections to `yield`; thus `resume` returns them. If all connections time out, the dispatcher calls `select` to wait for any of these connections to change status. This final implementation runs as fast as the first implementation with coroutines. Moreover, as it does no busy waits, it uses just a little more CPU than the sequential implementation.

10

Complete Examples

To end this introduction about the language, we show two complete programs that illustrate different facilities of Lua. The first example illustrates the use of Lua as a data description language. The second example is an implementation of the *Markov chain algorithm*, described by Kernighan & Pike in their book *The Practice of Programming* (Addison-Wesley, 1999).

10.1 Data Description

The Lua web site keeps a database containing a sample of projects around the world that use Lua. We represent each entry in the database by a constructor in an auto-documented way, as Listing 10.1 shows. The interesting thing about this representation is that a file with a sequence of such entries is a Lua program, which performs a sequence of calls to a function entry, using the tables as arguments.

Our goal is to write a program that shows those data in HTML, so that the data becomes the web page http://www.lua.org/uses.html. Because there are many projects, the final page first shows a list of all project titles, and then shows the details of each project. Listing 10.2 is a typical output of the program.

To read the data, the program simply gives a proper definition for entry, and then runs the data file as a program (with dofile). Note that we have to traverse all the entries twice, first for the title list, and again for the project descriptions. A first approach would be to collect all entries in an array. However, there is a second attractive solution: to run the data file twice, each time with a different definition for entry. We follow this approach in the next program.

Listing 10.1. A typical database entry:

```
entry{
  title = "Tecgraf",
  org = "Computer Graphics Technology Group, PUC-Rio",
  url = "http://www.tecgraf.puc-rio.br/",
  contact = "Waldemar Celes",
  description = [[
    Tecgraf is the result of a partnership between PUC-Rio,
    the Pontifical Catholic University of Rio de Janeiro,
    and <a HREF="http://www.petrobras.com.br/">PETROBRAS</a>,
    the Brazilian Oil Company.
    Tecgraf is Lua's birthplace,
    and the language has been used there since 1993.
    Currently, more than thirty programmers in Tecgraf use
    Lua regularly; they have written more than two hundred
    thousand lines of code, distributed among dozens of
    final products.]]
}
```

First, we define an auxiliary function for writing formatted text (we already saw this function in Section 5.2):

```
function fwrite (fmt, ...)
  return io.write(string.format(fmt, ...))
end
```

The writeheader function simply writes the page header, which is always the same:

```
function writeheader()
  io.write([[
    <html>
    <head><title>Projects using Lua</title></head>
    <body bgcolor="#FFFFFF">
    Here are brief descriptions of some projects around the
    world that use <a href="home.html">Lua</a>.
    <br>
  ]])
end
```

The first definition for entry writes each title project as a list item. The argument o will be the table describing the project:

```
function entry1 (o)
  count = count + 1
  local title = o.title or '(no title)'
  fwrite('<li><a href="#%d">%s</a>\n', count, title)
end
```

Listing 10.2. A typical HTML page listing Lua projects:

```
<html>
<head><title>Projects using Lua</title></head>
<body bgcolor="#FFFFFF">
Here are brief descriptions of some projects around the
world that use <a href="home.html">Lua</a>.
<br>
<ul>
<li><a href="#1">Tecgraf</a>
<li>  <other entries>
</ul>

<h3>
<a name="1" href="http://www.tecgraf.puc-rio.br/">Tecgraf</a>
<br>
<small><em>Computer Graphics Technology Group,
           PUC-Rio</em></small>
</h3>

    Tecgraf is the result of a partnership between
    ...
    distributed among dozens of final products.<p>
Contact: Waldemar Celes

<a name="2"></a><hr>

<other entries>

</body></html>
```

If `o.title` is **nil** (that is, the field was not provided), the function uses a fixed string "(no title)".

The second definition (Listing 10.3) writes all useful data about a project. It is a little more complex, because all items are optional. (To avoid conflict with HTML, which uses double quotes, we have used only single quotes in this program.)

The last function closes the page:

```
function writetail ()
  fwrite('</body></html>\n')
end
```

The main program is in Listing 10.4. It starts the page, loads the data file, runs it with the first definition for entry (entry1) to create the list of titles, then resets the counter and runs the data file again with the second definition for entry, and finally closes the page.

Listing 10.3. Callback function to format a full entry:

```
function entry2 (o)
  count = count + 1
  fwrite('<hr>\n<h3>\n')

  local href = o.url and string.format(' href="%s"', o.url) or ''
  local title = o.title or o.org or 'org'
  fwrite('<a name="%d"%s>%s</a>\n', count, href, title)

  if o.title and o.org then
    fwrite('<br>\n<small><em>%s</em></small>', o.org)
  end
  fwrite('\n</h3>\n')

  if o.description then
    fwrite('%s<p>\n',
           string.gsub(o.description, '\n\n+', '<p>\n'))
  end

  if o.email then
    fwrite('Contact: <a href="mailto:%s">%s</a>\n',
           o.email, o.contact or o.email)
  elseif o.contact then
    fwrite('Contact: %s\n', o.contact)
  end
end
```

Listing 10.4. The main program:

```
local inputfile = 'db.lua'
writeheader()

count = 0
f = loadfile(inputfile)         -- loads data file

entry = entry1                  -- defines 'entry'
fwrite('<ul>\n')
f()                             -- runs data file
fwrite('</ul>\n')

count = 0
entry = entry2                  -- redefines 'entry'
f()                             -- runs data file again

writetail()
```

10.2   Markov Chain Algorithm

Our second example is an implementation of the *Markov chain algorithm*. The program generates random text, based on what words may follow a sequence of n previous words in a base text. For this implementation, we will assume 2 for the value of n.

The first part of the program reads the base text and builds a table that, for each prefix of two words, gives a list of the words that follow that prefix in the text. After building the table, the program uses the table to generate random text, wherein each word follows two previous words with the same probability as in the base text. As a result, we have text that is very, but not quite, random. For instance, when applied to this book, the output of the program has pieces like *"Constructors can also traverse a table constructor, then the parentheses in the following line does the whole file in a field n to store the contents of each function, but to show its only argument. If you want to find the maximum element in an array can return both the maximum value and continues showing the prompt and running the code. The following words are reserved and cannot be used to convert between degrees and radians."*

We will code each prefix by its two words concatenated with a space in between:

```
function prefix (w1, w2)
  return w1 .. " " .. w2
end
```

We use the string NOWORD ("\n") to initialize the prefix words and to mark the end of the text. For instance, for the following text

```
the more we try the more we do
```

the table of following words would be

```
{ ["\n \n"] = {"the"},
  ["\n the"] = {"more"},
  ["the more"] = {"we", "we"},
  ["more we"] = {"try", "do"},
  ["we try"] = {"the"},
  ["try the"] = {"more"},
  ["we do"] = {"\n"},
}
```

The program keeps its table in the variable statetab. To insert a new word in a prefix list of this table, we use the following function:

```
function insert (index, value)
  local list = statetab[index]
  if list == nil then
    statetab[index] = {value}
  else
    list[#list + 1] = value
  end
end
```

It first checks whether that prefix already has a list; if not, it creates a new one with the new value. Otherwise, it inserts the new value at the end of the existing list.

To build the statetab table, we keep two variables, w1 and w2, with the last two words read. For each new word read, we add it to the list associated with w1–w2 and then update w1 and w2.

After building the table, the program starts to generate a text with MAXGEN words. First, it re-initializes variables w1 and w2. Then, for each prefix, it chooses a next word randomly from the list of valid next words, prints this word, and updates w1 and w2. Listing 10.5 and Listing 10.6 show the complete program.

Listing 10.5. Auxiliary definitions for the Markov program:

```lua
function allwords ()
  local line = io.read()     -- current line
  local pos = 1              -- current position in the line
  return function ()         -- iterator function
    while line do            -- repeat while there are lines
      local s, e = string.find(line, "%w+", pos)
      if s then                       -- found a word?
        pos = e + 1                   -- update next position
        return string.sub(line, s, e)   -- return the word
      else
        line = io.read()              -- word not found; try next line
        pos = 1                       -- restart from first position
      end
    end
    return nil               -- no more lines: end of traversal
  end
end

function prefix (w1, w2)
  return w1 .. " " .. w2
end

local statetab = {}

function insert (index, value)
  local list = statetab[index]
  if list == nil then
    statetab[index] = {value}
  else
    list[#list + 1] = value
  end
end
```

Listing 10.6. The Markov program:

```
local N  = 2
local MAXGEN = 10000
local NOWORD = "\n"

-- build table
local w1, w2 = NOWORD, NOWORD
for w in allwords() do
  insert(prefix(w1, w2), w)
  w1 = w2; w2 = w;
end
insert(prefix(w1, w2), NOWORD)

-- generate text
w1 = NOWORD; w2 = NOWORD      -- reinitialize
for i=1, MAXGEN do
  local list = statetab[prefix(w1, w2)]
  -- choose a random item from list
  local r = math.random(#list)
  local nextword = list[r]
  if nextword == NOWORD then return end
  io.write(nextword, " ")
  w1 = w2; w2 = nextword
end
```

Part II
**Tables and
Objects**

11

Data Structures

Tables in Lua are not a data structure; they are *the* data structure. All structures that other languages offer — arrays, records, lists, queues, sets — can be represented with tables in Lua. More to the point, Lua tables implement all these structures efficiently.

In traditional languages, such as C and Pascal, we implement most data structures with arrays and lists (where lists = records + pointers). Although we can implement arrays and lists using Lua tables (and sometimes we do this), tables are more powerful than arrays and lists; many algorithms are simplified to the point of triviality with the use of tables. For instance, we seldom write a search in Lua, because tables offer direct access to any type.

It takes a while to learn how to use tables efficiently. Here, I will show how to implement typical data structures with tables and will provide some examples of their use. We will start with arrays and lists, not because we need them for the other structures, but because most programmers are already familiar with them. We have already seen the basics of this material in the chapters about the language, but I will repeat it here for completeness.

11.1 Arrays

We implement arrays in Lua simply by indexing tables with integers. Therefore, arrays do not have a fixed size, but grow as needed. Usually, when we initialize the array we define its size indirectly. For instance, after the following code, any attempt to access a field outside the range 1–1000 will return **nil**, instead of zero:

```
a = {}     -- new array
for i=1, 1000 do
  a[i] = 0
end
```

The length operator ('#') uses this fact to find the size of an array:

```
print(#a)          --> 1000
```

You can start an array at index 0, 1, or any other value:

```
-- creates an array with indices from -5 to 5
a = {}
for i=-5, 5 do
  a[i] = 0
end
```

However, it is customary in Lua to start arrays with index 1. The Lua libraries adhere to this convention; so does the length operator. If your arrays do not start with 1, you will not be able to use these facilities.

We can use a constructor to create and initialize arrays in a single expression:

```
squares = {1, 4, 9, 16, 25, 36, 49, 64, 81}
```

Such constructors can be as large as you need (well, up to a few million elements).

11.2   Matrices and Multi-Dimensional Arrays

There are two main ways to represent matrices in Lua. The first one is to use an array of arrays, that is, a table wherein each element is another table. For instance, you can create a matrix of zeros with dimensions N by M with the following code:

```
mt = {}            -- create the matrix
for i=1,N do
  mt[i] = {}       -- create a new row
  for j=1,M do
    mt[i][j] = 0
  end
end
```

Because tables are objects in Lua, you have to create each row explicitly to create a matrix. On the one hand, this is certainly more verbose than simply declaring a matrix, as you do in C or Pascal. On the other hand, it gives you more flexibility. For instance, you can create a triangular matrix changing the loop for j=1,M do ... end in the previous example to for j=1,i do ... end. With this code, the triangular matrix uses only half the memory of the original one.

The second way to represent a matrix in Lua is by composing the two indices into a single one. If the two indices are integers, you can multiply the first one by a suitable constant and then add the second index. With this approach, the following code would create our matrix of zeros with dimensions N by M:

```
mt = {}                 -- create the matrix
for i=1,N do
  for j=1,M do
    mt[(i-1)*M + j] = 0
  end
end
```

If the indices are strings, you can create a single index concatenating both indices with a character in between to separate them. For instance, you can index a matrix m with string indices s and t with the code m[s.."::"..t], provided that both s and t do not contain colons; otherwise, pairs like ("a:","b") and ("a",":b") would collapse into a single index "a::b". When in doubt, you can use a control character like '\0' to separate the indices.

Quite often, applications use a *sparse matrix*, a matrix wherein most elements are 0 or **nil**. For instance, you can represent a graph by its adjacency matrix, which has the value x in position m,n when the nodes m and n are connected with cost x; when these nodes are not connected, the value in position m,n is **nil**. To represent a graph with ten thousand nodes, where each node has about five neighbors, you will need a matrix with a hundred million entries (a square matrix with 10000 columns and 10000 rows), but approximately only fifty thousand of them will not be **nil** (five non-nil columns for each row, corresponding to the five neighbors of each node). Many books on data structures discuss at length how to implement such sparse matrices without wasting 400 Mbytes of memory, but you do not need these techniques when programming in Lua. Because arrays are represented by tables, they are naturally sparse. With our first representation (tables of tables), you will need ten thousand tables, each one with about five elements, with a grand total of fifty thousand entries. With the second representation, you will have a single table, with fifty thousand entries in it. Whatever the representation, you need space only for the non-nil elements.

We cannot use the length operator over sparse matrices, because of the holes (nil values) between active entries. This is not a big loss; even if we could use it, we should not. For most operations, it would be quite inefficient to traverse all these empty entries. Instead, we can use pairs to traverse only the non-nil elements. For instance, to multiply a row by a constant, we can use the following code:

```
function mult (a, rowindex, k)
  local row = a[rowindex]
  for i, v in pairs(row) do
    row[i] = v * k
  end
end
```

Be aware, however, that keys have no intrinsic order in a table, so the iteration with `pairs` does not ensure that we visit the columns in increasing order. For some tasks (like our previous example), this is not a problem. For other tasks, you may need an alternative approach, such as linked lists.

11.3   Linked Lists

Because tables are dynamic entities, it is easy to implement linked lists in Lua. Each node is represented by a table and links are simply table fields that contain references to other tables. For instance, to implement a basic list, where each node has two fields, `next` and `value`, we create a variable to be the list root:

```
list = nil
```

To insert an element at the beginning of the list, with a value `v`, we do:

```
list = {next = list, value = v}
```

To traverse the list, we write:

```
local l = list
while l do
  <visit l.value>
  l = l.next
end
```

Other kinds of lists, such as double-linked lists or circular lists, are also implemented easily. However, you seldom need those structures in Lua, because usually there is a simpler way to represent your data without using linked lists. For instance, we can represent a stack with an (unbounded) array.

11.4   Queues and Double Queues

A simple way to implement queues in Lua is with functions `insert` and `remove` (from the `table` library). These functions insert and remove elements in any position of an array, moving other elements to accommodate the operation. However, these moves can be expensive for large structures. A more efficient implementation uses two indices, one for the first element and another for the last:

```
function ListNew ()
  return {first = 0, last = -1}
end
```

To avoid polluting the global space, we will define all list operations inside a table, properly called `List` (that is, we will create a *module*). Therefore, we rewrite our last example like this:

```
List = {}
function List.new ()
  return {first = 0, last = -1}
end
```

Now, we can insert or remove an element at both ends in constant time:

```
function List.pushfirst (list, value)
  local first = list.first - 1
  list.first = first
  list[first] = value
end

function List.pushlast (list, value)
  local last = list.last + 1
  list.last = last
  list[last] = value
end

function List.popfirst (list)
  local first = list.first
  if first > list.last then error("list is empty") end
  local value = list[first]
  list[first] = nil          -- to allow garbage collection
  list.first = first + 1
  return value
end

function List.poplast (list)
  local last = list.last
  if list.first > last then error("list is empty") end
  local value = list[last]
  list[last] = nil          -- to allow garbage collection
  list.last = last - 1
  return value
end
```

If you use this structure in a strict queue discipline, calling only pushlast and popfirst, both first and last will increase continually. However, because we represent arrays in Lua with tables, you can index them either from 1 to 20 or from 16 777 216 to 16 777 236. Because Lua uses double precision to represent numbers, your program can run for two hundred years, doing one million insertions per second, before it has problems with overflows.

11.5 Sets and Bags

Suppose you want to list all identifiers used in a program source; somehow you need to filter the reserved words out of your listing. Some C programmers could be tempted to represent the set of reserved words as an array of strings, and then to search this array to know whether a given word is in the set. To speed up the search, they could even use a binary tree to represent the set.

In Lua, an efficient and simple way to represent such sets is to put the set elements as *indices* in a table. Then, instead of searching the table for a given element, you just index the table and test whether the result is **nil** or not. In our example, we could write the next code:

```
reserved = {
  ["while"] = true,      ["end"] = true,
  ["function"] = true,   ["local"] = true,
}

for w in allwords() do
  if not reserved[w] then
    <do something with 'w'>    -- 'w' is not a reserved word
  end
end
```

(Because these words are reserved in Lua, we cannot use them as identifiers; for instance, we cannot write while=true. Instead, we use the ["while"]=true notation.)

You can have a clearer initialization using an auxiliary function to build the set:

```
function Set (list)
  local set = {}
  for _, l in ipairs(list) do set[l] = true end
  return set
end

reserved = Set{"while", "end", "function", "local", }
```

Bags, also called *multisets*, differ from regular sets in that each element may appear multiple times. An easy representation for bags in Lua is similar to the previous representation for sets, but where we associate a counter with each key. To insert an element we increment its counter:

```
function insert (bag, element)
  bag[element] = (bag[element] or 0) + 1
end
```

To remove an element we decrement its counter:

```
function remove (bag, element)
  local count = bag[element]
  bag[element] = (count and count > 1) and count - 1 or nil
end
```

We only keep the counter if it already exists and it is still greater than zero.

11.6 String Buffers

Suppose you are building a string piecemeal, for instance reading a file line by line. Your typical code would look like this:

```
local buff = ""
for line in io.lines() do
  buff = buff .. line .. "\n"
end
```

Despite its innocent look, this code in Lua can cause a huge performance penalty for large files: for instance, it takes almost a minute to read a 350 Kbyte file.

Why is that? To understand what happens, let us assume that we are in the middle of the read loop; each line has 20 bytes and we have already read some 2500 lines, so `buff` is a string with 50 Kbytes. When Lua concatenates `buff..line.."\n"`, it creates a new string with 50020 bytes and copies 50000 bytes from `buff` into this new string. That is, for each new line, Lua moves 50 Kbytes of memory, and growing. After reading 100 new lines (only 2 Kbytes), Lua has already moved more than 5 Mbytes of memory. More to the point, the algorithm is quadratic. When Lua finishes reading 350 Kbytes, it has moved around more than 50 Gbytes.

This problem is not peculiar to Lua: other languages wherein strings are immutable values present a similar behavior, Java being the most famous example.

Before we continue, we should remark that, despite all I said, this situation is not a common problem. For small strings, the above loop is fine. To read an entire file, Lua provides the `io.read("*all")` option, which reads the file at once. However, sometimes we must face this problem. Java offers the structure `StringBuffer` to ameliorate the problem. In Lua, we can use a table as the string buffer. The key to this approach is the `table.concat` function, which returns the concatenation of all the strings of a given list. Using `concat`, we can write our previous loop as follows:

```
local t = {}
for line in io.lines() do
  t[#t + 1] = line .. "\n"
end
local s = table.concat(t)
```

This algorithm takes less than 0.5 seconds to read the file that took almost a minute to read with the original code. (Of course, for reading a whole file it is better to use `io.read` with the "*all" option.)

We can do even better. The `concat` function accepts an optional second argument, which is a separator to be inserted between the strings. Using this separator, we do not need to insert a newline after each line:

```
local t = {}
for line in io.lines() do
  t[#t + 1] = line
end
s = table.concat(t, "\n") .. "\n"
```

Function `concat` inserts the separator between the strings, but we still have to add the last newline. This last concatenation duplicates the resulting string, which can be quite long. There is no option to make `concat` insert this extra separator, but we can deceive it, inserting an extra empty string in `t`:

```
t[#t + 1] = ""
s = table.concat(t, "\n")
```

The extra newline that `concat` adds before this empty string is at the end of the resulting string, as we wanted.

Internally, both `concat` and `io.read("*all")` use the same algorithm to concatenate many small strings. Several other functions from the standard libraries also use this algorithm to create large strings. Let us have a look at how it works.

Our original loop took a linear approach to the problem, concatenating small strings one by one into the accumulator. This new algorithm avoids this, using a binary approach instead. It concatenates several small strings among them and, occasionally, it concatenates the resulting large strings into larger ones. The heart of the algorithm is a stack that keeps the large strings already created in its bottom, while small strings enter through the top. The main invariant of this stack is similar to that of the popular (among programmers, at least) *Tower of Hanoi*: a string in the stack can never sit over a shorter string. Whenever a new string is pushed over a shorter one, then (and only then) the algorithm concatenates both. This concatenation creates a larger string, which now may be larger than its neighbor in the previous floor. If this happens, they are joined too. These concatenations go down the stack until the loop reaches a larger string or the stack bottom.

```
function addString (stack, s)
  stack[#stack + 1] = s        -- push 's' into the the stack
  for i = #stack-1, 1, -1 do
    if #stack[i] > #stack[i+1] then
      break
    end
    stack[i] = stack[i] .. stack[i + 1]
    stack[i + 1] = nil
  end
end
```

To get the final contents of the buffer, we just concatenate all strings down to the bottom.

11.7 Graphs

Like any reasonable language, Lua allows multiple implementations for graphs, each one better adapted to some particular algorithms. Here we will see a simple

Listing 11.1. Reading a graph from a file:

```
function readgraph ()
  local graph = {}
  for line in io.lines() do
    -- split line in two names
    local namefrom, nameto = string.match(line, "(%S+)%s+(%S+)")
    -- find corresponding nodes
    local from = name2node(graph, namefrom)
    local to = name2node(graph, nameto)
    -- adds 'to' to the adjacent set of 'from'
    from.adj[to] = true
  end
  return graph
end
```

object-oriented implementation, where we represent nodes as objects (actually tables, of course) and arcs as references between nodes.

We will represent each node as a table with two fields: name, with the node's name; and adj, the set of nodes adjacent to this one. Because we will read the graph from a text file, we need a way to find a node given its name. So, we will use an extra table mapping names to nodes. Given a name, function name2node returns the corresponding node:

```
local function name2node (graph, name)
  if not graph[name] then
    -- node does not exist; create a new one
    graph[name] = {name = name, adj = {}}
  end
  return graph[name]
end
```

Listing 11.1 shows the function that builds a graph. It reads a file where each line has two node names, meaning that there is an arc from the first node to the second. For each line, it uses string.match to split the line in two names, finds the nodes corresponding to these names (creating the nodes if needed), and connects the nodes.

Listing 11.2 illustrates an algorithm using such graphs. Function findpath searches for a path between two nodes using a depth-first traversal. Its first parameter is the current node; the second is its goal; the third parameter keeps the path from the origin to the current node; the last parameter is a set with all the nodes already visited (to avoid loops). Note how the algorithm manipulates nodes directly, without using their names. For instance, visited is a set of nodes, not of node names. Similarly, path is a list of nodes.

Listing 11.2. Finding a path between two nodes:

```
function findpath (curr, to, path, visited)
  path = path or {}
  visited = visited or {}
  if visited[curr] then        -- node already visited?
    return nil                 -- no path here
  end
  visited[curr] = true         -- mark node as visited
  path[#path + 1] = curr       -- add it to path
  if curr == to then           -- final node?
    return path
  end
  -- try all adjacent nodes
  for node in pairs(curr.adj) do
    local p = findpath(node, to, path, visited)
    if p then return p end
  end
  path[#path] = nil            -- remove node from path
end
```

To test this code, we add a function to print a path and some code to put it all to work:

```
function printpath (path)
  for i=1, #path do
    print(path[i].name)
  end
end

g = readgraph()
a = name2node(g, "a")
b = name2node(g, "b")
p = findpath(a, b)
if p then printpath(p) end
```

12

Data Files and Persistence

When dealing with data files, it is usually much easier to write the data than to read them back. When we write a file, we have full control of what is going on. When we read a file, on the other hand, we do not know what to expect. Besides all kinds of data that a correct file may contain, a robust program should also handle bad files gracefully. Therefore, coding robust input routines is always difficult.

In this chapter we will see how we can use Lua to eliminate all code for reading data from our programs, simply by writing the data in an appropriate format.

12.1 Data Files

As we saw in the example of Section 10.1, table constructors provide an interesting alternative for file formats. With a little extra work when writing data, reading becomes trivial. The technique is to write our data file as Lua code that, when run, builds the data into the program. With table constructors, these chunks can look remarkably like a plain data file.

As usual, let us see an example to make things clear. If our data file is in a predefined format, such as CSV (Comma-Separated Values) or XML, we have little choice. However, if we are going to create the file for our own use, we can use Lua constructors as our format. In this format, we represent each data record as a Lua constructor. Instead of writing in our data file something like

```
Donald E. Knuth,Literate Programming,CSLI,1992
Jon Bentley,More Programming Pearls,Addison-Wesley,1990
```

we write

```
Entry{"Donald E. Knuth",
      "Literate Programming",
      "CSLI",
      1992}

Entry{"Jon Bentley",
      "More Programming Pearls",
      "Addison-Wesley",
      1990}
```

Remember that Entry{*code*} is the same as Entry({*code*}), that is, a call to function Entry with a table as its single argument. So, that previous piece of data is a Lua program. To read that file, we only need to run it, with a sensible definition for Entry. For instance, the following program counts the number of entries in a data file:

```
local count = 0
function Entry (_) count = count + 1 end
dofile("data")
print("number of entries: " .. count)
```

The next program collects in a set the names of all authors found in the file, and then prints them (not necessarily in the same order as in the file):

```
local authors = {}        -- a set to collect authors
function Entry (b) authors[b[1]] = true end
dofile("data")
for name in pairs(authors) do print(name) end
```

Notice the event-driven approach in these program fragments: the Entry function acts as a callback function, which is called during the dofile for each entry in the data file.

When file size is not a big concern, we can use name-value pairs for our representation:[10]

```
Entry{
  author = "Donald E. Knuth",
  title = "Literate Programming",
  publisher = "CSLI",
  year = 1992
}

Entry{
  author = "Jon Bentley",
  title = "More Programming Pearls",
  year = 1990,
  publisher = "Addison-Wesley",
}
```

---

[10]If this format reminds you of BibTeX, it is not a coincidence. BibTeX was one of the inspirations for the constructor syntax in Lua.

This format is what we call a *self-describing data* format, because each piece of data has attached to it a short description of its meaning. Self-describing data are more readable (by humans, at least) than CSV or other compact notations; they are easy to edit by hand, when necessary; and they allow us to make small modifications in the basic format without having to change the data file. For instance, if we add a new field we need only a small change in the reading program, so that it supplies a default value when the field is absent.

With the name-value format, our program to collect authors becomes

```
local authors = {}        -- a set to collect authors
function Entry (b) authors[b.author] = true end
dofile("data")
for name in pairs(authors) do print(name) end
```

Now the order of fields is irrelevant. Even if some entries do not have an author, we have to adapt only the Entry function:

```
function Entry (b)
  if b.author then authors[b.author] = true end
end
```

Lua not only runs fast, but it also compiles fast. For instance, the above program for listing authors processes 2 Mbytes of data in less than one second. This is not by chance. Data description has been one of the main applications of Lua since its creation and we took great care to make its compiler fast for large programs.

12.2 Serialization

Frequently we need to serialize some data, that is, to convert the data into a stream of bytes or characters, so that we can save it into a file or send it through a network connection. We can represent serialized data as Lua code in such a way that, when we run the code, it reconstructs the saved values into the reading program.

Usually, if we want to restore the value of a global variable, our chunk will be something like varname=*exp*, where *exp* is the Lua code to create the value. The varname is the easy part, so let us see how to write the code that creates a value. For a numeric value, the task is easy:

```
function serialize (o)
  if type(o) == "number" then
    io.write(o)
  else <other cases>
  end
end
```

For a string value, a naive approach would be something like this:

```
if type(o) == "string" then
  io.write("'", o, "'")
```

However, if the string contains special characters (such as quotes or newlines) the resulting code will not be a valid Lua program.

You may be tempted to solve this problem changing quotes:

```
if type(o) == "string" then
  io.write("[[", o, "]]")
```

Beware! If a malicious user manages to direct your program to save something like "]]..os.execute('rm *')..[[" (for instance, she can supply this string as her address), your final chunk will be

```
varname = [[ ]]..os.execute('rm *')..[[ ]]
```

You will have a bad surprise trying to load this "data".

A simple way to quote a string in a secure way is with the option "%q" from the string.format function. It surrounds the string with double quotes and properly escapes double quotes, newlines, and some other characters inside the string:

```
a = 'a "problematic" \\string'
print(string.format("%q", a))     --> "a \"problematic\" \\string"
```

Using this feature, our serialize function now looks like this:

```
function serialize (o)
  if type(o) == "number" then
    io.write(o)
  elseif type(o) == "string" then
    io.write(string.format("%q", o))
  else <other cases>
  end
end
```

Lua 5.1 offers another option to quote arbitrary strings in a secure way, with the new notation [=[...]=] for long strings. However, this new notation is mainly intended for hand-written code, where we do not want to change a literal string in any way. In automatically generated code, it is easier to escape problematic characters, as the option "%q" from string.format does.

If you nevertheless want to use the long-string notation for automatically generated code, you must take care of some details. The first one is that you must choose a proper number of equal signs. A good proper number is one more than the maximum that appears in the original string. Because strings containing long sequences of equal signs are not uncommon (e.g., comments delimiting parts of a source code), we can limit our attention to sequences of equal signs preceded by a closing square bracket; other sequences cannot produce an erroneous end-of-string mark. The second detail is that a newline at the beginning of a long string is always ignored; a simple way to avoid this problem is to always add a newline to be ignored.

Listing 12.1. Quoting arbitrary literal strings:

```
function quote (s)
  -- find maximum length of sequences of equal signs
  local n = -1
  for w in string.gmatch(s, "]=*") do
    n = math.max(n, #w - 1)
  end

  -- produce a string with 'n' plus one equal signs
  local eq = string.rep("=", n + 1)

  -- build quoted string
  return string.format(" [%s[\n%s]%s] ", eq, s, eq)
end
```

The quote function (Listing 12.1) is the result of our previous remarks. It receives an arbitrary string and returns it formatted as a long string. The call to string.gmatch creates an iterator to traverse all occurrences of the pattern ']=*' (that is, a closing square bracket followed by a sequence of zero or more equal signs) in the string s.[11] For each occurrence, the loop updates n with the maximum number of equal signs so far. After the loop we use string.rep to replicate an equal sign n+1 times, which is one more than the maximum occurring in the string. Finally, string.format encloses s with pairs of brackets with the correct number of equal signs in between and adds extra spaces around the quoted string plus a newline at the beginning of the enclosed string.

Saving tables without cycles

Our next (and harder) task is to save tables. There are several ways to save them, according to what restrictions we assume about the table structure. No single algorithm is appropriate for all cases. Simple tables not only need simpler algorithms, but the resulting files can be more aesthetic, too.

Our first attempt is in Listing 12.2. Despite its simplicity, that function does a reasonable job. It even handles nested tables (that is, tables within other tables), as long as the table structure is a tree (that is, there are no shared subtables and no cycles). A small aesthetic improvement would be to indent occasional nested tables; you can try it as an exercise. (Hint: add an extra parameter to serialize with the indentation string.)

The previous function assumes that all keys in a table are valid identifiers. If a table has numeric keys, or string keys which are not syntactic valid Lua identifiers, we are in trouble. A simple way to solve this difficulty is to change the line

```
        io.write("  ", k, " = ")
```

[11]We will discuss pattern matching in Chapter 20.

Listing 12.2. Serializing tables without cycles:

```
function serialize (o)
  if type(o) == "number" then
    io.write(o)
  elseif type(o) == "string" then
    io.write(string.format("%q", o))
  elseif type(o) == "table" then
    io.write("{\n")
    for k,v in pairs(o) do
      io.write("  ", k, " = ")
      serialize(v)
      io.write(",\n")
    end
    io.write("}\n")
  else
    error("cannot serialize a " .. type(o))
  end
end
```

to

```
      io.write("  ["); serialize(k); io.write("] = ")
```

With this change, we improve the robustness of our function, at the cost of the aesthetics of the resulting file. The result of

```
serialize{a=12, b='Lua', key='another "one"'}
```

with the first version of serialize is this:

```
{
  a = 12,
  b = "Lua",
  key = "another \"one\"",
}
```

Compare it to the second version:

```
{
  ["a"] = 12,
  ["b"] = "Lua",
  ["key"] = "another \"one\"",
}
```

We can improve this result by testing for each case whether it needs the square brackets; again, we will leave this improvement as an exercise.

Listing 12.3. Saving tables with cycles:

```
function basicSerialize (o)
  if type(o) == "number" then
    return tostring(o)
  else    -- assume it is a string
    return string.format("%q", o)
  end
end

function save (name, value, saved)
  saved = saved or {}                    -- initial value
  io.write(name, " = ")
  if type(value) == "number" or type(value) == "string" then
    io.write(basicSerialize(value), "\n")
  elseif type(value) == "table" then
    if saved[value] then                 -- value already saved?
      io.write(saved[value], "\n")       -- use its previous name
    else
      saved[value] = name                -- save name for next time
      io.write("{}\n")                    -- create a new table
      for k,v in pairs(value) do         -- save its fields
        k = basicSerialize(k)
        local fname = string.format("%s[%s]", name, k)
        save(fname, v, saved)
      end
    end
  else
    error("cannot save a " .. type(value))
  end
end
```

Saving tables with cycles

To handle tables with generic topology (i.e., with cycles and shared subtables)
we need a different approach. Constructors cannot represent such tables, so we
will not use them. To represent cycles we need names, so our next function will
get as arguments the value to be saved plus its name. Moreover, we must keep
track of the names of the tables already saved, to reuse them when we detect a
cycle. We will use an extra table for this tracking. This table will have tables as
indices and their names as the associated values.

The resulting code is in Listing 12.3. We keep the restriction that the tables
we want to save have only strings and numbers as keys. The basicSerialize
function serializes these basic types, returning the result. The next function,
save, does the hard work. The saved parameter is the table that keeps track of

tables already saved. As an example, if we build a table like

```
a = {x=1, y=2; {3,4,5}}
a[2] = a    -- cycle
a.z = a[1]  -- shared subtable
```

then the call save("a", a) will save it as follows:

```
a = {}
a[1] = {}
a[1][1] = 3
a[1][2] = 4
a[1][3] = 5

a[2] = a
a["y"] = 2
a["x"] = 1
a["z"] = a[1]
```

The actual order of these assignments may vary, as it depends on a table traversal. Nevertheless, the algorithm ensures that any previous node needed in a new definition is already defined.

If we want to save several values with shared parts, we can make the calls to save using the same saved table. For instance, assume the following two tables:

```
a = {{"one", "two"}, 3}
b = {k = a[1]}
```

If we save them independently, the result will not have common parts:

```
save("a", a)
save("b", b)

  --> a = {}
  --> a[1] = {}
  --> a[1][1] = "one"
  --> a[1][2] = "two"
  --> a[2] = 3
  --> b = {}
  --> b["k"] = {}
  --> b["k"][1] = "one"
  --> b["k"][2] = "two"
```

However, if we use the same saved table for both calls to save, then the result will share common parts:

```
local t = {}
save("a", a, t)
save("b", b, t)
```

```
--> a = {}
--> a[1] = {}
--> a[1][1] = "one"
--> a[1][2] = "two"
--> a[2] = 3
--> b = {}
--> b["k"] = a[1]
```

As is usual in Lua, there are several other alternatives. Among them, we can save a value without giving it a global name (instead, the chunk builds a local value and returns it), we can handle functions (by building an auxiliary table that associates each function to its name), and so on. Lua gives you the power; you build the mechanisms.

13

Metatables and Metamethods

Usually, each value in Lua has a quite predictable set of operations. We can add numbers, we can concatenate strings, we can insert key–value pairs into tables, and so on. But we cannot add tables, we cannot compare functions, and we cannot call a string.

Metatables allow us to change the behavior of a value when confronted with an undefined operation. For instance, using metatables, we can define how Lua computes the expression a+b, where a and b are tables. Whenever Lua tries to add two tables, it checks whether either of them has a *metatable* and whether this metatable has an __add field. If Lua finds this field, it calls the corresponding value — the so-called *metamethod*, which should be a function — to compute the sum.

Each value in Lua may have a metatable. Tables and userdata have individual metatables; values of other types share one single metatable for all values of that type.[12] Lua always creates new tables without metatables:

```
t = {}
print(getmetatable(t))    --> nil
```

We can use setmetatable to set or change the metatable of any table:

```
t1 = {}
setmetatable(t, t1)
assert(getmetatable(t) == t1)
```

---

[12] In Lua 5.0, only tables and userdata could have metatables. More often than not, these are the types that we want to control with metatables.

Any table can be the metatable of any value; a group of related tables may share a common metatable, which describes their common behavior; a table can be its own metatable, so that it describes its own individual behavior. Any configuration is valid.

From Lua we can set the metatables only of tables; to manipulate the metatables of values of other types we must use C code. (The main reason for this restriction is to curb excessive use of type-wide metatables. Experience with older versions of Lua has shown that those settings frequently lead to non-reusable code.) As we will see later, in Chapter 20, the string library sets a metatable for strings. All other types by default have no metatable:

```
print(getmetatable("hi"))              --> table: 0x80772e0
print(getmetatable(10))                --> nil
```

13.1 Arithmetic Metamethods

In this section, we will introduce a simple example to explain how to use metatables. Suppose we are using tables to represent sets, with functions to compute the union of two sets, intersection, and the like. To keep our namespace clean, we store these functions inside a table called Set:

```
Set = {}

-- create a new set with the values of the given list
function Set.new (l)
  local set = {}
  for _, v in ipairs(l) do set[v] = true end
  return set
end

function Set.union (a, b)
  local res = Set.new{}
  for k in pairs(a) do res[k] = true end
  for k in pairs(b) do res[k] = true end
  return res
end

function Set.intersection (a, b)
  local res = Set.new{}
  for k in pairs(a) do
    res[k] = b[k]
  end
  return res
end
```

To help checking our examples, we also define a function to print sets:

```
function Set.tostring (set)
  local l = {}     -- list to put all elements from the set
  for e in pairs(set) do
    l[#l + 1] = e
  end
  return "{" .. table.concat(l, ", ") .. "}"
end

function Set.print (s)
  print(Set.tostring(s))
end
```

Now, we want to make the addition operator ('+') compute the union of two sets. For that, we will arrange for all tables representing sets to share a metatable, which will define how they react to the addition operator. Our first step is to create a regular table that we will use as the metatable for sets:

```
local mt = {}     -- metatable for sets
```

The next step is to modify the Set.new function, which creates sets. The new version has only one extra line, which sets mt as the metatable for the tables that it creates:

```
function Set.new (l)    -- 2nd version
  local set = {}
  setmetatable(set, mt)
  for _, v in ipairs(l) do set[v] = true end
  return set
end
```

After that, every set we create with Set.new will have that same table as its metatable:

```
s1 = Set.new{10, 20, 30, 50}
s2 = Set.new{30, 1}
print(getmetatable(s1))         --> table: 00672B60
print(getmetatable(s2))         --> table: 00672B60
```

Finally, we add to the metatable the metamethod, a field __add that describes how to perform the addition:

```
mt.__add = Set.union
```

After that, whenever Lua tries to add two sets it will call the Set.union function, with the two operands as arguments.

With the metamethod in place, we can use the addition operator to do set unions:

```
s3 = s1 + s2
Set.print(s3)   --> {1, 10, 20, 30, 50}
```

Similarly, we may set the multiplication operator to perform set intersection:

```
mt.__mul = Set.intersection

Set.print((s1 + s2)*s1)     --> {10, 20, 30, 50}
```

For each arithmetic operator there is a corresponding field name in a metatable. Besides `__add` and `__mul`, there are `__sub` (for subtraction), `__div` (for division), `__unm` (for negation), `__mod` (for modulo), and `__pow` (for exponentiation). We may define also the field `__concat`, to describe a behavior for the concatenation operator.

When we add two sets, there is no question about what metatable to use. However, we may write an expression that mixes two values with different metatables, for instance like this:

```
s = Set.new{1,2,3}
s = s + 8
```

When looking for a metamethod, Lua does the following steps: if the first value has a metatable with an `__add` field, Lua uses this field as the metamethod, independently of the second value; otherwise, if the second value has a metatable with an `__add` field, Lua uses this field as the metamethod; otherwise, Lua raises an error. Therefore, the last example will call `Set.union`, as will the expressions `10+s` and `"hello"+s`.

Lua does not care about these mixed types, but our implementation does. If we run the `s=s+8` example, the error we get will be inside `Set.union`:

```
bad argument #1 to 'pairs' (table expected, got number)
```

If we want more lucid error messages, we must check the type of the operands explicitly before attempting to perform the operation:

```
function Set.union (a, b)
  if getmetatable(a) ~= mt or getmetatable(b) ~= mt then
    error("attempt to 'add' a set with a non-set value", 2)
  end
  <as before>
```

Remember that the second argument to `error` (2, in this example) directs the error message to where the operation was called.

13.2   Relational Metamethods

Metatables also allow us to give meaning to the relational operators, through the metamethods `__eq` (*equal to*), `__lt` (*less than*), and `__le` (*less than or equal to*). There are no separate metamethods for the other three relational operators, as Lua translates `a~=b` to `not (a==b)`, `a>b` to `b<a`, and `a>=b` to `b<=a`.

Until Lua 4.0, all order operators were translated to a single one, by translating `a<=b` to `not (b<a)`. However, this translation is incorrect when we have

a *partial order*, that is, when not all elements in our type are properly ordered. For instance, floating-point numbers are not totally ordered in most machines, because of the value *Not a Number* (*NaN*). According to the IEEE 754 standard, currently adopted by virtually all floating-point hardware, NaN represents undefined values, such as the result of 0/0. The standard specifies that any comparison that involves NaN should result in false. This means that NaN<=x is always false, but x<NaN is also false. It also implies that the translation from a<=b to not (b<a) is not valid in this case.

In our example with sets, we have a similar problem. An obvious (and useful) meaning for <= in sets is set containment: a<=b means that a is a subset of b. With this meaning, again it is possible that both a<=b and b<a are false; therefore, we need separate implementations for __le (*less or equal*) and __lt (*less than*):

```
mt.__le = function (a, b)    -- set containment
  for k in pairs(a) do
    if not b[k] then return false end
  end
  return true
end
mt.__lt = function (a, b)
  return a <= b and not (b <= a)
end
```

Finally, we can define set equality through set containment:

```
mt.__eq = function (a, b)
  return a <= b and b <= a
end
```

After these definitions, we are ready to compare sets:

```
s1 = Set.new{2, 4}
s2 = Set.new{4, 10, 2}
print(s1 <= s2)       --> true
print(s1 < s2)        --> true
print(s1 >= s1)       --> true
print(s1 > s1)        --> false
print(s1 == s2 * s1)  --> true
```

Unlike arithmetic metamethods, relational metamethods cannot be applied to mixed types. Their behavior for mixed types mimics the common behavior of these operators in Lua. If you try to compare a string with a number for order, Lua raises an error. Similarly, if you try to compare two objects with different metamethods for order, Lua raises an error.

An equality comparison never raises an error, but if two objects have different metamethods, the equality operation results in false, without even calling any metamethod. Again, this behavior mimics the common behavior of Lua, which always classifies strings as different from numbers, regardless of their values. Lua calls an equality metamethod only when the two objects being compared share that metamethod.

13.3 Library-Defined Metamethods

It is a common practice for libraries to define their own fields in metatables. So far, all the metamethods we have seen are for the Lua core. It is the virtual machine that detects that the values involved in an operation have metatables and that these metatables define metamethods for that operation. However, because metatables are regular tables, anyone can use them.

Function `tostring` provides a typical example. As we saw earlier, `tostring` represents tables in a rather simple format:

```
print({})        --> table: 0x8062ac0
```

(Function `print` always calls `tostring` to format its output.) However, when formatting any value, `tostring` first checks whether the value has a `__tostring` metamethod. In this case, `tostring` calls the metamethod to do its job, passing the object as an argument. Whatever this metamethod returns is the result of `tostring`.

In our example with sets, we have already defined a function to present a set as a string. So, we need only to set the `__tostring` field in the metatable:

```
mt.__tostring = Set.tostring
```

After that, whenever we call `print` with a set as its argument, `print` calls `tostring` that calls `Set.tostring`:

```
s1 = Set.new{10, 4, 5}
print(s1)      --> {4, 5, 10}
```

Functions `setmetatable` and `getmetatable` also use a metafield, in this case to protect metatables. Suppose you want to protect your sets, so that users can neither see nor change their metatables. If you set a `__metatable` field in the metatable, `getmetatable` will return the value of this field, whereas `setmetatable` will raise an error:

```
mt.__metatable = "not your business"

s1 = Set.new{}
print(getmetatable(s1))      --> not your business
setmetatable(s1, {})
  stdin:1: cannot change protected metatable
```

13.4 Table-Access Metamethods

The metamethods for arithmetic and relational operators all define behavior for otherwise erroneous situations. They do not change the normal behavior of the language. But Lua also offers a way to change the behavior of tables for two normal situations, the query and modification of absent fields in a table.

The __index metamethod

I said earlier that, when we access an absent field in a table, the result is **nil**. This is true, but it is not the whole truth. Actually, such accesses trigger the interpreter to look for an __index metamethod: if there is no such method, as usually happens, then the access results in **nil**; otherwise, the metamethod will provide the result.

The archetypal example here is inheritance. Suppose we want to create several tables describing windows. Each table must describe several window parameters, such as position, size, color scheme, and the like. All these parameters have default values and so we want to build window objects giving only the non-default parameters. A first alternative is to provide a constructor that fills in the absent fields. A second alternative is to arrange for the new windows to *inherit* any absent field from a prototype window. First, we declare the prototype and a constructor function, which creates new windows sharing a metatable:

```
Window = {}          -- create a namespace
-- create the prototype with default values
Window.prototype = {x=0, y=0, width=100, height=100}
Window.mt = {}       -- create a metatable
-- declare the constructor function
function Window.new (o)
  setmetatable(o, Window.mt)
  return o
end
```

Now, we define the __index metamethod:

```
Window.mt.__index = function (table, key)
  return Window.prototype[key]
end
```

After this code, we create a new window and query it for an absent field:

```
w = Window.new{x=10, y=20}
print(w.width)     --> 100
```

When Lua detects that w does not have the requested field, but has a metatable with an __index field, Lua calls this __index metamethod, with arguments w (the table) and "width" (the absent key). The metamethod then indexes the prototype with the given key and returns the result.

The use of the __index metamethod for inheritance is so common that Lua provides a shortcut. Despite the name, the __index metamethod does not need to be a function: it can be a table, instead. When it is a function, Lua calls it with the table and the absent key as its arguments, as we have just seen. When it is a table, Lua redoes the access in this table. Therefore, in our previous example, we could declare __index simply like this:

```
Window.mt.__index = Window.prototype
```

Now, when Lua looks for the metatable's `__index` field, it finds the value of `Window.prototype`, which is a table. Consequently, Lua repeats the access in this table, that is, it executes the equivalent of the following code:

```
Window.prototype["width"]
```

This access then gives the desired result.

The use of a table as an `__index` metamethod provides a fast and simple way of implementing single inheritance. A function, although more expensive, provides more flexibility: we can implement multiple inheritance, caching, and several other variations. We will discuss these forms of inheritance in Chapter 16.

When we want to access a table without invoking its `__index` metamethod, we use the `rawget` function. The call `rawget(t,i)` does a *raw* access to table t, that is, a primitive access without considering metatables. Doing a raw access will not speed up your code (the overhead of a function call kills any gain you could have), but sometimes you need it, as we will see later.

The `__newindex` metamethod

The `__newindex` metamethod does for table updates what `__index` does for table accesses. When you assign a value to an absent index in a table, the interpreter looks for a `__newindex` metamethod: if there is one, the interpreter calls it instead of making the assignment. Like `__index`, if the metamethod is a table, the interpreter does the assignment in this table, instead of in the original one. Moreover, there is a raw function that allows you to bypass the metamethod: the call `rawset(t,k,v)` sets the value v associated with key k in table t without invoking any metamethod.

The combined use of `__index` and `__newindex` metamethods allows several powerful constructs in Lua, such as read-only tables, tables with default values, and inheritance for object-oriented programming. In this chapter we will see some of these uses. Object-oriented programming has its own chapter.

Tables with default values

The default value of any field in a regular table is **nil**. It is easy to change this default value with metatables:

```
function setDefault (t, d)
  local mt = {__index = function () return d end}
  setmetatable(t, mt)
end

tab = {x=10, y=20}
print(tab.x, tab.z)      --> 10    nil
setDefault(tab, 0)
print(tab.x, tab.z)      --> 10    0
```

After the call to `setDefault`, any access to an absent field in `tab` calls its `__index` metamethod, which returns zero (the value of `d` for this metamethod).

The `setDefault` function creates a new metatable for each table that needs a default value. This may be expensive if we have many tables that need default values. However, the metatable has the default value `d` wired into its metamethod, so the function cannot use a single metatable for all tables. To allow the use of a single metatable for tables with different default values, we can store the default value of each table in the table itself, using an exclusive field. If we are not worried about name clashes, we can use a key like "`___`" for our exclusive field:

```
local mt = {__index = function (t) return t.___ end}
function setDefault (t, d)
  t.___ = d
  setmetatable(t, mt)
end
```

If we are worried about name clashes, it is easy to ensure the uniqueness of this special key. All we need is to create a new table and use it as the key:

```
local key = {}     -- unique key
local mt = {__index = function (t) return t[key] end}
function setDefault (t, d)
  t[key] = d
  setmetatable(t, mt)
end
```

An alternative approach for associating each table with its default value is to use a separate table, where the indices are the tables and the values are their default values. However, for the correct implementation of this approach we need a special breed of table, called *weak tables*, and so we will not use it here; we will return to the subject in Chapter 17.

Another alternative is to *memoize* metatables in order to reuse the same metatable for tables with the same default. However, that needs weak tables too, so that again we will have to wait until Chapter 17.

Tracking table accesses

Both `__index` and `__newindex` are relevant only when the index does not exist in the table. The only way to catch all accesses to a table is to keep it empty. So, if we want to monitor all accesses to a table, we should create a *proxy* for the real table. This proxy is an empty table, with proper `__index` and `__newindex` metamethods that track all accesses and redirect them to the original table. Suppose that `t` is the original table we want to track. We can write something like this:

```
t = {}   -- original table (created somewhere)

-- keep a private access to the original table
local _t = t
```

```
-- create proxy
t = {}

-- create metatable
local mt = {
  __index = function (t, k)
    print("*access to element " .. tostring(k))
    return _t[k]    -- access the original table
  end,

  __newindex = function (t, k, v)
    print("*update of element " .. tostring(k) ..
          " to " .. tostring(v))
    _t[k] = v    -- update original table
  end
}
setmetatable(t, mt)
```

This code tracks every access to t:

```
> t[2] = "hello"
*update of element 2 to hello
> print(t[2])
*access to element 2
hello
```

(Notice that, unfortunately, this scheme does not allow us to traverse tables. The pairs function will operate on the proxy, not on the original table.)

If we want to monitor several tables, we do not need a different metatable for each one. Instead, we can somehow associate each proxy to its original table and share a common metatable for all proxies. This problem is similar to the problem of associating tables to their default values, which we discussed in the previous section. For instance, we can keep the original table in a proxy's field, using an exclusive key. The result is the following code:

```
local index = {}              -- create private index

local mt = {                  -- create metatable
  __index = function (t, k)
    print("*access to element " .. tostring(k))
    return t[index][k]    -- access the original table
  end,

  __newindex = function (t, k, v)
    print("*update of element " .. tostring(k) ..
                    " to " .. tostring(v))
    t[index][k] = v    -- update original table
  end
}
```

```
function track (t)
  local proxy = {}
  proxy[index] = t
  setmetatable(proxy, mt)
  return proxy
end
```

Now, whenever we want to monitor a table t, all we have to do is to execute t=track(t).

Read-only tables

It is easy to adapt the concept of proxies to implement read-only tables. All we have to do is to raise an error whenever we track any attempt to update the table. For the __index metamethod, we can use a table—the original table itself—instead of a function, as we do not need to track queries; it is simpler and rather more efficient to redirect all queries to the original table. This use, however, demands a new metatable for each read-only proxy, with __index pointing to the original table:

```
function readOnly (t)
  local proxy = {}
  local mt = {        -- create metatable
    __index = t,
    __newindex = function (t, k, v)
      error("attempt to update a read-only table", 2)
    end
  }
  setmetatable(proxy, mt)
  return proxy
end
```

As an example of use, we can create a read-only table for weekdays:

```
days = readOnly{"Sunday", "Monday", "Tuesday", "Wednesday",
        "Thursday", "Friday", "Saturday"}

print(days[1])      --> Sunday
days[2] = "Noday"
stdin:1: attempt to update a read-only table
```

14

The Environment

Lua keeps all its global variables in a regular table, called the *environment*. (To be more precise, Lua keeps its "global" variables in several environments, but we will ignore this multiplicity for a while.) One advantage of this structure is that it simplifies the internal implementation of Lua, because there is no need for a different data structure for global variables. The other (actually the main) advantage is that we can manipulate this table as any other table. To facilitate such manipulations, Lua stores the environment itself in a global variable _G. (Yes, _G._G is equal to _G.) For instance, the following code prints the names of all global variables defined in the current environment:

```
for n in pairs(_G) do print(n) end
```

In this chapter, we will see several useful techniques for manipulating the environment.

14.1   Global Variables with Dynamic Names

Usually, assignment is enough for accessing and setting global variables. However, often we need some form of meta-programming, such as when we need to manipulate a global variable whose name is stored in another variable, or somehow computed at run time. To get the value of this variable, many programmers are tempted to write something like this:

```
value = loadstring("return " .. varname)()
```

If varname is x, for example, the concatenation will result in "return x", which when run achieves the desired result. However, this code involves the creation and compilation of a new chunk. You can accomplish the same effect with the following code, which is more than an order of magnitude more efficient than the previous one:

```
value = _G[varname]
```

Because the environment is a regular table, you can simply index it with the desired key (the variable name).

In a similar way, you can assign a value to a global variable whose name is computed dynamically, writing _G[varname]=value. Beware, however: some programmers get a little excited with these facilities and end up writing code like _G["a"]=_G["var1"], which is just a complicated way to write a=var1.

A generalization of the previous problem is to allow fields in the dynamic name, such as "io.read" or "a.b.c.d". If we write _G["io.read"], we do not get the read field from the io table. But we can write a function getfield such that getfield("io.read") returns the expected result. This function is mainly a loop, which starts at _G and evolves field by field:

```
function getfield (f)
  local v = _G     -- start with the table of globals
  for w in string.gmatch(f, "[%w_]+") do
    v = v[w]
  end
  return v
end
```

We rely on gmatch, from the string library, to iterate over all words in f (where "word" is a sequence of one or more alphanumeric characters and underscores).

The corresponding function to set fields is a little more complex. An assignment like a.b.c.d=v is equivalent to the following code:

```
local temp = a.b.c
temp.d = v
```

That is, we must retrieve up to the last name and then handle it separately. The next setfield function does the task, and also creates intermediate tables in a path when they do not exist:

```
function setfield (f, v)
  local t = _G               -- start with the table of globals
  for w, d in string.gmatch(f, "([%w_]+)(.?)") do
    if d == "." then         -- not last field?
      t[w] = t[w] or {}      -- create table if absent
      t = t[w]               -- get the table
    else                     -- last field
      t[w] = v               -- do the assignment
    end
  end
end
```

This new pattern captures the field name in variable w and an optional following dot in variable d.[13] If a field name is not followed by a dot then it is the last name.

With the previous functions in place, the call

```
setfield("t.x.y", 10)
```

creates a global table t, another table t.x, and assigns 10 to t.x.y:

```
print(t.x.y)      --> 10
print(getfield("t.x.y"))   --> 10
```

14.2 Global-Variable Declarations

Global variables in Lua do not need declarations. Although this is handy for small programs, in larger programs a simple typo can cause bugs that are difficult to find. However, we can change this behavior if we like. Because Lua keeps its global variables in a regular table, we can use metatables to change its behavior when accessing global variables.

A first approach simply detects any access to absent keys in the global table:

```
setmetatable(_G, {
  __newindex = function (_, n)
    error("attempt to write to undeclared variable " .. n, 2)
  end,
  __index = function (_, n)
    error("attempt to read undeclared variable " .. n, 2)
  end,
})
```

After this code, any attempt to access a non-existent global variable will trigger an error:

```
> print(a)
stdin:1: attempt to read undeclared variable a
```

But how do we declare new variables? One option is to use rawset, which bypasses the metamethod:

```
function declare (name, initval)
  rawset(_G, name, initval or false)
end
```

(The **or** with **false** ensures that the new global always gets a value different from **nil**.) A simpler way is to allow assignments to global variables in the main chunk, so that we declare variables as here:

```
a = 1
```

---

[13]We will discuss pattern matching at great length in Chapter 20.

To check whether the assignment is in the main chunk, we can use the debug library. The call `debug.getinfo(2, "S")` returns a table whose field `what` tells whether the function that called the metamethod is a main chunk, a regular Lua function, or a C function.[14] Using this function, we can rewrite the `__newindex` metamethod like this:

```
__newindex = function (t, n, v)
  local w = debug.getinfo(2, "S").what
  if w ~= "main" and w ~= "C" then
    error("attempt to write to undeclared variable " .. n, 2)
  end
  rawset(t, n, v)
end
```

This new version also accepts assignments from C code, as this kind of code usually knows what it is doing.

To test whether a variable exists, we cannot simply compare it to **nil** because, if it is **nil**, the access will throw an error. Instead, we use `rawget`, which avoids the metamethod:

```
if rawget(_G, var) == nil then
  -- 'var' is undeclared
  ...
end
```

As it is, our scheme does not allow global variables with nil values, as they would be automatically considered undeclared. But it is not difficult to correct this problem. All we need is an auxiliary table that keeps the names of declared variables. Whenever a metamethod is called, it checks in this table whether the variable is undeclared or not. The code may be like in Listing 14.1. Now even an assignment like `x=nil` is enough to declare a global variable.

For both solutions, the overhead is negligible. With the first solution, the metamethods are never called during normal operation. In the second, they may be called, but only when the program accesses a variable holding a **nil**.

The Lua distribution comes with a module `strict.lua` that implements a global-variable check that uses essentially the code we just reviewed. It is a good habit to use it when developing Lua code.

14.3   Non-Global Environments

One of the problems with the environment is that it is global. Any modification you do on it affects all parts of your program. For instance, when you install a metatable to control global access, your whole program must follow the guidelines. If you want to use a library that uses global variables without declaring them, you are in bad luck.

---

[14]We will see `debug.getinfo` in more detail in Chapter 23.

Listing 14.1. Checking global-variable declaration:

```
local declaredNames = {}

setmetatable(_G, {
  __newindex = function (t, n, v)
    if not declaredNames[n] then
      local w = debug.getinfo(2, "S").what
      if w ~= "main" and w ~= "C" then
        error("attempt to write to undeclared variable "..n, 2)
      end
      declaredNames[n] = true
    end
    rawset(t, n, v)   -- do the actual set
  end,

  __index = function (_, n)
    if not declaredNames[n] then
      error("attempt to read undeclared variable "..n, 2)
    else
      return nil
    end
  end,
})
```

Lua 5 ameliorated this problem by allowing each function to have its own environment, wherein it looks for global variables. This facility may sound strange at first; after all, the goal of a table of global variables is to be global. However, in Section 15.3 we will see that this facility allows several interesting constructions, where global values are still available everywhere.

You can change the environment of a function with the setfenv function (*set function environment*). It takes as arguments the function and the new environment. Instead of the function itself, you can also give a number, meaning the active function at that given stack level. Number 1 means the current function, number 2 means the function calling the current function (which is handy to write auxiliary functions that change the environment of their caller), and so on.

A naive first attempt to use setfenv fails miserably. The code

```
a = 1   -- create a global variable
-- change current environment to a new empty table
setfenv(1, {})
print(a)
```

results in

```
stdin:5: attempt to call global 'print' (a nil value)
```

(You must run this code in a single chunk. If you enter it line by line in interactive mode, each line is a different function and the call to setfenv affects only its own line.) Once you change your environment, all global accesses will use the new table. If it is empty, you have lost all your global variables, even _G. So, you should first populate it with some useful values, such as the old environment:

```
a = 1                       -- create a global variable
setfenv(1, {g = _G})        -- change current environment
g.print(a)                  --> nil
g.print(g.a)                --> 1
```

Now, when you access the "global" g, its value is the old environment, wherein you will find the field print.

We can rewrite the previous example using the name _G instead of g:

```
setfenv(1, {_G = _G})
_G.print(a)                 --> nil
_G.print(_G.a)              --> 1
```

For Lua, _G is a name like any other. Its only special status happens when Lua creates the initial global table and assigns this table to the global variable _G. Lua does not care about the current value of this variable; setfenv does not set it in new environments. But it is customary to use this same name whenever we have a reference to the initial global table, as we did in the rewritten example.

Another way to populate your new environment is with inheritance:

```
a = 1
local newgt = {}            -- create new environment
setmetatable(newgt, {__index = _G})
setfenv(1, newgt)           -- set it
print(a)                    --> 1
```

In this code, the new environment inherits both print and a from the old one. Nevertheless, any assignment goes to the new table. There is no danger of changing a really global variable by mistake, although you still can change them through _G:

```
-- continuing previous code
a = 10
print(a)                    --> 10
print(_G.a)                 --> 1
_G.a = 20
print(_G.a)                 --> 20
```

Each function, or more specifically each closure, has an independent environment. The next chunk illustrates this mechanism:

```
function factory ()
  return function ()
          return a          -- "global" a
        end
end
```

```
a = 3
f1 = factory()
f2 = factory()
print(f1())          --> 3
print(f2())          --> 3

setfenv(f1, {a = 10})
print(f1())          --> 10
print(f2())          --> 3
```

The factory function creates simple closures that return the value of their global a. Each call to factory creates a new closure with its own environment. When you create a new function, it inherits its environment from the function creating it. So, when created, these closures share the global environment, where the value of a is 3. The call setfenv(f1,{a=10}) changes the environment of f1 to a new environment where the value of a is 10, without affecting the environment of f2.

Because new functions inherit their environments from the function creating them, if a chunk changes its own environment, all functions it defines afterward will share this new environment. This is a useful mechanism for creating namespaces, as we will see in the next chapter.

15

Modules and Packages

Usually, Lua does not set policies. Instead, Lua provides mechanisms that are powerful enough for groups of developers to implement the policies that best suit them. However, this approach does not work well for modules. One of the main goals of a module system is to allow different groups to share code. The lack of a common policy impedes this sharing.

Starting in version 5.1, Lua defines a set of policies for modules and packages (a package being a collection of modules). These policies do not demand any extra facility from the language; programmers can implement them using what we have seen so far: tables, functions, metatables, and environments. However, two important functions ease the adoption of these policies: `require`, for using modules, and `module`, for building modules. Programmers are free to re-implement these functions with different policies. Of course, alternative implementations may lead to programs that cannot use foreign modules and modules that cannot be used by foreign programs.

From the user point of view, a *module* is a library that can be loaded through `require` and that defines one single global name containing a table. Everything that the module exports, such as functions and constants, it defines inside this table, which works as a namespace. A well-behaved module also arranges for `require` to return this table.

An obvious benefit of using tables to implement modules is that we can manipulate modules like any other table and use the whole power of Lua to create extra facilities. In most languages, modules are not first-class values (that is, they cannot be stored in variables, passed as arguments to functions, etc.), so those languages need special mechanisms for each extra facility they want to offer for modules. In Lua, you get extra facilities for free.

For instance, there are several ways for a user to call a function from a module. The simplest is this:

```
require "mod"
mod.foo()
```

If she prefers a shorter name for the module, she can set a local name for it:

```
local m = require "mod"
m.foo()
```

She can also rename individual functions:

```
require "mod"
local f = mod.foo
f()
```

The nice thing about these facilities is that they involve no explicit support from the language. They use what the language already offers.

15.1   The require **Function**

Lua offers a high-level function to load modules, called require. This function tries to keep to a minimum its assumptions about what a module is. For require, a module is just any chunk of code that defines some values (such as functions or tables containing functions).

To load a module, we simply call require "*modname*". Typically, this call returns a table comprising the module functions, and it also defines a global variable containing this table. However, these actions are done by the module, not by require, so some modules may choose to return other values or to have different side effects.

It is a good programming practice always to require the modules you need, even if you know that they would be already loaded. You may exclude the standard libraries from this rule, because they are pre-loaded in Lua. Nevertheless, some people prefer to use an explicit require even for them:

```
local m = require "io"
m.write("hello world\n")
```

Listing 15.1 details the behavior of require. Its first step is to check in table package.loaded whether the module is already loaded. If so, require returns its corresponding value. Therefore, once a module is loaded, other calls to require simply return the same value, without loading the module again.

If the module is not loaded yet, require tries to find a *loader* for this module. (This step is illustrated by the abstract function findloader in Listing 15.1.) Its first attempt is to query the given library name in table package.preload. If it finds a function there, it uses this function as the module loader. This preload table provides a generic method to handle some non-conventional situations (e.g., C libraries statically linked to Lua). Usually, this table does not have an entry for the module, so require will search first for a Lua file and then for a C library to load the module from.

If require finds a Lua file for the given module, it loads it with loadfile; otherwise, if it finds a C library, it loads it with loadlib. Remember that both

Listing 15.1. The require function:

```
function require (name)
  if not package.loaded[name] then      -- module not loaded yet?
    local loader = findloader(name)
    if loader == nil then
      error("unable to load module " .. name)
    end
    package.loaded[name] = true          -- mark module as loaded
    local res = loader(name)             -- initialize module
    if res ~= nil then
      package.loaded[name] = res
    end
  end
  return package.loaded[name]
end
```

loadfile and loadlib only load some code, without running it. To run the code, require calls it with a single argument, the module name. If the loader returns any value, require returns this value and stores it in table package.loaded to return the same value in future calls for this same library. If the loader returns no value, require returns whatever value is in table package.loaded. As we will see later in this chapter, a module can put the value to be returned by require directly into package.loaded.

An important detail of that previous code is that, before calling the loader, require marks the module as already loaded, assigning **true** to the respective field in package.loaded. Therefore, if the module requires another module and that in turn recursively requires the original module, this last call to require returns immediately, avoiding an infinite loop.

To force require into loading the same library twice, we simply erase the library entry from package.loaded. For instance, after a successful require "foo", package.loaded["foo"] will not be **nil**. The following code will load the library again:

```
package.loaded["foo"] = nil
require "foo"
```

When searching for a file, require uses a path that is a little different from typical paths. The path used by most programs is a list of directories wherein to search for a given file. However, ANSI C (the abstract platform where Lua runs) does not have the concept of directories. Therefore, the path used by require is a list of *patterns*, each of them specifying an alternative way to transform a module name (the argument to require) into a file name. More specifically, each component in the path is a file name containing optional question marks. For each component, require replaces the module name for each '?' and checks whether there is a file with the resulting name; if not, it goes to the next component. The components in a path are separated by semicolons (a character seldom used for file names in most operating systems). For instance, if the path is

```
?;?.lua;c:\windows\?;/usr/local/lua/?/?.lua
```

then the call `require "sql"` will try to open the following files:

```
sql
sql.lua
c:\windows\sql
/usr/local/lua/sql/sql.lua
```

The `require` function assumes only the semicolon (as the component separator) and the question mark; everything else, such as directory separators or file extensions, is defined by the path itself.

The path that `require` uses to search for Lua files is always the current value of the variable `package.path`. When Lua starts, it initializes this variable with the value of the environment variable LUA_PATH or with a compiled-defined default path, if this environment variable is not defined. When using LUA_PATH, Lua substitutes the default path for any substring "; ;". For instance, if you set LUA_PATH to "mydir/?.lua; ;", the final path will be the component "mydir/?.lua" followed by the default path.

If `require` cannot find a Lua file compatible with the module name, it looks for a C library. For this search, it gets the path from variable `package.cpath` (instead of `package.path`). This variable gets its initial value from the environment variable LUA_CPATH (instead of LUA_PATH). A typical value for this variable in Unix is like this:

```
./?.so;/usr/local/lib/lua/5.1/?.so
```

Note that the file extension is defined by the path (e.g., the previous example uses `.so` for all templates). In Windows, a typical path is more like this one:

```
.\?.dll;C:\Program Files\Lua501\dll\?.dll
```

Once it finds a C library, `require` loads it with `package.loadlib`, which we discussed in Section 8.2. Unlike Lua chunks, C libraries do not define one single main function. Instead, they can export several C functions. Well-behaved C libraries should export one function called luaopen_*modname*, which is the function that `require` tries to call after linking the library. In Section 26.2 we will discuss how to write C libraries.

Usually, we use modules with their original names, but sometimes we must rename a module to avoid name clashes. A typical situation is when we need to load different versions of the same module, for instance for testing. For a Lua module, either it does not have its name fixed internally (as we will see later) or we can easily edit it to change its name. But we cannot edit a binary module to correct the name of its luaopen_* function. To allow for such renamings, `require` uses a small trick: if the module name contains a hyphen, `require`

strips from the name its prefix up to the hyphen when creating the `luaopen_*`
function name. For instance, if a module is named a-b, `require` expects its open
function to be named `luaopen_b`, instead of `luaopen_a-b` (which would not be a
valid C name anyway). So, if we need to use two modules named `mod`, we can
rename one of them to v1-mod (or -mod, or anything like that). When we call
`m1 = require "v1-mod"`, `require` will find both the renamed file v1-mod and, inside
this file, the function with the original name `luaopen_mod`.

15.2   The Basic Approach for Writing Modules

The simplest way to create a module in Lua is really simple: we create a table,
put all functions we want to export inside it, and return this table. Listing 15.2
illustrates this approach. Note how we define `inv` as a private name simply by
declaring it local to the chunk.

The use of tables for modules does not provide exactly the same functionality
as provided by real modules. First, we must explicitly put the module name
in every function definition. Second, a function that calls another function
inside the same module must qualify the name of the called function. We
can ameliorate these problems using a fixed local name for the module (M,
for instance), and then assigning this local to the final name of the module.
Following this guideline, we would write our previous module like this:

```
local M = {}
complex = M              -- module name

M.i = {r=0, i=1}
function M.new (r, i) return {r=r, i=i} end

function M.add (c1, c2)
  return M.new(c1.r + c2.r, c1.i + c2.i)
end

    <as before>
```

Whenever a function calls another function inside the same module (or whenever it calls itself recursively), it still needs to prefix the name. At least, the
connection between the two functions does not depend on the module name anymore. Moreover, there is only one place in the whole module where we write
the module name. Actually, we can avoid writing the module name altogether,
because `require` passes it as an argument to the module:

```
local modname = ...
local M = {}
_G[modname] = M

M.i = {r=0, i=1}
    <as before>
```

Listing 15.2. A simple module:

```
complex = {}

function complex.new (r, i) return {r=r, i=i} end

-- defines a constant 'i'
complex.i = complex.new(0, 1)

function complex.add (c1, c2)
  return complex.new(c1.r + c2.r, c1.i + c2.i)
end

function complex.sub (c1, c2)
  return complex.new(c1.r - c2.r, c1.i - c2.i)
end

function complex.mul (c1, c2)
  return complex.new(c1.r*c2.r - c1.i*c2.i,
                     c1.r*c2.i + c1.i*c2.r)
end

local function inv (c)
  local n = c.r^2 + c.i^2
  return complex.new(c.r/n, -c.i/n)
end

function complex.div (c1, c2)
  return complex.mul(c1, inv(c2))
end

return complex
```

With this change, all we have to do to rename a module is to rename the file that defines it.

Another small improvement relates to the closing return statement. It would be nice if we could concentrate all module-related setup tasks at the beginning of the module. One way of eliminating the need for the return statement is to assign the module table directly into package.loaded:

```
local modname = ...
local M = {}
_G[modname] = M
package.loaded[modname] = M
  <as before>
```

With this assignment, we do not need to return M at the end of the module: remember that, if a module does not return a value, require returns the current value of package.loaded[modname].

15.3 Using Environments

A major drawback of that basic method for creating modules is that it calls for special attention from the programmer. She must qualify names when accessing other public entities inside the same module. She has to change the calls whenever she changes the status of a function from private to public (or from public to private). Moreover, it is all too easy to forget a **local** in a private declaration.

Function environments offer an interesting technique for creating modules that solves all these problems. Once the module main chunk has an exclusive environment, not only all its functions share this table, but also all its global variables go to this table. Therefore, we can declare all public functions as global variables and they will go to a separate table automatically. All the module has to do is to assign this table to the module name and also to package.loaded. The next code fragment illustrates this technique:

```
local modname = ...
local M = {}
_G[modname] = M
package.loaded[modname] = M
setfenv(1, M)
```

Now, when we declare function add, it goes to complex.add:

```
function add (c1, c2)
  return new(c1.r + c2.r, c1.i + c2.i)
end
```

Moreover, we can call other functions from the same module without any prefix. For instance, add gets new from its environment, that is, it gets complex.new.

This method offers a good support for modules, with little extra work for the programmer. It needs no prefixes at all. There is no difference between calling an exported and a private function. If the programmer forgets a **local**, he does not pollute the global namespace; instead, a private function simply becomes public.

What is missing, of course, is access to other modules. Once we make the empty table M our environment, we lose access to all previous global variables. There are several ways to recover this access, each with its pros and cons.

The simplest solution is inheritance, as we saw earlier:

```
local modname = ...
local M = {}
_G[modname] = M
package.loaded[modname] = M
setmetatable(M, {__index = _G})
setfenv(1, M)
```

(You must call `setmetatable` before calling `setfenv`; can you tell why?) With this construction, the module has direct access to any global identifier, paying a small overhead for each access. A funny consequence of this solution is that, conceptually, your module now contains all global variables. For instance, someone using your module may call the standard sine function by writing `complex.math.sin(x)`. (Perl's package system has this peculiarity, too.)

Another quick method of accessing other modules is to declare a local that holds the old environment:

```
local modname = ...
local M = {}
_G[modname] = M
package.loaded[modname] = M
local _G = _G
setfenv(1, M)
```

Now you must prefix any global-variable name with `_G.`, but the access is a little faster, because there is no metamethod involved.

A more disciplined approach is to declare as locals only the functions you need, or at most the modules you need:

```
-- module setup
local modname = ...
local M = {}
_G[modname] = M
package.loaded[modname] = M

-- Import Section:
-- declare everything this module needs from outside
local sqrt = math.sqrt
local io = io

-- no more external access after this point
setfenv(1, M)
```

This technique demands more work, but it documents your module dependencies better. It also results in code that runs faster than code with the previous schemes.

15.4   The `module` Function

Probably you noticed the repetitions of code in our previous examples. All of them started with this same pattern:

```
local modname = ...
local M = {}
_G[modname] = M
package.loaded[modname] = M
   <setup for external access>
setfenv(1, M)
```

Lua 5.1 provides a new function, called `module`, that packs this functionality. Instead of this previous setup code, we can start a module simply like this:

```
module(...)
```

This call creates a new table, assigns it to the appropriate global variable and to the `loaded` table, and then sets the table as the environment of the main chunk.

By default, `module` does not provide external access: before calling it, you must declare appropriate local variables with the external functions or modules you want to access. You can also use inheritance for external access adding the option `package.seeall` to the call to `module`. This option does the equivalent of the following code:

```
setmetatable(M, {__index = _G})
```

Therefore, simply adding the statement

```
module(..., package.seeall)
```

in the beginning of a file turns it into a module; you can write everything else like regular Lua code. You need to qualify neither module names nor external names. You do not need to write the module name (actually, you do not even need to know the module name). You do not need to worry about returning the module table. All you have to do is to add that single statement.

The `module` function provides some extra facilities. Most modules do not need these facilities, but some distributions need some special treatment (e.g., to create a module that contains both C functions and Lua functions). Before creating the module table, `module` checks whether `package.loaded` already contains a table for this module, or whether a variable with the given name already exists. If it finds a table in one of these places, `module` reuses this table for the module; this means we can use `module` for reopening a module already created. If the module does not exist yet, then `module` creates the module table. After that, it populates the table with some predefined variables: `_M` contains the module table itself (it is an equivalent of `_G`); `_NAME` contains the module name (the first argument passed to `module`); and `_PACKAGE` contains the package name (the name without the last component; see next section).

15.5 Submodules and Packages

Lua allows module names to be hierarchical, using a dot to separate name levels. For instance, a module named `mod.sub` is a *submodule* of `mod`. Accordingly, you may assume that module `mod.sub` will define all its values inside a table `mod.sub`, that is, inside a table stored with key `sub` in table `mod`. A *package* is a complete tree of modules; it is the unit of distribution in Lua.

When you require a module called `mod.sub`, `require` queries first the table `package.loaded` and then the table `package.preload` using the original module name "`mod.sub`" as the key; the dot has no significance whatsoever in this search.

However, when searching for a file that defines that submodule, `require` translates the dot into another character, usually the system's directory separator (e.g., '/' for Unix or '\' for Windows). After the translation, `require` searches for the resulting name like any other name. For instance, assuming the path

```
./?.lua;/usr/local/lua/?.lua;/usr/local/lua/?/init.lua
```

and '/' as the directory separator, the call `require "a.b"` will try to open the following files:

```
./a/b.lua
/usr/local/lua/a/b.lua
/usr/local/lua/a/b/init.lua
```

This behavior allows all modules of a package to live in a single directory. For instance, if a package has modules p, p.a, and p.b, their respective files can be named p/init.lua, p/a.lua, and p/b.lua, with the directory p within some appropriate directory.

The directory separator used by Lua is configured at compile time and can be any string (remember, Lua knows nothing about directories). For instance, systems without hierarchical directories can use a '_' as the "directory" separator, so that `require "a.b"` will search for a file a_b.lua.

C-function names cannot contain dots, so a C library for submodule a.b cannot export a function `luaopen_a.b`. Here `require` translates the dot into another character, an underscore. So, a C library named a.b should name its initialization function `luaopen_a_b`. We can use the hyphen trick here too, with some subtle results. For instance, if we have a C library a and we want to make it a submodule of mod, we can rename the file to mod/-a. When we write `require "mod.-a"`, `require` correctly finds the new file mod/-a as well as the function `luaopen_a` inside it.

As an extra facility, `require` has one more option for loading C submodules. When it cannot find either a Lua file or a C file for a submodule, it again searches the C path, but this time looking for the package name. For example, if the program requires a submodule a.b.c, and `require` cannot find a file when looking for a/b/c, this last search will look for a. If it finds a C library with this name, then `require` looks into this library for an appropriate open function, `luaopen_a_b_c` in this example. This facility allows a distribution to put several submodules together into a single C library, each with its own open function.

The `module` function also offers explicit support for submodules. When we create a submodule, with a call like `module("a.b.c")`, `module` puts the environment table into variable a.b.c, that is, into a field c of a table in field b of a table a. If any of these intermediate tables do not exist, `module` creates them. Otherwise, it reuses them.

From the Lua point of view, submodules in the same package have no explicit relationship other than that their environment tables may be nested. Requiring a module a does not automatically load any of its submodules; similarly, requiring a.b does not automatically load a. Of course, the package implementer is free to create these links if she wants. For instance, a particular module a may start by explicitly requiring one or all of its submodules.

16

Object-Oriented Programming

A table in Lua is an object in more than one sense. Like objects, tables have a state. Like objects, tables have an identity (a *self*) that is independent of their values; specifically, two objects (tables) with the same value are different objects, whereas an object can have different values at different times. Like objects, tables have a life cycle that is independent of who created them or where they were created.

Objects have their own operations. Tables also can have operations:

```
Account = {balance = 0}
function Account.withdraw (v)
  Account.balance = Account.balance - v
end
```

This definition creates a new function and stores it in field `withdraw` of the Account object. Then, we can call it as

```
Account.withdraw(100.00)
```

This kind of function is almost what we call a *method*. However, the use of the global name `Account` inside the function is a bad programming practice. First, this function will work only for this particular object. Second, even for this particular object, the function will work only as long as the object is stored in that particular global variable. If we change the object's name, `withdraw` does not work any more:

```
a = Account; Account = nil
a.withdraw(100.00)      -- ERROR!
```

Such behavior violates the previous principle that objects have independent life cycles.

A more flexible approach is to operate on the *receiver* of the operation. For that, our method would need an extra parameter with the value of the receiver. This parameter usually has the name *self* or *this*:

```
function Account.withdraw (self, v)
  self.balance = self.balance - v
end
```

Now, when we call the method we have to specify the object it has to operate on:

```
a1 = Account; Account = nil
...
a1.withdraw(a1, 100.00)    -- OK
```

With the use of a *self* parameter, we can use the same method for many objects:

```
a2 = {balance=0, withdraw = Account.withdraw}
...
a2.withdraw(a2, 260.00)
```

This use of a *self* parameter is a central point in any object-oriented language. Most OO languages have this mechanism partly hidden from the programmer, so that she does not have to declare this parameter (although she still can use the name *self* or *this* inside a method). Lua also can hide this parameter, using the *colon operator*. We can rewrite the previous method definition as

```
function Account:withdraw (v)
  self.balance = self.balance - v
end
```

and the method call as

```
a:withdraw(100.00)
```

The effect of the colon is to add an extra hidden parameter in a method definition and to add an extra argument in a method call. The colon is only a syntactic facility, although a convenient one; there is nothing really new here. We can define a function with the dot syntax and call it with the colon syntax, or vice-versa, as long as we handle the extra parameter correctly:

```
Account = { balance=0,
            withdraw = function (self, v)
                         self.balance = self.balance - v
                       end
          }
function Account:deposit (v)
  self.balance = self.balance + v
end
```

```
Account.deposit(Account, 200.00)
Account:withdraw(100.00)
```

Our objects have an identity, a state, and operations over this state. They still lack a class system, inheritance, and privacy. Let us tackle the first problem: how can we create several objects with similar behavior? Specifically, how can we create several accounts?

16.1 Classes

A *class* works as a mold for the creation of objects. Several object-oriented languages offer the concept of class. In such languages, each object is an instance of a specific class. Lua does not have the concept of class; each object defines its own behavior and has a shape of its own. Nevertheless, it is not difficult to emulate classes in Lua, following the lead from prototype-based languages like Self and NewtonScript. In these languages, objects have no classes. Instead, each object may have a prototype, which is a regular object where the first object looks up any operation that it does not know about. To represent a class in such languages, we simply create an object to be used exclusively as a prototype for other objects (its instances). Both classes and prototypes work as a place to put behavior to be shared by several objects.

In Lua, it is trivial to implement prototypes, using the idea of inheritance that we saw in Section 13.4. More specifically, if we have two objects a and b, all we have to do to make b a prototype for a is this:

```
setmetatable(a, {__index = b})
```

After that, a looks up in b for any operation that it does not have. To see b as the class of object a is not much more than a change in terminology.

Let us go back to our example of a bank account. To create other accounts with behavior similar to Account, we arrange for these new objects to inherit their operations from Account, using the __index metamethod. A small optimization is that we do not need to create an extra table to be the metatable of the account objects; instead, we use the Account table itself for this purpose:

```
function Account:new (o)
  o = o or {}   -- create table if user does not provide one
  setmetatable(o, self)
  self.__index = self
  return o
end
```

(When we call Account:new, self is equal to Account; so, we could have used Account directly, instead of self. However, the use of self will fit nicely when we introduce class inheritance, in the next section.) After this code, what happens when we create a new account and call a method on it?

```
a = Account:new{balance = 0}
a:deposit(100.00)
```

When we create the new account, a will have `Account` (the *self* in the call to `Account:new`) as its metatable. Then, when we call a:deposit(100.00), we are actually calling a.deposit(a, 100.00); the colon is only syntactic sugar. However, Lua cannot find a "deposit" entry in table a; so, it looks into the metatable's __index entry. The situation now is more or less like this:

```
getmetatable(a).__index.deposit(a, 100.00)
```

The metatable of a is `Account` and `Account.__index` is also `Account` (because the new method did self.__index=self). Therefore, the previous expression reduces to

```
Account.deposit(a, 100.00)
```

That is, Lua calls the original deposit function, but passing a as the *self* parameter. So, the new account a inherited the deposit function from `Account`. By the same mechanism, it can inherit all fields from `Account`.

The inheritance works not only for methods, but also for other fields that are absent in the new account. Therefore, a class can provide not only methods, but also default values for its instance fields. Remember that, in our first definition of `Account`, we provided a field balance with value 0. So, if we create a new account without an initial balance, it will inherit this default value:

```
b = Account:new()
print(b.balance)      --> 0
```

When we call the deposit method on b, it runs the equivalent of

```
b.balance = b.balance + v
```

(because `self` is b). The expression b.balance evaluates to zero and an initial deposit is assigned to b.balance. Subsequent accesses to b.balance will not invoke the index metamethod, because now b has its own balance field.

16.2   Inheritance

Because classes are objects, they can get methods from other classes, too. This behavior makes inheritance (in the usual object-oriented meaning) quite easy to implement in Lua.

Let us assume we have a base class like `Account`:

```
Account = {balance = 0}

function Account:new (o)
  o = o or {}
  setmetatable(o, self)
  self.__index = self
  return o
end
```

```
function Account:deposit (v)
  self.balance = self.balance + v
end

function Account:withdraw (v)
  if v > self.balance then error"insufficient funds" end
  self.balance = self.balance - v
end
```

From this class, we want to derive a subclass SpecialAccount that allows the customer to withdraw more than his balance. We start with an empty class that simply inherits all its operations from its base class:

```
SpecialAccount = Account:new()
```

Up to now, SpecialAccount is just an instance of Account. The nice thing happens now:

```
s = SpecialAccount:new{limit=1000.00}
```

SpecialAccount inherits new from Account like any other method. This time, however, when new executes, its self parameter will refer to SpecialAccount. Therefore, the metatable of s will be SpecialAccount, whose value at field __index is also SpecialAccount. So, s inherits from SpecialAccount, which inherits from Account. When we evaluate

```
s:deposit(100.00)
```

Lua cannot find a deposit field in s, so it looks into SpecialAccount; it cannot find a deposit field there, too, so it looks into Account and there it finds the original implementation for a deposit.

What makes a SpecialAccount special is that we can redefine any method inherited from its superclass. All we have to do is to write the new method:

```
function SpecialAccount:withdraw (v)
  if v - self.balance >= self:getLimit() then
    error"insufficient funds"
  end
  self.balance = self.balance - v
end

function SpecialAccount:getLimit ()
  return self.limit or 0
end
```

Now, when we call s:withdraw(200.00), Lua does not go to Account, because it finds the new withdraw method in SpecialAccount first. Because s.limit is 1000.00 (remember that we set this field when we created s), the program does the withdrawal, leaving s with a negative balance.

An interesting aspect of objects in Lua is that you do not need to create a new class to specify a new behavior. If only a single object needs a specific behavior, you can implement that behavior directly in the object. For instance, if the account s represents some special client whose limit is always 10% of her balance, you can modify only this single account:

```
function s:getLimit ()
  return self.balance * 0.10
end
```

After this declaration, the call s:withdraw(200.00) runs the withdraw method from SpecialAccount, but when withdraw calls self:getLimit, it is this last definition that it invokes.

16.3   Multiple Inheritance

Because objects are not primitive in Lua, there are several ways to do object-oriented programming in Lua. The approach that we have seen, using the index metamethod, is probably the best combination of simplicity, performance, and flexibility. Nevertheless, there are other implementations, which may be more appropriate for some particular cases. Here we will see an alternative implementation that allows multiple inheritance in Lua.

The key to this implementation is the use of a function for the metafield __index. Remember that, when a table's metatable has a function in the __index field, Lua will call this function whenever it cannot find a key in the original table. Then, __index can look up for the missing key in how many parents it wants.

Multiple inheritance means that a class may have more than one superclass. Therefore, we cannot use a class method to create subclasses. Instead, we will define a specific function for this purpose, createClass, which has as arguments the superclasses of the new class (see Listing 16.1). This function creates a table to represent the new class, and sets its metatable with an __index metamethod that does the multiple inheritance. Despite the multiple inheritance, each object instance still belongs to one single class, where it looks for all its methods. Therefore, the relationship between classes and superclasses is different from the relationship between classes and instances. Particularly, a class cannot be the metatable for its instances and for its subclasses at the same time. In Listing 16.1, we keep the class as the metatable for its instances, and create another table to be the class' metatable.

Let us illustrate the use of createClass with a small example. Assume our previous class Account and another class, Named, with only two methods, setname and getname:

```
Named = {}
function Named:getname ()
  return self.name
end
function Named:setname (n)
  self.name = n
end
```

Listing 16.1. An implementation of Multiple Inheritance:

```
-- look up for 'k' in list of tables 'plist'
local function search (k, plist)
  for i=1, #plist do
    local v = plist[i][k]      -- try 'i'-th superclass
    if v then return v end
  end
end

function createClass (...)
  local c = {}          -- new class
  local parents = {...}

  -- class will search for each method in the list of its parents
  setmetatable(c, {__index = function (t, k)
    return search(k, parents)
  end})

  -- prepare 'c' to be the metatable of its instances
  c.__index = c

  -- define a new constructor for this new class
  function c:new (o)
    o = o or {}
    setmetatable(o, c)
    return o
  end

  return c                -- return new class
end
```

To create a new class NamedAccount that is a subclass of both Account and Named, we simply call createClass:

```
NamedAccount = createClass(Account, Named)
```

To create and to use instances, we do as usual:

```
account = NamedAccount:new{name = "Paul"}
print(account:getname())    --> Paul
```

Now let us follow how this last statement works. Lua cannot find the field "getname" in account; so, it looks for the field __index of account's metatable, which is NamedAccount. But NamedAccount also cannot provide a "getname" field, so Lua looks for the field __index of NamedAccount's metatable. Because this field contains a function, Lua calls it. This function then looks for "getname" first in Account, without success, and then in Named, where it finds a non-nil value, which is the final result of the search.

Of course, due to the underlying complexity of this search, the performance of multiple inheritance is not the same as single inheritance. A simple way to improve this performance is to copy inherited methods into the subclasses. Using this technique, the index metamethod for classes would be like this:

```
setmetatable(c, {__index = function (t, k)
  local v = search(k, parents)
  t[k] = v          -- save for next access
  return v
end})
```

With this trick, accesses to inherited methods are as fast as to local methods (except for the first access). The drawback is that it is difficult to change method definitions after the system is running, because these changes do not propagate down the hierarchy chain.

16.4   Privacy

Many people consider privacy to be an integral part of an object-oriented language; the state of each object should be its own internal affair. In some object-oriented languages, such as C++ and Java, you can control whether an object field (also called an *instance variable*) or a method is visible outside the object. Other languages, such as Smalltalk, make all variables private and all methods public. The first object-oriented language, Simula, did not offer any kind of protection.

The main design for objects in Lua, which we have shown previously, does not offer privacy mechanisms. Partly, this is a consequence of our use of a general structure (tables) to represent objects. But this also reflects some basic design decisions behind Lua. Lua is not intended for building huge programs, where many programmers are involved for long periods. Quite the opposite, Lua aims at small to medium programs, usually part of a larger system, typically developed by one or a few programmers, or even by non programmers. Therefore, Lua avoids too much redundancy and artificial restrictions. If you do not want to access something inside an object, just *do not do it*.

Nevertheless, another aim of Lua is to be flexible, offering to the programmer meta-mechanisms that enable her to emulate many different mechanisms. Although the basic design for objects in Lua does not offer privacy mechanisms, we can implement objects in a different way, so as to have access control. Although this implementation is not used frequently, it is instructive to know about it, both because it explores some interesting corners of Lua and because it can be a good solution for other problems.

The basic idea of this alternative design is to represent each object through two tables: one for its state; another for its operations, or its *interface*. The object itself is accessed through the second table, that is, through the operations that compose its interface. To avoid unauthorized access, the table that represents the state of an object is not kept in a field of the other table; instead, it is kept only in the closure of the methods. For instance, to represent our bank account with this design, we could create new objects running the following factory function:

```
function newAccount (initialBalance)
  local self = {balance = initialBalance}

  local withdraw = function (v)
                     self.balance = self.balance - v
                   end
  local deposit = function (v)
                    self.balance = self.balance + v
                  end

  local getBalance = function () return self.balance end

  return {
    withdraw = withdraw,
    deposit = deposit,
    getBalance = getBalance
  }
end
```

First, the function creates a table to keep the internal object state and stores it in the local variable self. Then, the function creates the methods of the object. Finally, the function creates and returns the external object, which maps method names to the actual method implementations. The key point here is that these methods do not get self as an extra parameter; instead, they access self directly. Because there is no extra argument, we do not use the colon syntax to manipulate such objects. The methods are called just like regular functions:

```
acc1 = newAccount(100.00)
acc1.withdraw(40.00)
print(acc1.getBalance())     --> 60
```

This design gives full privacy to anything stored in the self table. After newAccount returns, there is no way to gain direct access to this table. We can access it only through the functions created inside newAccount. Although our example puts only one instance variable into the private table, we can store all private parts of an object in this table. We can also define private methods: they are like public methods, but we do not put them in the interface. For instance, our accounts may give an extra credit of 10% for users with balances above a certain limit, but we do not want the users to have access to the details of that computation. We can implement this functionality as follows:

```
function newAccount (initialBalance)
  local self = {
    balance = initialBalance,
    LIM = 10000.00,
  }
```

```
local extra = function ()
  if self.balance > self.LIM then
    return self.balance*0.10
  else
    return 0
  end
end

local getBalance = function ()
  return self.balance + extra()
end
```

<as before>

Again, there is no way for any user to access the extra function directly.

16.5   The Single-Method Approach

A particular case of the previous approach for object-oriented programming
occurs when an object has a single method. In such cases, we do not need to
create an interface table; instead, we can return this single method as the object
representation. If this sounds a little weird, it is worth remembering Section 7.1,
where we saw how to construct iterator functions that keep state as closures. An
iterator that keeps state is nothing more than a single-method object.

Another interesting case of single-method objects occurs when this single-
method is actually a dispatch method that performs different tasks based on
a distinguished argument. A possible implementation for such an object is as
follows:

```
function newObject (value)
  return function (action, v)
    if action == "get" then return value
    elseif action == "set" then value = v
    else error("invalid action")
    end
  end
end
```

Its use is straightforward:

```
d = newObject(0)
print(d("get"))     --> 0
d("set", 10)
print(d("get"))     --> 10
```

This unconventional implementation for objects is quite effective. The syntax
d("set",10), although peculiar, is only two characters longer than the more
conventional d:set(10). Each object uses one single closure, which is cheaper

than one table. There is no inheritance, but we have full privacy: the only way to access an object state is through its sole method.

Tcl/Tk uses a similar approach for its widgets. The name of a widget in Tk denotes a function (a *widget command*) that can perform all kinds of operations over the widget.

17

Weak Tables

Lua does automatic memory management. A program only creates objects (tables, functions, etc.); there is no function to delete objects. Lua automatically deletes objects that become garbage, using *garbage collection*. This frees you from most of the burden of memory management and, more important, frees you from most of the bugs related to this activity, such as dangling pointers and memory leaks.

Unlike some other collectors, Lua's garbage collector has no problems with cycles. You do not need to take any special action when using cyclic data structures; they are collected like any other data. Nevertheless, sometimes even the smarter collector needs your help. No garbage collector allows you to forget all worries about memory management.

A garbage collector can collect only what it can be sure is garbage; it cannot guess what you consider garbage. A typical example is a stack, implemented with an array and an index to the top. You know that the valid part of the array goes only up to the top, but Lua does not. If you pop an element by simply decrementing the top, the object left in the array is not garbage for Lua. Similarly, any object stored in a global variable is not garbage for Lua, even if your program will never use it again. In both cases, it is up to you (i.e., your program) to assign **nil** to these positions so that they do not lock an otherwise free object.

However, simply cleaning your references is not always enough. Some constructions need extra collaboration between the program and the collector. A typical example happens when you want to keep a collection of all live objects of some kind (e.g., files) in your program. This task seems simple: all you have to do is to insert each new object into the collection. However, once the object is inside the collection, it will never be collected! Even if no one else points to it, the collection does. Lua cannot know that this reference should not prevent the reclamation of the object, unless you tell Lua about this fact.

Weak tables are the mechanism that you use to tell Lua that a reference should not prevent the reclamation of an object. A *weak reference* is a reference to an object that is not considered by the garbage collector. If all references pointing to an object are weak, the object is collected and somehow these weak references are deleted. Lua implements weak references as weak tables: A *weak table* is a table whose entries are weak. This means that, if an object is held only inside weak tables, Lua will eventually collect the object.

Tables have keys and values, and both may contain any kind of object. Under normal circumstances, the garbage collector does not collect objects that appear as keys or as values of an accessible table. That is, both keys and values are *strong* references, as they prevent the reclamation of objects they refer to. In a weak table, keys and values may be weak. This means that there are three kinds of weak tables: tables with weak keys, tables with weak values, and fully weak tables, where both keys and values are weak. Irrespective of the table kind, when a key or a value is collected the whole entry disappears from the table.

The weakness of a table is given by the field __mode of its metatable. The value of this field, when present, should be a string: if this string contains the letter 'k', the keys in the table are weak; if this string contains the letter 'v', the values in the table are weak. The following example, although artificial, illustrates the basic behavior of weak tables:

```
a = {}
b = {__mode = "k"}
setmetatable(a, b)      -- now 'a' has weak keys
key = {}                -- creates first key
a[key] = 1
key = {}                -- creates second key
a[key] = 2
collectgarbage()        -- forces a garbage collection cycle
for k, v in pairs(a) do print(v) end
   --> 2
```

In this example, the second assignment key={} overwrites the first key. When the collector runs, there is no other reference to the first key, so it is collected and the corresponding entry in the table is removed. The second key, however, is still anchored in variable key, so it is not collected.

Notice that only objects can be collected from a weak table. Values, such as numbers and booleans, are not collectible. For instance, if we insert a numeric key in table a (from our previous example), it will never be removed by the collector. Of course, if the value corresponding to a numeric key is collected, then the whole entry is removed from the weak table.

Strings present a subtlety here: although strings are collectible, from an implementation point of view, they are not like other collectible objects. Other objects, such as tables and functions, are created explicitly. For instance, whenever

Lua evaluates the expression {}, it creates a new table. Whenever it evaluates function() ... end, it creates a new function (a closure, actually). However, does Lua create a new string when it evaluates "a".."b"? What if there is already a string "ab" in the system? Does Lua create a new one? Can the compiler create this string before running the program? It does not matter: these are implementation details. From the programmer's point of view, strings are values, not objects. Therefore, like a number or a boolean, a string is not removed from weak tables (unless its associated value is collected).

17.1 Memoize Functions

A common programming technique is to trade space for time. You can speed up some functions by *memoizing* their results so that, later, when you call the function with the same argument, it can reuse the result.

Imagine a generic server that receives requests containing strings with Lua code. Each time it gets a request, it runs loadstring on the string, and then calls the resulting function. However, loadstring is an expensive function, and some commands to the server may be quite frequent. Instead of calling loadstring repeatedly each time it receives a common command like "closeconnection()", the server can *memoize* the results from loadstring using an auxiliary table. Before calling loadstring, the server checks in the table whether the given string already has a translation. If it cannot find the string, then (and only then) the server calls loadstring and stores the result into the table. We can pack this behavior in a new function:

```
local results = {}
function mem_loadstring (s)
  local res = results[s]
  if res == nil then                 -- result not available?
    res = assert(loadstring(s))      -- compute new result
    results[s] = res                 -- save for later reuse
  end
  return res
end
```

The savings with this scheme can be huge. However, it may also cause unsuspected waste. Although some commands repeat over and over, many other commands happen only once. Gradually, the table results accumulates all commands the server has ever received plus their respective codes; after enough time, this behavior will exhaust the server's memory. A weak table provides a simple solution to this problem. If the results table has weak values, each garbage-collection cycle will remove all translations not in use at that moment (which means virtually all of them):

```
local results = {}
setmetatable(results, {__mode = "v"})  -- make values weak
function mem_loadstring (s)
  <as before>
```

Actually, because the indices are always strings, we can make this table fully weak, if we want:

```
setmetatable(results, {__mode = "kv"})
```

The net result is the same.

The memoize technique is useful also to ensure the uniqueness of some kind of object. For instance, assume a system that represents colors as tables, with fields red, green, and blue in some range. A naive color factory generates a new color for each new request:

```
function createRGB (r, g, b)
   return {red = r, green = g, blue = b}
end
```

Using the memoize technique, we can reuse the same table for the same color. To create a unique key for each color, we simply concatenate the color indices with a separator in between:

```
local results = {}
setmetatable(results, {__mode = "v"})   -- make values weak
function createRGB (r, g, b)
  local key = r .. "-" .. g .. "-" .. b
  local color = results[key]
  if color == nil then
    color = {red = r, green = g, blue = b}
    results[key] = color
  end
  return color
end
```

An interesting consequence of this implementation is that the user can compare colors using the primitive equality operator, because two coexistent equal colors are always represented by the same table. Note that the same color may be represented by different tables at different times, because from time to time a garbage-collector cycle clears the results table. However, as long as a given color is in use, it is not removed from results. So, whenever a color survives long enough to be compared with a new one, its representation also survives long enough to be reused by the new color.

17.2   Object Attributes

Another important use of weak tables is to associate attributes with objects. There are endless situations where we need to attach some attribute to an object: names to functions, default values to tables, sizes to arrays, and so on.

When the object is a table, we can store the attribute in the table itself, with an appropriate unique key. As we saw before, a simple and error-proof way to create a unique key is to create a new object (typically a table) and use it as the key. However, if the object is not a table, it cannot keep its own attributes. Even for tables, sometimes we may not want to store the attribute in the original object. For instance, we may want to keep the attribute private, or we do not want the attribute to disturb a table traversal. In all these cases, we need an alternative way to associate attributes to objects. Of course, an external table provides an ideal way to associate attributes to objects (it is not by chance that tables are sometimes called *associative arrays*). We use the objects as keys, and their attributes as values. An external table can keep attributes of any type of object, as Lua allows us to use any type of object as a key. Moreover, attributes kept in an external table do not interfere with other objects, and can be as private as the table itself.

However, this seemingly perfect solution has a huge drawback: once we use an object as a key in a table, we lock the object into existence. Lua cannot collect an object that is being used as a key. If we use a regular table to associate functions to its names, none of these functions will ever be collected. As you might expect, we can avoid this drawback by using a weak table. This time, however, we need weak keys. The use of weak keys does not prevent any key from being collected, once there are no other references to it. On the other hand, the table cannot have weak values; otherwise, attributes of live objects could be collected.

17.3   Revisiting Tables with Default Values

In Section 13.4, we discussed how to implement tables with non-nil default values. We saw one particular technique and commented that two other techniques needed weak tables so we postponed them. Now it is time to revisit the subject. As we will see, these two techniques for default values are actually particular applications of the two general techniques that we have seen here: object attributes and memoizing.

In the first solution, we use a weak table to associate to each table its default value:

```
local defaults = {}
setmetatable(defaults, {__mode = "k"})
local mt = {__index = function (t) return defaults[t] end}
function setDefault (t, d)
  defaults[t] = d
  setmetatable(t, mt)
end
```

If `defaults` did not have weak keys, it would anchor all tables with default values into permanent existence.

In the second solution, we use distinct metatables for distinct default values, but we reuse the same metatable whenever we repeat a default value. This is a typical use of memoizing:

```
local metas = {}
setmetatable(metas, {__mode = "v"})
function setDefault (t, d)
  local mt = metas[d]
  if mt == nil then
    mt = {__index = function () return d end}
    metas[d] = mt      -- memoize
  end
  setmetatable(t, mt)
end
```

We use weak values, in this case, to allow the collection of metatables that are not being used anymore.

Given these two implementations for default values, which is best? As usual, it depends. Both have similar complexity and similar performance. The first implementation needs a few memory words for each table with a default value (an entry in defaults). The second implementation needs a few dozen memory words for each distinct default value (a new table, a new closure, plus an entry in metas). So, if your application has thousands of tables with a few distinct default values, the second implementation is clearly superior. On the other hand, if few tables share common defaults, then you should favor the first implementation.

Part III
**The Standard
Libraries**

18

The Mathematical Library

In this and the next chapters about the standard libraries, my purpose is not to give the complete specification of each function, but to show you what kind of functionality the library can provide. I may omit some subtle options or behaviors for clarity of exposition. The main idea is to spark your curiosity, which can then be satisfied by the Lua reference manual.

The math library comprises a standard set of mathematical functions, such as trigonometric functions (sin, cos, tan, asin, acos, etc.), exponentiation and logarithms (exp, log, log10), rounding functions (floor, ceil), max, min, functions for generating pseudo-random numbers (random, randomseed), plus the variables pi and huge, which is the largest representable number. (huge may be the special value *inf* in some platforms.)

All trigonometric functions work in radians. You can use the functions deg and rad to convert between degrees and radians. If you want to work in degrees, you can redefine the trigonometric functions:

```
local sin, asin, ... = math.sin, math.asin, ...
local deg, rad = math.deg, math.rad
math.sin = function (x) return sin(rad(x)) end
math.asin = function (x) return deg(asin(x)) end
...
```

The math.random function generates pseudo-random numbers. We can call it in three ways. When we call it without arguments, it returns a pseudo-random real number with uniform distribution in the interval $[0, 1)$. When we call it with only one argument, an integer n, it returns a pseudo-random integer x such that $1 \leq x \leq n$. For instance, you can simulate the result of tossing a die with random(6). Finally, we can call random with two integer arguments, l and u, to get a pseudo-random integer x such that $l \leq x \leq u$.

You can set a seed for the pseudo-random generator with the `randomseed` function; its numeric sole argument is the seed. Usually, when a program starts, it initializes the generator with a fixed seed. This means that, every time you run your program, it generates the same sequence of pseudo-random numbers. For debugging, this is a nice property; but in a game, you will have the same scenario over and over. A common trick to solve this problem is to use the current time as a seed:

```
math.randomseed(os.time())
```

The `os.time` function returns a number that represents the current time, usually as the number of seconds since some epoch.

The `math.random` function uses the `rand` function from the standard C library. In some implementations, this function produces numbers with not-so-good statistical properties. You can check for independent distributions of better pseudo-random generators for Lua. (The standard Lua distribution does not include any such generator to avoid copyright problems. It contains only code written by the Lua authors.)

19

The Table Library

The table library comprises auxiliary functions to manipulate tables as arrays. It provides functions to insert and remove elements from lists, to sort the elements of an array, and to concatenate all strings in an array.

19.1 Insert and Remove

The table.insert function inserts an element in a given position of an array, moving up other elements to open space. For instance, if t is the array {10, 20, 30}, after the call table.insert(t, 1, 15) t will be {15, 10, 20, 30}. As a special (and frequent) case, if we call insert without a position, it inserts the element in the last position of the array (and, therefore, moves no elements). As an example, the following code reads the program input line by line, storing all lines in an array:

```
t = {}
for line in io.lines() do
  table.insert(t, line)
end
print(#t)          --> (number of lines read)
```

(In Lua 5.0 this idiom was common. In Lua 5.1, I prefer the idiom t[#t+1]=line to append elements to a list.)

The table.remove function removes (and returns) an element from a given position in an array, moving down other elements to close space. When called without a position, it removes the last element of the array.

With these two functions, it is straightforward to implement stacks, queues, and double queues. We can initialize such structures as `t = {}`. A push operation is equivalent to `table.insert(t, x)`; a pop operation is equivalent to `table.remove(t)`. The call `table.insert(t, 1, x)` inserts at the other end of the structure (its beginning, actually), and `table.remove(t, 1)` removes from this end. The last two operations are not particularly efficient, as they must move elements up and down. However, because the `table` library implements these functions in C, these loops are not too expensive, so that this implementation is good enough for small arrays (up to some hundred elements, say).

19.2   Sort

Another useful function on arrays is `table.sort`, which we have seen before. It takes the array to be sorted, plus an optional order function. This order function takes two arguments and must return true when the first argument should come first in the sorted array. If this function is not provided, `sort` uses the default less-than operation (corresponding to the '<' operator).

A common mistake is to try to order the indices of a table. In a table, the indices form a set, and have no order whatsoever. If you want to order them, you have to copy them to an array and then sort the array. Let us see an example. Suppose that you read a source file and build a table that gives, for each function name, the line where this function is defined; something like this:

```
lines = {
  luaH_set = 10,
  luaH_get = 24,
  luaH_present = 48,
}
```

Now you want to print these function names in alphabetical order. If you traverse this table with `pairs`, the names appear in an arbitrary order. You cannot sort them directly, because these names are keys of the table. However, when you put them into an array, then you can sort them. First, you must create an array with these names, then sort it, and finally print the result:

```
a = {}
for n in pairs(lines) do a[#a + 1] = n end
table.sort(a)
for i,n in ipairs(a) do print(n) end
```

Note that, for Lua, arrays also have no order (they are tables, after all). But we know how to count, so we get ordered values as long as we access the array with ordered indices. That is why you should always traverse arrays with `ipairs`, rather than `pairs`. The first imposes the key order 1, 2, ..., whereas the latter uses the natural arbitrary order of the table.

As a more advanced solution, we can write an iterator that traverses a table following the order of its keys. An optional parameter `f` allows the specification of an alternative order. It first sorts the keys into an array, and then iterates on the array. At each step, it returns the key and value from the original table:

```
function pairsByKeys (t, f)
  local a = {}
  for n in pairs(t) do a[#a + 1] = n end
  table.sort(a, f)
  local i = 0        -- iterator variable
  return function ()   -- iterator function
    i = i + 1
    return a[i], t[a[i]]
  end
end
```

With this function, it is easy to print those function names in alphabetical order:

```
for name, line in pairsByKeys(lines) do
  print(name, line)
end
```

19.3 Concatenation

We have already seen table.concat in Section 11.6. It takes a list of strings and returns the result of concatenating all these strings. An optional second argument specifies a string separator to be inserted between the strings of the list. The function also accepts two other optional arguments that specify the indices of the first and the last string to concatenate.

The next function is an interesting generalization of table.concat. It accepts nested lists of strings:

```
function rconcat (l)
  if type(l) ~= "table" then return l end
  local res = {}
  for i=1, #l do
    res[i] = rconcat(l[i])
  end
  return table.concat(res)
end
```

For each list element, rconcat calls itself recursively to concatenate a possible nested list. Then it calls the original table.concat to concatenate all partial results.

```
print(rconcat{{"a", {" nice"}}, " and", {{" long"}, {" list"}}})
  --> a nice and long list
```

20

The String Library

The power of a raw Lua interpreter to manipulate strings is quite limited. A program can create string literals, concatenate them, and get string lengths. But it cannot extract substrings or examine their contents. The full power to manipulate strings in Lua comes from its string library.

The string library exports its functions as a module, called string. In Lua 5.1, it also exports its functions as methods of the string type (using the metatable of that type). So, for instance, to translate a string to upper case we can write either string.upper(s) or s:upper(). Pick your choice. To avoid unnecessary incompatibilities with Lua 5.0, I am using the module notation in most examples in this book.

20.1 Basic String Functions

Some functions in the string library are quite simple: string.len(s) returns the length of a string s. string.rep(s,n) (or s:rep(n)) returns the string s repeated n times. You can create a string with 1 Mbytes (e.g., for tests) with string.rep("a",2^20). string.lower(s) returns a copy of s with the upper-case letters converted to lower case; all other characters in the string are unchanged. (string.upper converts to upper case.) As a typical use, if you want to sort an array of strings regardless of case, you may write something like this:

```
table.sort(a, function (a, b)
  return string.lower(a) < string.lower(b)
end)
```

Both string.upper and string.lower follow the current locale. Therefore, if you work with the European Latin-1 locale, the expression string.upper("ação") results in "AÇÃO".

The call string.sub(s,i,j) extracts a piece of the string s, from the i-th to the j-th character inclusive. In Lua, the first character of a string has index 1. You can also use negative indices, which count from the end of the string: the index –1 refers to the last character in a string, –2 to the previous one, and so on. Therefore, the call string.sub(s,1,j) (or s:sub(1,j)) gets a *prefix* of the string s with length j; string.sub(s,j,-1) (or simply s:sub(j), since the default for the last argument is –1) gets a *suffix* of the string, starting at the j-th character; and string.sub(s,2,-2) returns a copy of the string s with the first and last characters removed:

```
s = "[in brackets]"
print(string.sub(s, 2, -2))    --> in brackets
```

Remember that strings in Lua are immutable. The string.sub function, like any other function in Lua, does not change the value of a string, but returns a new string. A common mistake is to write something like

```
string.sub(s, 2, -2)
```

and to assume that the value of s will be modified. If you want to modify the value of a variable, you must assign the new value to it:

```
s = string.sub(s, 2, -2)
```

The string.char and string.byte functions convert between characters and their internal numeric representations. The function string.char gets zero or more integers, converts each one to a character, and returns a string concatenating all these characters. The function string.byte(s,i) returns the internal numeric representation of the i-th character of the string s; the second argument is optional, so that the call string.byte(s) returns the internal numeric representation of the first (or single) character of s. In the following examples, we assume that characters are represented in ASCII:

```
print(string.char(97))                 --> a
i = 99; print(string.char(i, i+1, i+2))   --> cde
print(string.byte("abc"))              --> 97
print(string.byte("abc", 2))           --> 98
print(string.byte("abc", -1))          --> 99
```

In the last line, we used a negative index to access the last character of the string.

In Lua 5.1, string.byte accepts an optional third argument. A call like string.byte(s,i,j) returns multiple values with the numeric representation of all characters between indices i and j (inclusive):

```
print(string.byte("abc", 1, 2))        --> 97 98
```

The default value for j is i, so a call without this argument returns only the i-th character, as in Lua 5.0. A nice idiom is {s:byte(1,-1)}, which creates a table with the codes of all characters in s. Given this table, we can recreate the original string by calling string.char(unpack(t)). Unfortunately, these techniques do not work for long strings (say, longer than 2 Kbytes), because Lua puts a limit on how many values a function can return.

The function string.format is a powerful tool for formatting strings, typically for output. It returns a formatted version of its variable number of arguments following the description given by its first argument, the so-called *format string*. The format string has rules similar to those of the printf function of standard C: it is composed of regular text and *directives*, which control where and how each argument must be placed in the formatted string. A directive is the character '%' plus a letter that tells how to format the argument: 'd' for a decimal number, 'x' for hexadecimal, 'o' for octal, 'f' for a floating-point number, 's' for strings, plus other variants. Between the '%' and the letter, a directive can include other options that control the details of the format, such as the number of decimal digits of a floating-point number:

```
print(string.format("pi = %.4f", math.pi))      --> pi = 3.1416
d = 5; m = 11; y = 1990
print(string.format("%02d/%02d/%04d", d, m, y))    --> 05/11/1990
tag, title = "h1", "a title"
print(string.format("<%s>%s</%s>", tag, title, tag))
   --> <h1>a title</h1>
```

In the first example, the %.4f means a floating-point number with four digits after the decimal point. In the second example, the %02d means a decimal number, with at least two digits and zero padding; the directive %2d, without the zero, would use blanks for padding. For a complete description of these directives, see the Lua reference manual. Or, better yet, see a C manual, as Lua calls the standard C library to do the hard work here.

20.2 Pattern-Matching Functions

The most powerful functions in the string library are find, match, gsub (*Global Substitution*), and gmatch (*Global Match*). They all are based on *patterns*.

Unlike several other scripting languages, Lua uses neither POSIX (regexp) nor Perl regular expressions for pattern matching. The main reason for this decision is size: a typical implementation of POSIX regular expressions takes more than 4000 lines of code. This is about the size of all Lua standard libraries together. In comparison, the implementation of pattern matching in Lua has less than 500 lines. Of course, the pattern matching in Lua cannot do all that a full POSIX implementation does. Nevertheless, pattern matching in Lua is a powerful tool, and includes some features that are difficult to match with standard POSIX implementations.

The `string.find` **function**

The `string.find` function searches for a pattern inside a given subject string. The simplest form of a pattern is a word, which matches only a copy of itself. For instance, the pattern 'hello' will search for the substring "hello" inside the subject string. When `find` finds its pattern, it returns two values: the index where the match begins and the index where the match ends. If it does not find a match, it returns **nil**:

```
s = "hello world"
i, j = string.find(s, "hello")
print(i, j)                        --> 1     5
print(string.sub(s, i, j))      --> hello
print(string.find(s, "world"))   --> 7     11
i, j = string.find(s, "l")
print(i, j)                        --> 3     3
print(string.find(s, "lll"))     --> nil
```

When a match succeeds, we can call `string.sub` with the values returned by `string.find` to get the part of the subject string that matched the pattern. (For simple patterns, this is the pattern itself.)

The `string.find` function has an optional third parameter: an index that tells where in the subject string to start the search. This parameter is useful when we want to process all the indices where a given pattern appears: we search for a new match repeatedly, each time starting after the position where we found the previous one. As an example, the following code makes a table with the positions of all newlines in a string:

```
local t = {}                          -- table to store the indices
local i = 0
while true do
  i = string.find(s, "\n", i+1)    -- find next newline
  if i == nil then break end
  t[#t + 1] = i
end
```

We will see later a simpler way to write such loops, using the `string.gmatch` iterator.

The `string.match` **function**

The `string.match` function is similar to `string.find`, in the sense that it also searches for a pattern in a string. However, instead of returning the position where it found the pattern, it returns the part of the subject string that matched the pattern:

```
print(string.match("hello world", "hello"))   --> hello
```

For fixed patterns like 'hello', this function is pointless. It shows its power when used with variable patterns, as in the next example:

```
date = "Today is 17/7/1990"
d = string.match(date, "%d+/%d+/%d+")
print(d)   --> 17/7/1990
```

Shortly we will discuss the meaning of the pattern '%d+/%d+/%d+' and more advanced uses for string.match.

The string.gsub **function**

The string.gsub function has three parameters: a subject string, a pattern, and a replacement string. Its basic use is to substitute the replacement string for all occurrences of the pattern inside the subject string:

```
s = string.gsub("Lua is cute", "cute", "great")
print(s)          --> Lua is great
s = string.gsub("all lii", "l", "x")
print(s)          --> axx xii
s = string.gsub("Lua is great", "Sol", "Sun")
print(s)          --> Lua is great
```

An optional fourth parameter limits the number of substitutions to be made:

```
s = string.gsub("all lii", "l", "x", 1)
print(s)          --> axl lii
s = string.gsub("all lii", "l", "x", 2)
print(s)          --> axx lii
```

The string.gsub function also returns as a second result the number of times it made the substitution. For instance, an easy way to count the number of spaces in a string is

```
count = select(2, string.gsub(str, " ", " "))
```

The string.gmatch **function**

The string.gmatch function returns a function that iterates over all occurrences of a pattern in a string. For instance, the following example collects all words in a given string s:

```
words = {}
for w in string.gmatch(s, "%a+") do
  words[#words + 1] = w
end
```

As we will discuss shortly, the pattern '%a+' matches sequences of one or more alphabetic characters (that is, words). So, the **for** loop will iterate over all words of the subject string, storing them in the list words.

Using gmatch and gsub, it is not difficult to emulate in Lua the search strategy that require uses when looking for modules:

```
function search (modname, path)
  modname = string.gsub(modname, "%.", "/")
  for c in string.gmatch(path, "[^;]+") do
    local fname = string.gsub(c, "?", modname)
    local f = io.open(fname)
    if f then
      f:close()
      return fname
    end
  end
  return nil    -- not found
end
```

The fist step is to substitute the directory separator, assumed to be '/' for this example, for any dots. (As we will see later, a dot has a special meaning in a pattern. To get a dot without other meanings we must write '%.'.) Then the function loops over all components of the path, wherein each component is a maximum expansion of non-semicolon characters. For each component, it replaces the module name for the question marks to get the final file name, and then checks whether there is such a file. If so, the function closes the file and returns its name.

20.3 Patterns

You can make patterns more useful with *character classes*. A character class is an item in a pattern that can match any character in a specific set. For instance, the class %d matches any digit. Therefore, you can search for a date in the format dd/mm/yyyy with the pattern '%d%d/%d%d/%d%d%d%d':

```
s = "Deadline is 30/05/1999, firm"
date = "%d%d/%d%d/%d%d%d%d"
print(string.sub(s, string.find(s, date)))   --> 30/05/1999
```

The following table lists all character classes:

.	all characters
%a	letters
%c	control characters
%d	digits
%l	lower-case letters
%p	punctuation characters
%s	space characters
%u	upper-case letters
%w	alphanumeric characters
%x	hexadecimal digits
%z	the character whose representation is 0

An upper-case version of any of these classes represents the complement of the class. For instance, '%A' represents all non-letter characters:

```
print(string.gsub("hello, up-down!", "%A", "."))
  --> hello..up.down. 4
```

(The 4 is not part of the result string. It is the second result of gsub, the total number of substitutions. I will omit this count in other examples that print the result of gsub.)

Some characters, called *magic characters*, have special meanings when used in a pattern. The magic characters are

$$( ) \, . \, \% + - * ? \, [\,] \, \hat{} \, \$$$

The character '%' works as an escape for these magic characters. So, '%.' matches a dot; '%%' matches the character '%' itself. You can use the escape '%' not only for the magic characters, but also for all other non-alphanumeric characters. When in doubt, play safe and put an escape.

For Lua, patterns are regular strings. They have no special treatment, following the same rules as other strings. Only the pattern functions interpret them as patterns, and only then does the '%' work as an escape. To put a quote inside a pattern, you use the same techniques that you use to put a quote inside other strings; for instance, you can escape the quote with a '\', which is the escape character for Lua.

A *char-set* allows you to create your own character classes, combining different classes and single characters between square brackets. For instance, the char-set '[%w_]' matches both alphanumeric characters and underscores; the char-set '[01]' matches binary digits; and the char-set '[%[%]]' matches square brackets. To count the number of vowels in a text, you can write

```
nvow = select(2, string.gsub(text, "[AEIOUaeiou]", ""))
```

You can also include character ranges in a char-set, by writing the first and the last characters of the range separated by a hyphen. I seldom use this facility, because most useful ranges are already predefined; for instance, '[0-9]' is the same as '%d', and '[0-9a-fA-F]' is the same as '%x'. However, if you need to find an octal digit, then you may prefer '[0-7]' instead of an explicit enumeration like '[01234567]'. You can get the complement of any char-set by starting it with '^': the pattern '[^0-7]' finds any character that is not an octal digit and '[^\n]' matches any character different from newline. But remember that you can negate simple classes with its upper-case version: '%S' is simpler than '[^%s]'.

Character classes follow the current locale set for Lua. Therefore, the class '[a-z]' can be different from '%l'. In a proper locale, the latter form includes letters such as 'ç' and 'ã'. You should always use the latter form, unless you have a strong reason to do otherwise: it is simpler, more portable, and slightly more efficient.

You can make patterns still more useful with modifiers for repetitions and optional parts. Patterns in Lua offer four modifiers:

+	1 or more repetitions
*	0 or more repetitions
-	also 0 or more repetitions
?	optional (0 or 1 occurrence)

The '+' modifier matches one or more characters of the original class. It will always get the longest sequence that matches the pattern. For instance, the pattern '%a+' means one or more letters, or a word:

```
print(string.gsub("one, and two; and three", "%a+", "word"))
  --> word, word word; word word
```

The pattern '%d+' matches one or more digits (an integer):

```
print(string.match("the number 1298 is even", "%d+"))   --> 1298
```

The modifier '*' is similar to '+', but it also accepts zero occurrences of characters of the class. A typical use is to match optional spaces between parts of a pattern. For instance, to match an empty parenthesis pair, such as () or ( ), you use the pattern '%(%s*%)': the pattern '%s*' matches zero or more spaces. (Parentheses also have a special meaning in a pattern, so we must escape them with a '%'.) As another example, the pattern '[_%a][_%w]*' matches identifiers in a Lua program: a sequence starting with a letter or an underscore, followed by zero or more underscores or alphanumeric characters.

Like '*', the modifier '-' also matches zero or more occurrences of characters of the original class. However, instead of matching the longest sequence, it matches the shortest one. Sometimes, there is no difference between '*' and '-', but usually they present rather different results. For instance, if you try to find an identifier with the pattern '[_%a][_%w]-', you will find only the first letter, because the '[_%w]-' will always match the empty sequence. On the other hand, suppose you want to find comments in a C program. Many people would first try '/%*.*%*/' (that is, a "/*" followed by a sequence of any characters followed by "*/", written with the appropriate escapes). However, because the '.*' expands as far as it can, the first "/*" in the program would close only with the last "*/":

```
test = "int x; /* x */  int y; /* y */"
print(string.gsub(test, "/%*.*%*/", "<COMMENT>"))
  --> int x; <COMMENT>
```

The pattern '.-', instead, will expand the least amount necessary to find the first "*/", so that you get the desired result:

```
test = "int x; /* x */  int y; /* y */"
print(string.gsub(test, "/%*.-%*/", "<COMMENT>"))
  --> int x; <COMMENT>  int y; <COMMENT>
```

The last modifier, '?', matches an optional character. As an example, suppose we want to find an integer in a text, where the number may contain an optional sign. The pattern '[+-]?%d+' does the job, matching numerals like "-12", "23", and "+1009". The '[+-]' is a character class that matches both a '+' and a '-' sign; the following '?' makes this sign optional.

Unlike some other systems, in Lua a modifier can be applied only to a character class; there is no way to group patterns under a modifier. For instance, there is no pattern that matches an optional word (unless the word has only one letter). Usually you can circumvent this limitation using some of the advanced techniques that we will see in the end of this chapter.

If a pattern begins with a '^', it will match only at the beginning of the subject string. Similarly, if it ends with a '$', it will match only at the end of the subject string. These marks can be used both to restrict the patterns that you find and to anchor patterns. For instance, the test

```
if string.find(s, "^%d") then ...
```

checks whether the string s starts with a digit, and the test

```
if string.find(s, "^[+-]?%d+$") then ...
```

checks whether this string represents an integer number, without other leading or trailing characters.

Another item in a pattern is '%b', which matches balanced strings. Such item is written as '%bxy', where x and y are any two distinct characters; the x acts as an opening character and the y as the closing one. For instance, the pattern '%b()' matches parts of the string that start with a '(' and finish at the respective ')':

```
s = "a (enclosed (in) parentheses) line"
print(string.gsub(s, "%b()", ""))      --> a  line
```

Typically, this pattern is used as '%b()', '%b[]', '%b{}', or '%b<>', but you can use any characters as delimiters.

20.4 Captures

The *capture* mechanism allows a pattern to yank parts of the subject string that match parts of the pattern for further use. You specify a capture by writing the parts of the pattern that you want to capture between parentheses.

When a pattern has captures, the function string.match returns each captured value as a separate result; in other words, it breaks a string into its captured parts:[15]

```
pair = "name = Anna"
key, value = string.match(pair, "(%a+)%s*=%s*(%a+)")
print(key, value)  --> name  Anna
```

The pattern '%a+' specifies a non-empty sequence of letters; the pattern '%s*' specifies a possibly empty sequence of spaces. So, in the example above, the whole pattern specifies a sequence of letters, followed by a sequence of spaces, followed by '=', again followed by spaces, plus another sequence of letters. Both sequences of letters have their patterns enclosed by parentheses, so that they will be captured if a match occurs. Below is a similar example:

```
date = "Today is 17/7/1990"
d, m, y = string.match(date, "(%d+)/(%d+)/(%d+)")
print(d, m, y)  --> 17  7  1990
```

---

[15]In Lua 5.0 string.find did this task.

We can use captures in the pattern itself. In a pattern, an item like '%d', where d is a single digit, matches only a copy of the d-th capture. As a typical use, suppose you want to find, inside a string, a substring enclosed between single or double quotes. You could try a pattern such as '["']·-["']', that is, a quote followed by anything followed by another quote; but you would have problems with strings like "it's all right". To solve this problem, you can capture the first quote and use it to specify the second one:

```
s = [[then he said: "it's all right"!]]
q, quotedPart = string.match(s, "([\"'])(.-)%1")
print(quotedPart)    --> it's all right
print(q)             --> "
```

The first capture is the quote character itself and the second capture is the contents of the quote (the substring matching the '.-').

A similar example is the pattern that matches long strings in Lua:

```
%[(=*)%[(.-)%]%1%]
```

It will match an opening square bracket followed by zero or more equal signs, followed by another opening square bracket, followed by anything (the string content), followed by a closing square bracket, followed by the same number of equal signs, followed by another closing square bracket:

```
p = "%[(=*)%[(.-)%]%1%]"
s = "a = [=[[[ something ]] ]==] ]=]; print(a)"
print(string.match(s, p))    --> =          [[ something ]] ]==]
```

The first capture is the sequence of equal signs (only one in this example); the second is the string content.

The third use of captured values is in the replacement string of gsub. Like the pattern, also the replacement string may contain items like "%d", which are changed to the respective captures when the substitution is made. In particular, the item "%0" is changed to the whole match. (By the way, a '%' in the replacement string must be escaped as "%%".) As an example, the following command duplicates every letter in a string, with a hyphen between the copies:

```
print(string.gsub("hello Lua!", "%a", "%0-%0"))
  --> h-he-el-ll-lo-o L-Lu-ua-a!
```

This one interchanges adjacent characters:

```
print(string.gsub("hello Lua", "(.)(.)", "%2%1"))   --> ehll ouLa
```

As a more useful example, let us write a primitive format converter, which gets a string with commands written in a LaTeX style, such as

```
\command{some text}
```

and changes them to a format in XML style,

```
<command>some text</command>
```

If we disallow nested commands, the following line does the job:

```
s = string.gsub(s, "\\(%a+){(.-)}", "<%1>%2</%1>")
```

For instance, if s is the string

```
the \quote{task} is to \em{change} that.
```

that call to gsub will change s to

```
the <quote>task</quote> is to <em>change</em> that.
```

(In the next section we will see how to handle nested commands.)
   Another useful example is how to trim a string:

```
function trim (s)
  return (string.gsub(s, "^%s*(.-)%s*$", "%1"))
end
```

Note the judicious use of pattern formats. The two anchors ('^' and '$') ensure that we get the whole string. Because the '. -' tries to expand as little as possible, the two patterns '%s*' match all spaces at both extremities. Note also that, because gsub returns two values, we use extra parentheses to discard the extra result (the count).

20.5 Replacements

Instead of a string, we can use either a function or a table as the third argument to string.gsub. When invoked with a function, string.gsub calls the function every time it finds a match; the arguments to each call are the captures, and the value that the function returns is used as the replacement string. When invoked with a table, string.gsub looks up the table using the first capture as the key, and the associated value is used as the replacement string. If the table does not have this key, gsub does not change this match.
   As a first example, the following function does *variable expansion*: it substitutes the value of the global variable varname for every occurrence of $varname in a string:

```
function expand (s)
  return (string.gsub(s, "$(%w+)", _G))
end

name = "Lua"; status = "great"
print(expand("$name is $status, isn't it?"))
  --> Lua is great, isn't it?
```

For each match with '$(%w+)' (a dollar sign followed by a name), gsub looks up the captured name in the global table _G; the result replaces the match. When the table does not have the key, there is no replacement:

```
print(expand("$othername is $status, isn't it?"))
  --> $othername is great, isn't it?
```

If you are not sure whether the given variables have string values, you may want to apply `tostring` to their values. In this case, you can use a function as the replacement value:

```
function expand (s)
  return (string.gsub(s, "$(%w+)", function (n)
            return tostring(_G[n])
          end))
end

print(expand("print = $print; a = $a"))
  --> print = function: 0x8050ce0; a = nil
```

Now, for each match with '`$(%w+)`', gsub calls the given function with the captured name as argument; the return replaces the match. If the function returns **nil**, there is no replacement. (This case cannot happen in this example, because `tostring` never returns **nil**.)

This last example goes back to our format converter, from the previous section. Again we want to convert commands in LaTeX style (\example{text}) to XML style (<example>text</example>), but allowing nested commands this time. The next function uses recursion to do the job:

```
function toxml (s)
  s = string.gsub(s, "\\(%a+)(%b{})", function (tag, body)
        body = string.sub(body, 2, -2)  -- remove brackets
        body = toxml(body)              -- handle nested commands
        return string.format("<%s>%s</%s>", tag, body, tag)
      end)
  return s
end

print(toxml("\\title{The \\bold{big} example}"))
  --> <title>The <bold>big</bold> example</title>
```

URL encoding

For our next example, we use *URL encoding*, which is the encoding used by HTTP to send parameters in a URL. This encoding encodes special characters (such as '=', '&', and '+') as "%xx", where xx is the hexadecimal representation of the character. After that, it changes spaces to '+'. For instance, it encodes the string "a+b = c" as "a%2Bb+%3D+c". Finally, it writes each parameter name and parameter value with an '=' in between and appends all resulting pairs name=value with an ampersand in between. For instance, the values

```
name = "al";  query = "a+b = c"; q="yes or no"
```

are encoded as "name=al&query=a%2Bb+%3D+c&q=yes+or+no".

Now, suppose we want to decode this URL and store each value in a table, indexed by its corresponding name. The following function does the basic decoding:

```
function unescape (s)
  s = string.gsub(s, "+", " ")
  s = string.gsub(s, "%%(%x%x)", function (h)
        return string.char(tonumber(h, 16))
      end)
  return s
end
```

The first statement changes each '+' in the string to a space. The second gsub matches all two-digit hexadecimal numerals preceded by '%' and calls an anonymous function for each match. This function converts the hexadecimal numeral into a number (tonumber, with base 16) and returns the corresponding character (string.char). For instance,

```
print(unescape("a%2Bb+%3D+c"))   --> a+b = c
```

To decode the pairs name=value we use gmatch. Because both names and values cannot contain either '&' or '=', we can match them with the pattern '[^&=]+':

```
cgi = {}
function decode (s)
  for name, value in string.gmatch(s, "([^&=]+)=([^&=]+)") do
    name = unescape(name)
    value = unescape(value)
    cgi[name] = value
  end
end
```

The call to gmatch matches all pairs in the form name=value. For each pair, the iterator returns the corresponding captures (as marked by the parentheses in the matching string) as the values for name and value. The loop body simply calls unescape on both strings and stores the pair in the cgi table.

The corresponding encoding is also easy to write. First, we write the escape function; this function encodes all special characters as a '%' followed by the character code in hexadecimal (the format option "%02X" makes a hexadecimal number with two digits, using 0 for padding), and then changes spaces to '+':

```
function escape (s)
  s = string.gsub(s, "[&=+%%%c]", function (c)
        return string.format("%%%02X", string.byte(c))
      end)
  s = string.gsub(s, " ", "+")
  return s
end
```

The encode function traverses the table to be encoded, building the resulting string:

```
function encode (t)
  local b = {}
  for k,v in pairs(t) do
    b[#b + 1] = (escape(k) .. "=" .. escape(v))
  end
  return table.concat(b, "&")
end

t = {name = "al",  query = "a+b = c", q = "yes or no"}
print(encode(t)) --> q=yes+or+no&query=a%2Bb+%3D+c&name=al
```

Tab expansion

An empty capture like '()' has a special meaning in Lua. Instead of capturing nothing (a quite useless task), this pattern captures its position in the subject string, as a number:

```
print(string.match("hello", "()ll()"))   --> 3  5
```

(Note that the result of this example is not the same as what you get from string.find, because the position of the second empty capture is *after* the match.)

A nice example of the use of empty captures is for expanding tabs in a string:

```
function expandTabs (s, tab)
  tab = tab or 8       -- tab "size" (default is 8)
  local corr = 0
  s = string.gsub(s, "()\t", function (p)
      local sp = tab - (p - 1 + corr)%tab
      corr = corr - 1 + sp
      return string.rep(" ", sp)
    end)
  return s
end
```

The gsub pattern matches all tabs in the string, capturing their positions. For each tab, the inner function uses this position to compute the number of spaces needed to arrive at a column that is a multiple of tab: it subtracts one from the position to make it relative to zero and adds corr to compensate for previous tabs (the expansion of each tab affects the position of the next ones). It then updates the correction to be used for the next tab: minus one for the tab being removed, plus sp for the spaces being added. Finally it returns the appropriate number of spaces.

Just for completeness, let us see how to reverse this operation, converting spaces to tabs. A first approach could also involve the use of empty captures to manipulate positions, but there is a simpler solution. At every eighth character we insert a mark in the string. Then, wherever the mark is preceded by spaces we replace it by a tab:

```
function unexpandTabs (s, tab)
  tab = tab or 8
  s = expandTabs(s)
  local pat = string.rep(".", tab)
  s = string.gsub(s, pat, "%0\1")
  s = string.gsub(s, " +\1", "\t")
  s = string.gsub(s, "\1", "")
  return s
end
```

The function starts by expanding the string to remove any previous tabs. Then it computes an auxiliary pattern for matching all sequences of tab characters, and uses this pattern to add a mark (the control character \1) after every tab characters. It then substitutes a tab for all sequences of spaces followed by a mark. Finally, it removes the marks left (those not preceded by spaces).

20.6 Tricks of the Trade

Pattern matching is a powerful tool for manipulating strings. You can perform many complex operations with only a few calls to string.gsub. However, as with any power, you must use it carefully.

Pattern matching is not a replacement for a proper parser. For quick-and-dirty programs, you can do useful manipulations on source code, but it is hard to build a product with quality. As a good example, consider the pattern we used to match comments in a C program: '/%*.-%*/'. If your program has a literal string containing "/*", you may get a wrong result:

```
test = [[char s[] = "a /* here";  /* a tricky string */]]
print(string.gsub(test, "/%*.-%*/", "<COMMENT>"))
  --> char s[] = "a <COMMENT>
```

Strings with such contents are rare and, for your own use, that pattern will probably do its job. But you should not distribute a program with such a flaw.

Usually, pattern matching is efficient enough for Lua programs: a Pentium 333 MHz (which is an ancient machine) takes less than a tenth of a second to match all words in a text with 200K characters (30K words). But you can take precautions. You should always make the pattern as specific as possible; loose patterns are slower than specific ones. An extreme example is '(.-)%$', to get all text in a string up to the first dollar sign. If the subject string has a dollar sign, everything goes fine; but suppose that the string does not contain any dollar signs. The algorithm will first try to match the pattern starting at the first position of the string. It will go through all the string, looking for a dollar. When the string ends, the pattern fails *for the first position* of the string. Then, the algorithm will do the whole search again, starting at the second position of the string, only to discover that the pattern does not match there, too; and so on. This will take a quadratic time, which results in more than three hours in a Pentium 333 MHz for a string with 200K characters. You can correct this problem simply by anchoring the pattern at the first position of the string, with '^(.-)%$'. The anchor tells the algorithm to stop the search if it cannot find a match at the first position. With the anchor, the pattern runs in less than a tenth of a second.

Beware also of *empty* patterns, that is, patterns that match the empty string. For instance, if you try to match names with a pattern like '%a*', you will find names everywhere:

```
i, j = string.find(";$%  **#$hello13", "%a*")
print(i,j)    --> 1   0
```

In this example, the call to string.find has correctly found an empty sequence of letters at the beginning of the string.

It never makes sense to write a pattern that begins or ends with the modifier '-', because it will match only the empty string. This modifier always needs something around it to anchor its expansion. Similarly, a pattern that includes '.*' is tricky, because this construction can expand much more than you intended.

Sometimes, it is useful to use Lua itself to build a pattern. We already used this trick in our function to convert spaces to tabs. As another example, let us see how we can find long lines in a text, say lines with more than 70 characters. Well, a long line is a sequence of 70 or more characters different from newline. We can match a single character different from newline with the character class '[^\n]'. Therefore, we can match a long line with a pattern that repeats 70 times the pattern for one character, followed by zero or more of these characters. Instead of writing this pattern by hand, we can create it with string.rep:

```
pattern = string.rep("[^\n]", 70) .. "[^\n]*"
```

As another example, suppose you want to make a case-insensitive search. A way of doing this is to change any letter x in the pattern for the class '$[xX]$', that is, a class including both the lower and the upper-case versions of the original letter. We can automate this conversion with a function:

```
function nocase (s)
  s = string.gsub(s, "%a", function (c)
        return "[" .. string.lower(c) .. string.upper(c) .. "]"
      end)
  return s
end

print(nocase("Hi there!"))   --> [hH][iI] [tT][hH][eE][rR][eE]!
```

Sometimes, you want to change every plain occurrence of s1 to s2, without regarding any character as magic. If the strings s1 and s2 are literals, you can add proper escapes to magic characters while you write the strings. But if these strings are variable values, you can use another gsub to put the escapes for you:

```
s1 = string.gsub(s1, "(%W)", "%%%1")
s2 = string.gsub(s2, "%%", "%%%%")
```

In the search string, we escape all non-alphanumeric characters (thus the upper-case 'W'). In the replacement string, we escape only the '%'.

Another useful technique for pattern matching is to pre-process the subject string before the real work. Suppose we want to change to upper case all quoted strings in a text, where a quoted string starts and ends with a double quote ('"'), but may contain escaped quotes ("\""):

```
follows a typical string: "This is \"great\"!".
```

Our approach to handling such cases is to pre-process the text so as to encode the problematic sequence to something else. For instance, we could code "\"" as "\1". However, if the original text already contains a "\1", we are in trouble. An easy way to do the encoding and avoid this problem is to code all sequences "\x" as "\ddd", where *ddd* is the decimal representation of the character *x*:

```
function code (s)
    return (string.gsub(s, "\\(.)", function (x)
             return string.format("\\%03d", string.byte(x))
           end))
end
```

Now any sequence "\ddd" in the encoded string must have come from the coding, because any "\ddd" in the original string has been coded, too. So, the decoding is an easy task:

```
function decode (s)
    return (string.gsub(s, "\\(%d%d%d)", function (d)
             return "\\" .. string.char(d)
           end))
end
```

Now we can complete our task. As the encoded string does not contain any escaped quote ("\""), we can search for quoted strings simply with '".-"':

```
s = [[follows a typical string: "This is \"great\"!".]]
s = code(s)
s = string.gsub(s, '".-"', string.upper)
s = decode(s)
print(s)    --> follows a typical string: "THIS IS \"GREAT\"!".
```

or, in a more compact notation,

```
print(decode(string.gsub(code(s), '".-"', string.upper)))
```

21

The I/O Library

The I/O library offers two different models for file manipulation. The simple model assumes a *current input file* and a *current output file*, and its I/O operations operate on these files. The complete model uses explicit file handles; it adopts an object-oriented style that defines all operations as methods on file handles.

The simple model is convenient for simple things; we have been using it throughout the book until now. But it is not enough for more advanced file manipulation, such as reading from several files simultaneously. For these manipulations, we need the complete model.

21.1   The Simple I/O Model

The simple model does all of its operations on two current files. The library initializes the current input file as the process standard input (stdin) and the current output file as the process standard output (stdout). Therefore, when we execute something like io.read(), we read a line from the standard input.

We can change these current files with the io.input and io.output functions. A call like io.input(filename) opens the given file in read mode and sets it as the current input file. From this point on, all input will come from this file, until another call to io.input; io.output does a similar job for output. In case of error, both functions raise the error. If you want to handle errors directly, you must use io.open, from the complete model.

As write is simpler than read, we will look at it first. The io.write function simply gets an arbitrary number of string arguments and writes them to the current output file. Numbers are converted to strings following the

usual conversion rules; for full control over this conversion, you should use the
`string.format` function:

```
> io.write("sin (3) = ", math.sin(3), "\n")
--> sin (3) = 0.14112000805987
> io.write(string.format("sin (3) = %.4f\n", math.sin(3)))
--> sin (3) = 0.1411
```

Avoid code like `io.write(a..b..c)`; the call `io.write(a,b,c)` accomplishes the
same effect with fewer resources, as it avoids the concatenations.

As a rule, you should use `print` for quick-and-dirty programs, or for debugging, and `write` when you need full control over your output:

```
> print("hello", "Lua"); print("Hi")
--> hello     Lua
--> Hi

> io.write("hello", "Lua"); io.write("Hi", "\n")
--> helloLuaHi
```

Unlike `print`, `write` adds no extra characters to the output, such as tabs or
newlines. Moreover, `write` uses the current output file, whereas `print` always
uses the standard output. Finally, `print` automatically applies `tostring` to its
arguments, so it can also show tables, functions, and **nil**.

The `io.read` function reads strings from the current input file. Its arguments
control what is read:

"*all"	reads the whole file
"*line"	reads the next line
"*number"	reads a number
num	reads a string with up to *num* characters

The call `io.read("*all")` reads the whole current input file, starting at its
current position. If we are at the end of the file, or if the file is empty, the call
returns an empty string.

Because Lua handles long strings efficiently, a simple technique for writing
filters in Lua is to read the whole file into a string, do the processing to the string
(typically with `gsub`), and then write the string to the output:

```
t = io.read("*all")            -- read the whole file
t = string.gsub(t, ...)     -- do the job
io.write(t)                    -- write the file
```

As an example, the following code is a complete program to code a file's content using the MIME *quoted-printable* encoding. In this encoding, non-ASCII
characters are coded as *=xx*, where *xx* is the numeric code of the character in
hexadecimal. To keep the consistency of the encoding, the '=' character must be
encoded as well:

```
t = io.read("*all")
t = string.gsub(t, "([\128-\255=])", function (c)
      return string.format("=%02X", string.byte(c))
    end)
io.write(t)
```

The pattern used in the gsub captures all characters with codes from 128 to 255, plus the equal sign.

The call io.read("*line") returns the next line from the current input file, without the newline character. When we reach the end of file, the call returns **nil** (as there is no next line to return). This pattern is the default for read. Usually, I use this pattern only when the algorithm naturally handles the file line by line; otherwise, I favor reading the whole file at once, with *all, or in blocks, as we will see later.

As a simple example of the use of this pattern, the following program copies its current input to the current output, numbering each line:

```
for count = 1, math.huge do
  local line = io.read()
  if line == nil then break end
  io.write(string.format("%6d  ", count), line, "\n")
end
```

However, to iterate on a whole file line by line, we do better to use the io.lines iterator. For instance, we can write a complete program to sort the lines of a file as follows:

```
local lines = {}
-- read the lines in table 'lines'
for line in io.lines() do  lines[#lines + 1] = line  end
-- sort
table.sort(lines)
-- write all the lines
for _, l in ipairs(lines) do  io.write(l, "\n")  end
```

The call io.read("*number") reads a number from the current input file. This is the only case where read returns a number, instead of a string. When a program needs to read many numbers from a file, the absence of the intermediate strings improves its performance. The *number option skips any spaces before the number and accepts number formats like -3, +5.2, 1000, and -3.4e-23. If it cannot find a number at the current file position (because of bad format or end of file), it returns **nil**.

You can call read with multiple options; for each argument, the function will return the respective result. Suppose you have a file with three numbers per line:

```
6.0        -3.23      15e12
4.3        234        1000001
...
```

Now you want to print the maximum value of each line. You can read all three
numbers with a single call to `read`:

```
while true do
  local n1, n2, n3 = io.read("*number", "*number", "*number")
  if not n1 then break end
  print(math.max(n1, n2, n3))
end
```

In any case, you should always consider the alternative of reading the whole file
with option "*all" and then using `gmatch` to break it up:

```
local pat = "(%S+)%s+(%S+)%s+(%S+)%s+"
for n1, n2, n3 in string.gmatch(io.read("*all"), pat) do
  print(math.max(tonumber(n1), tonumber(n2), tonumber(n3)))
end
```

Besides the basic read patterns, you can call `read` with a number n as an
argument: in this case, `read` tries to read n characters from the input file. If it
cannot read any character (end of file), `read` returns **nil**; otherwise, it returns
a string with at most n characters. As an example of this read pattern, the
following program is an efficient way (in Lua, of course) to copy a file from `stdin`
to `stdout`:

```
while true do
  local block = io.read(2^13)           -- buffer size is 8K
  if not block then break end
  io.write(block)
end
```

As a special case, `io.read(0)` works as a test for end of file: it returns an
empty string if there is more to be read or **nil** otherwise.

21.2   The Complete I/O Model

For more control over I/O, you can use the complete model. A central concept
in this model is the *file handle*, which is equivalent to streams (FILE*) in C: it
represents an open file with a current position.

To open a file, you use the `io.open` function, which mimics the `fopen` function
in C. It takes as arguments the name of the file to open plus a *mode* string. This
mode string may contain an 'r' for reading, a 'w' for writing (which also erases
any previous content of the file), or an 'a' for appending, plus an optional 'b' to
open binary files. The `open` function returns a new handle for the file. In case of
error, `open` returns **nil**, plus an error message and an error number:

```
print(io.open("non-existent-file", "r"))
  --> nil      non-existent-file: No such file or directory   2

print(io.open("/etc/passwd", "w"))
  --> nil      /etc/passwd: Permission denied  13
```

The interpretation of the error numbers is system dependent.

A typical idiom to check for errors is

```
local f = assert(io.open(filename, mode))
```

If the open fails, the error message goes as the second argument to assert, which then shows the message.

After you open a file, you can read from it or write to it with the methods read/write. They are similar to the read/write functions, but you call them as methods on the file handle, using the colon syntax. For instance, to open a file and read it all, you can use a chunk like this:

```
local f = assert(io.open(filename, "r"))
local t = f:read("*all")
f:close()
```

The I/O library offers handles for the three predefined C streams: io.stdin, io.stdout, and io.stderr. So, you can send a message directly to the error stream with a code like this:

```
io.stderr:write(message)
```

We can mix the complete model with the simple model. We get the current input file handle by calling io.input(), without arguments. We set this handle with the call io.input(handle). (Similar calls are also valid for io.output.) For instance, if you want to change the current input file temporarily, you can write something like this:

```
local temp = io.input()    -- save current file
io.input("newinput")       -- open a new current file
<do something with new input>
io.input():close()         -- close current file
io.input(temp)             -- restore previous current file
```

A small performance trick

Usually, in Lua, it is faster to read a file as a whole than to read it line by line. However, sometimes we must face a big file (say, tens or hundreds megabytes) for which it is not reasonable to read it all at once. If you want to handle such big files with maximum performance, the fastest way is to read them in reasonably large chunks (e.g., 8 Kbytes each). To avoid the problem of breaking lines in the middle, you simply ask to read a chunk plus a line:

```
local lines, rest = f:read(BUFSIZE, "*line")
```

The variable rest will get the rest of any line broken by the chunk. We then concatenate the chunk and this rest of line. This way, the resulting chunk will always break at line boundaries.

The example in Listing 21.1 uses this technique to implement wc, a program that counts the number of characters, words, and lines in a file.

Listing 21.1. The `wc` program:

```
local BUFSIZE = 2^13          -- 8K
local f = io.input(arg[1])    -- open input file
local cc, lc, wc = 0, 0, 0    -- char, line, and word counts
while true do
  local lines, rest = f:read(BUFSIZE, "*line")
  if not lines then break end
  if rest then lines = lines .. rest .. "\n" end
  cc = cc + #lines
  -- count words in the chunk
  local _, t = string.gsub(lines, "%S+", "")
  wc = wc + t
  -- count newlines in the chunk
  _,t = string.gsub(lines, "\n", "\n")
  lc = lc + t
end
print(lc, wc, cc)
```

Binary files

The simple-model functions `io.input` and `io.output` always open a file in text mode (the default). In Unix, there is no difference between binary files and text files. But in some systems, notably Windows, binary files must be opened with a special flag. To handle such binary files, you must use `io.open`, with the letter 'b' in the mode string.

Binary data in Lua are handled similarly to text. A string in Lua may contain any bytes, and almost all functions in the libraries can handle arbitrary bytes. You can even do pattern matching over binary data, as long as the pattern does not contain a zero byte. If you want to match this byte in the subject, you can use the class `%z` instead.

Typically, you read binary data either with the `*all` pattern, that reads the whole file, or with the pattern n, that reads n bytes. As a simple example, the following program converts a text file from DOS format to Unix format (that is, it translates sequences of carriage return–newlines to newlines). It does not use the standard I/O files (`stdin`–`stdout`), because these files are open in text mode. Instead, it assumes that the names of the input file and the output file are given as arguments to the program:

```
local inp = assert(io.open(arg[1], "rb"))
local out = assert(io.open(arg[2], "wb"))

local data = inp:read("*all")
data = string.gsub(data, "\r\n", "\n")
out:write(data)

assert(out:close())
```

You can call this program with the following command line:

```
> lua prog.lua file.dos file.unix
```

As another example, the following program prints all strings found in a binary file:

```
local f = assert(io.open(arg[1], "rb"))
local data = f:read("*all")
local validchars = "[%w%p%s]"
local pattern = string.rep(validchars, 6) .. "+%z"
for w in string.gmatch(data, pattern) do
  print(w)
end
```

The program assumes that a string is any zero-terminated sequence of six or more valid characters, where a valid character is any character accepted by the pattern validchars. In our example, this pattern comprises the alphanumeric, the punctuation, and the space characters. We use string.rep and concatenation to create a pattern that captures all sequences of six or more validchars. The %z at the end of the pattern matches the byte zero at the end of a string.

As a last example, the following program makes a dump of a binary file:

```
local f = assert(io.open(arg[1], "rb"))
local block = 16
while true do
  local bytes = f:read(block)
  if not bytes then break end
  for _, b in pairs{string.byte(bytes, 1, -1)} do
    io.write(string.format("%02X ", b))
  end
  io.write(string.rep("   ", block - string.len(bytes)))
  io.write(" ", string.gsub(bytes, "%c", "."), "\n")
end
```

Again, the first program argument is the input file name; the output goes to the standard output. The program reads the file in chunks of 16 bytes. For each chunk, it writes the hexadecimal representation of each byte, and then it writes the chunk as text, changing control characters to dots. (Note the use of the idiom {string.byte(bytes,1,-1)} to create a table with all bytes of the string bytes.)

Listing 21.2 shows the result of applying this program over itself (in a Unix machine).

21.3   Other Operations on Files

The tmpfile function returns a handle for a temporary file, open in read/write mode. This file is automatically removed (deleted) when your program ends. The flush function executes all pending writes to a file. Like the write function,

Listing 21.2. Dumping the `dump` program:

```
6C 6F 63 61 6C 20 66 20 3D 20 61 73 73 65 72 74    local f = assert
28 69 6F 2E 6F 70 65 6E 28 61 72 67 5B 31 5D 2C    (io.open(arg[1],
20 22 72 62 22 29 29 0A 6C 6F 63 61 6C 20 62 6C     "rb")).local bl
6F 63 6B 20 3D 20 31 36 0A 77 68 69 6C 65 20 74    ock = 16.while t
72 75 65 20 64 6F 0A 20 20 6C 6F 63 61 6C 20 62    rue do.  local b
   . . .
6E 67 2E 67 73 75 62 28 62 79 74 65 73 2C 20 22    ng.gsub(bytes, "
25 63 22 2C 20 22 2E 22 29 2C 20 22 5C 6E 22 29    %c", "."), "\n")
0A 65 6E 64 0A                                      .end.
```

you can call it as a function, `io.flush()`, to flush the current output file; or as a method, `f:flush()`, to flush a particular file `f`.

The `seek` function can both get and set the current position of a file. Its general form is `f:seek(whence,offset)`. The `whence` parameter is a string that specifies how to interpret the offset. Its valid values are "set", when offsets are interpreted from the beginning of the file; "cur", when offsets are interpreted from the current position of the file; and "end", when offsets are interpreted from the end of the file. Independently of the value of `whence`, the call returns the final current position of the file, measured in bytes from the beginning of the file.

The default value for `whence` is "cur" and for `offset` is zero. Therefore, the call `file:seek()` returns the current file position, without changing it; the call `file:seek("set")` resets the position to the beginning of the file (and returns zero); and the call `file:seek("end")` sets the position to the end of the file and returns its size. The following function gets the file size without changing its current position:

```
function fsize (file)
   local current = file:seek()      -- get current position
   local size = file:seek("end")    -- get file size
   file:seek("set", current)        -- restore position
   return size
end
```

All these functions return **nil** plus an error message in case of error.

22

The Operating System Library

The Operating System library includes functions for file manipulation, for getting the current date and time, and other facilities related to the operating system. It is defined in table os. This library pays a price for Lua portability: because Lua is written in ANSI C, it uses only the functions that the ANSI standard defines. Many OS facilities, such as directory manipulation and sockets, are not part of this standard; therefore, the system library does not provide them. There are other Lua libraries, not included in the main distribution, that provide extended OS access. Examples are the posix library, which offers all functionality of the POSIX.1 standard to Lua; and luasocket, for network support.

For file manipulation, all that this library provides is an os.rename function, that changes the name of a file; and os.remove, that removes (deletes) a file.

22.1 Date and Time

Two functions, time and date, provide all date and time functionality in Lua.

The time function, when called without arguments, returns the current date and time, coded as a number. (In most systems, this number is the number of seconds since some epoch.) When called with a table, it returns the number representing the date and time described by the table. Such *date tables* have the following significant fields:

year	a full year
month	01–12
day	01–31
hour	00–23
min	00–59
sec	00–59
isdst	a boolean, **true** if daylight saving is on

The first three fields are mandatory; the others default to noon (12:00:00) when not provided. In a Unix system (where the epoch is 00:00:00 UTC, January 1, 1970) running in Rio de Janeiro (which is three hours west of Greenwich), we have the following examples:

```
print(os.time{year=1970, month=1, day=1, hour=0})        --> 10800
print(os.time{year=1970, month=1, day=1, hour=0, sec=1})
   --> 10801
print(os.time{year=1970, month=1, day=1})                --> 54000
```

(Note that 10 800 is 3 hours in seconds, and 54 000 is 10 800 plus 12 hours in seconds.)

The `date` function, despite its name, is a kind of a reverse of the `time` function: it converts a number representing the date and time back to some higher-level representation. Its first parameter is a *format string*, describing the representation we want. The second is the numeric date–time; it defaults to the current date and time.

To produce a date table, we use the format string "*t". For instance, the call `os.date("*t", 906000490)` returns the following table:

```
{year = 1998, month = 9, day = 16, yday = 259, wday = 4,
   hour = 23, min = 48, sec = 10, isdst = false}
```

Notice that, besides the fields used by `os.time`, the table created by `os.date` also gives the week day (`wday`, 1 is Sunday) and the year day (`yday`, 1 is January 1st).

For other format strings, `os.date` formats the date as a string that is a copy of the format string where specific tags were replaced by information about time and date. All tags are represented by a '%' followed by a letter, as in the next examples:

```
print(os.date("today is %A, in %B")) --> today is Tuesday, in May
print(os.date("%x", 906000490))      --> 09/16/1998
```

All representations follow the current locale. For instance, in a locale for Brazil–Portuguese, %B would result in "setembro" and %x in "16/09/98".

The following table shows each tag, its meaning, and its value for September 16, 1998 (a Wednesday), at 23:48:10. For numeric values, the table shows also their range of possible values:

%a	abbreviated weekday name (e.g., Wed)
%A	full weekday name (e.g., Wednesday)
%b	abbreviated month name (e.g., Sep)
%B	full month name (e.g., September)
%c	date and time (e.g., 09/16/98 23:48:10)
%d	day of the month (16) [01–31]
%H	hour, using a 24-hour clock (23) [00–23]
%I	hour, using a 12-hour clock (11) [01–12]
%M	minute (48) [00–59]
%m	month (09) [01–12]
%p	either "am" or "pm" (pm)
%S	second (10) [00–61]
%w	weekday (3) [0–6 = Sunday–Saturday]
%x	date (e.g., 09/16/98)
%X	time (e.g., 23:48:10)
%Y	full year (1998)
%y	two-digit year (98) [00–99]
%%	the character '%'

If you call date without any arguments, it uses the %c format, that is, complete date and time information in a reasonable format. Note that the representations for %x, %X, and %c change according to the locale and the system. If you want a fixed representation, such as mm/dd/yyyy, use an explicit format string, such as "%m/%d/%Y".

The os.clock function returns the number of seconds of CPU time for the program. Its typical use is to benchmark a piece of code:

```
local x = os.clock()
local s = 0
for i=1,100000 do s = s + i end
print(string.format("elapsed time: %.2f\n", os.clock() - x))
```

22.2 Other System Calls

The os.exit function terminates the execution of a program. The os.getenv function gets the value of an environment variable. It takes the name of the variable and returns a string with its value:

```
print(os.getenv("HOME"))     --> /home/lua
```

If the variable is not defined, the call returns **nil**. The function os.execute runs a system command; it is equivalent to the system function in C. It takes a string with the command and returns an error code. For instance, both in Unix and in DOS-Windows, you can write the following function to create new directories:

```
function createDir (dirname)
  os.execute("mkdir " .. dirname)
end
```

The os.execute function is powerful, but it is also highly system dependent.

The os.setlocale function sets the current locale used by a Lua program. Locales define behavior that is sensitive to cultural or linguistic differences. The setlocale function has two string parameters: the locale name and a category that specifies what features the locale will affect. There are six categories of locales: "collate" controls the alphabetic order of strings; "ctype" controls the types of individual characters (e.g., what is a letter) and the conversion between lower and upper cases; "monetary" has no influence in Lua programs; "numeric" controls how numbers are formatted; "time" controls how date and time are formatted (i.e., function os.date); and "all" controls all the above functions. The default category is "all", so that if you call setlocale with only the locale name it will set all categories. The setlocale function returns the locale name or **nil** if it fails (usually because the system does not support the given locale).

```
print(os.setlocale("ISO-8859-1", "collate"))    --> ISO-8859-1
```

The category "numeric" is a little tricky. As Portuguese and other Latin languages use a comma instead of a point to represent decimal numbers, the locale changes the way Lua prints and reads these numbers. But the locale does not change the way that Lua parses numbers in programs (among other reasons because expressions like print(3,4) already have a meaning in Lua). If you are using Lua to create pieces of Lua code, you may have problems here:

```
print(os.setlocale("pt_BR"))     --> pt_BR
s = "return (" .. 3.4 .. ")"
print(s)                         --> return (3,4)
print(loadstring(s))
   --> nil    [string "return (3,4)"]:1: ')' expected near ','
```

23

The Debug Library

The debug library does not give you a debugger for Lua, but it offers all the primitives that you need for writing your own debugger. For performance reasons, the official interface to these primitives is through the C API. The debug library in Lua is a way to access them directly within Lua code.

Unlike the other libraries, you should use the debug library with parsimony. First, some of its functionality is not exactly famous for performance. Second, it breaks some sacred truths of the language, such as that you cannot access a local variable from outside the function that created it. Frequently, you may not want to open this library in your final version of a product, or else you may want to erase it, running debug=nil.

The debug library comprises two kinds of functions: *introspective functions* and *hooks*. Introspective functions allow us to inspect several aspects of the running program, such as its stack of active functions, current line of execution, and values and names of local variables. Hooks allow us to trace the execution of a program.

An important concept in the debug library is the *stack level*. A stack level is a number that refers to a particular function that is active at that moment, that is, it has been called and has not returned yet. The function calling the debug library has level 1, the function that called it has level 2, and so on.

23.1 Introspective Facilities

The main introspective function in the debug library is the debug.getinfo function. Its first parameter may be a function or a stack level. When you call debug.getinfo(foo) for some function foo, you get a table with some data about this function. The table may have the following fields:

source: where the function was defined. If the function was defined in a string (through loadstring), source is this string. If the function was defined in a file, source is the file name prefixed with a '@'.

short_src: a short version of source (up to 60 characters), useful for error messages.

linedefined: the first line of the source where the function was defined.

lastlinedefined: the last line of the source where the function was defined.

what: what this function is. Options are "Lua" if foo is a regular Lua function, "C" if it is a C function, or "main" if it is the main part of a Lua chunk.

name: a reasonable name for the function.

namewhat: what the previous field means. This field may be "global", "local", "method", "field", or "" (the empty string). The empty string means that Lua did not find a name for the function.

nups: number of upvalues of that function.

activelines: a table representing the set of active lines of the function. An *active line* is a line with some code, as opposed to empty lines or lines containing only comments. (A typical use of this information is for setting breakpoints. Most debuggers do not allow you to set a breakpoint outside an active line, as it would be unreachable.)[16]

func: the function itself; see later.

When foo is a C function, Lua does not have much data about it. For such functions, only the fields what, name, and namewhat are relevant.

When you call debug.getinfo(n) for some number *n*, you get data about the function active at that stack level. For instance, if *n* is 1, you get data about the function doing the call. (When *n* is 0, you get data about getinfo itself, a C function.) If *n* is larger than the number of active functions in the stack, debug.getinfo returns **nil**. When you query an active function, calling debug.getinfo with a number, the result table has an extra field, currentline, with the line where the function is at that moment. Moreover, func has the function that is active at that level.

The field name is tricky. Remember that, because functions are first-class values in Lua, a function may not have a name, or may have several names. Lua tries to find a name for a function by looking into the code that called the function, to see how it was called. This method works only when we call getinfo with a number, that is, we get information about a particular invocation.

The getinfo function is not efficient. Lua keeps debug information in a form that does not impair program execution; efficient retrieval is a secondary goal here. To achieve better performance, getinfo has an optional second parameter

---

[16]The activelines field is new in Lua 5.1.

that selects what information to get. With this parameter, the function does not waste time collecting data that the user does not need. The format of this parameter is a string, where each letter selects a group of fields, according to the following table:

'n'	selects name and namewhat
'f'	selects func
'S'	selects source, short_src, what, linedefined, and lastlinedefined
'l'	selects currentline
'L'	selects activelines
'u'	selects nup

The following function illustrates the use of debug.getinfo. It prints a primitive traceback of the active stack:

```
function traceback ()
  for level = 1, math.huge do
    local info = debug.getinfo(level, "Sl")
    if not info then break end
    if info.what == "C" then    -- is a C function?
      print(level, "C function")
    else    -- a Lua function
      print(string.format("[%s]:%d", info.short_src,
                                     info.currentline))
    end
  end
end
```

It is not difficult to improve this function, by including more data from getinfo. Actually, the debug library offers such an improved version, the traceback function. Unlike our version, debug.traceback does not print its result; instead, it returns a (usually long) string with the traceback.

Accessing local variables

We can inspect the local variables of any active function with debug.getlocal. This function has two parameters: the stack level of the function you are querying and a variable index. It returns two values: the name and the current value of this variable. If the variable index is larger than the number of active variables, getlocal returns **nil**. If the stack level is invalid, it raises an error. We can use debug.getinfo to check the validity of the stack level.

Lua numbers local variables in the order that they appear in a function, counting only the variables that are active in the current scope of the function. For instance, the code

```
function foo (a, b)
  local x
  do local c = a - b end
  local a = 1
  while true do
    local name, value = debug.getlocal(1, a)
    if not name then break end
    print(name, value)
    a = a + 1
  end
end

foo(10, 20)
```

will print

```
a        10
b        20
x        nil
a        4
```

The variable with index 1 is a (the first parameter), 2 is b, 3 is x, and 4 is the other a. At the point where getlocal is called, c is already out of scope, while name and value are not yet in scope. (Remember that local variables are only visible *after* their initialization code.)

You can also change the values of local variables, with debug.setlocal. Its first two parameters are a stack level and a variable index, like in getlocal. Its third parameter is the new value for this variable. It returns the variable name, or **nil** if the variable index is out of scope.

Accessing non-local variables

The debug library also allows us to access the non-local variables used by a Lua function, with getupvalue. Unlike local variables, the non-local variables referred by a function exist even when the function is not active (this is what closures are about, after all). Therefore, the first argument for getupvalue is not a stack level, but a function (a closure, more precisely). The second argument is the variable index. Lua numbers non-local variables in the order they are first referred in a function, but this order is not relevant, because a function cannot access two non-local variables with the same name.

You can also update non-local variables, with debug.setupvalue. As you might expect, it has three parameters: a closure, a variable index, and the new value. Like setlocal, it returns the name of the variable, or **nil** if the variable index is out of range.

Listing 23.1 shows how we can access the value of any given variable of a calling function, given the variable name. First, we try a local variable. If there is more than one variable with the given name, we must get the one with the highest index; so we must always go through the whole loop. If we cannot find

Listing 23.1. Getting the value of a variable:

```lua
function getvarvalue (name)
  local value, found

  -- try local variables
  for i = 1, math.huge do
    local n, v = debug.getlocal(2, i)
    if not n then break end
    if n == name then
      value = v
      found = true
    end
  end
  if found then return value end

  -- try non-local variables
  local func = debug.getinfo(2, "f").func
  for i = 1, math.huge do
    local n, v = debug.getupvalue(func, i)
    if not n then break end
    if n == name then return v end
  end

  -- not found; get from the environment
  return getfenv(func)[name]
end
```

any local variable with that name, then we try non-local variables. First, we get the calling function, with debug.getinfo, and then we traverse its non-local variables. Finally, if we cannot find a non-local variable with that name, then we get a global variable. Notice the use of the number 2 as the first argument in the calls to debug.getlocal and debug.getinfo to access the calling function.

Accessing other coroutines

All introspective functions from the debug library accept an optional coroutine as their first argument, so that we can inspect the coroutine from outside.[17] For instance, consider the next example:

```lua
co = coroutine.create(function ()
  local x = 10
  coroutine.yield()
  error("some error")
end)
```

---

[17]This facility is new in Lua 5.1.

```
coroutine.resume(co)
print(debug.traceback(co))
```

The call to `traceback` will work on coroutine `co`, resulting in something like this:

```
stack traceback:
        [C]: in function 'yield'
        temp:3: in function <temp:1>
```

The trace does not go through the call to `resume`, because the coroutine and the main program run in different stacks.

If a coroutine raises an error, it does not unwind its stack. This means that we can inspect it after the error. Continuing our example, if we resume the coroutine again it hits the error:

```
print(coroutine.resume(co))        --> false    temp:4: some error
```

Now if we print its traceback we get something like this:

```
stack traceback:
        [C]: in function 'error'
        temp:4: in function <temp:1>
```

We can also inspect local variables from a coroutine, even after an error:

```
print(debug.getlocal(co, 1, 1))     --> x        10
```

23.2 Hooks

The hook mechanism of the debug library allows us to register a function that will be called at specific events as a program runs. There are four kinds of events that can trigger a hook: *call* events happen every time Lua calls a function; *return* events happen every time a function returns; *line* events happen when Lua starts executing a new line of code; and *count* events happen after a given number of instructions. Lua calls hooks with a single argument, a string describing the event that generated the call: "call", "return", "line", or "count". For line events, it also passes a second argument, the new line number. To get more information inside a hook we must call `debug.getinfo`.

To register a hook, we call `debug.sethook` with two or three arguments: the first argument is the hook function; the second argument is a string that describes the events we want to monitor; and an optional third argument is a number that describes at what frequency we want to get count events. To monitor the call, return, and line events, we add their first letters ('c', 'r', or 'l') in the mask string. To monitor the count event, we simply supply a counter as the third argument. To turn off hooks, we call `sethook` with no arguments.

As a simple example, the following code installs a primitive tracer, which prints each line the interpreter executes:

```
debug.sethook(print, "l")
```

This call simply installs `print` as the hook function and instructs Lua to call it only at line events. A more elaborated tracer can use `getinfo` to add the current file name to the trace:

```
function trace (event, line)
  local s = debug.getinfo(2).short_src
  print(s .. ":" .. line)
end

debug.sethook(trace, "l")
```

23.3 Profiles

Despite its name, the debug library is useful also for tasks other than debugging. A common such task is profiling. For a profile with timing, it is better to use the C interface: the overhead of a Lua call for each hook is too high and may invalidate any measure. However, for counting profiles, Lua code does a decent job. In this section, we will develop a rudimentary profiler that lists the number of times each function in a program is called in a run.

The main data structures of our program are two tables: one that associates functions to their call counters, another that associates functions to their names. The indices to both tables are the functions themselves.

```
local Counters = {}
local Names = {}
```

We could retrieve the name data after the profiling, but remember that we get better results if we get the name of a function while it is active, because then Lua can look at the code that is calling the function to find its name.

Now we define the hook function. Its job is to get the function being called and increment the corresponding counter; it also collects the function name:

```
local function hook ()
  local f = debug.getinfo(2, "f").func
  if Counters[f] == nil then    -- first time 'f' is called?
    Counters[f] = 1
    Names[f] = debug.getinfo(2, "Sn")
  else     -- only increment the counter
    Counters[f] = Counters[f] + 1
  end
end
```

The next step is to run the program with this hook. We will assume that the main chunk of the program is in a file and that the user gives this file name as an argument to the profiler:

```
% lua profiler main-prog
```

With this scheme, the profiler can get the file name in `arg[1]`, turn on the hook, and run the file:

```
local f = assert(loadfile(arg[1]))
debug.sethook(hook, "c")  -- turn on the hook for calls
f()                       -- run the main program
debug.sethook()           -- turn off the hook
```

The last step is to show the results. The next function produces a name for a function. Because function names in Lua are so uncertain, we add to each function its location, given as a pair *file:line*. If a function has no name, then we use only its location. If a function is a C function, we use only its name (as it has no location).

```
function getname (func)
  local n = Names[func]
  if n.what == "C" then
    return n.name
  end
  local lc = string.format("[%s]:%s", n.short_src, n.linedefined)
  if n.namewhat ~= "" then
    return string.format("%s (%s)", lc, n.name)
  else
    return lc
  end
end
```

Finally, we print each function with its counter:

```
for func, count in pairs(Counters) do
  print(getname(func), count)
end
```

If we apply our profiler to the Markov example that we developed in Section 10.2, we get a result like this:

```
[markov.lua]:4 884723
write    10000
[markov.lua]:0 (f)        1
read     31103
sub      884722
[markov.lua]:1 (allwords)        1
[markov.lua]:20 (prefix)         894723
find     915824
[markov.lua]:26 (insert)         884723
random   10000
sethook 1
insert   884723
```

This result means that the anonymous function at line 4 (which is the iterator function defined inside `allwords`) was called 884 723 times, `write` (`io.write`) was called 10 000 times, and so on.

There are several improvements that you can make to this profiler, such as to sort the output, to print better function names, and to embellish the output format. Nevertheless, this basic profiler is already useful as it is, and can be used as a base for more advanced tools.

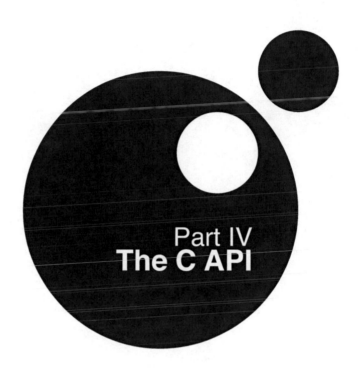

Part IV
The C API

24

An Overview of the C API

Lua is an *embedded language*. This means that Lua is not a stand-alone package, but a library that we can link with other applications to incorporate Lua facilities into them.

You may be wondering: if Lua is not a stand-alone program, how come we have been using Lua stand-alone through the whole book? The solution to this puzzle is the Lua interpreter (the executable lua). This interpreter is a tiny application (with less than four hundred lines of code) that uses the Lua library to implement the stand-alone interpreter. This program handles the interface with the user, taking her files and strings to feed them to the Lua library, which does the bulk of the work (such as actually running Lua code).

This ability to be used as a library to extend an application is what makes Lua an *extension language*. At the same time, a program that uses Lua can register new functions in the Lua environment; such functions are implemented in C (or another language), so that they can add facilities that cannot be written directly in Lua. This is what makes Lua an *extensible language*.

These two views of Lua (as an extension language and as an extensible language) correspond to two kinds of interaction between C and Lua. In the first kind, C has the control and Lua is the library. The C code in this kind of interaction is what we call *application code*. In the second kind, Lua has the control and C is the library. Here, the C code is called *library code*. Both application code and library code use the same API to communicate with Lua, the so-called C API.

The C API is the set of functions that allow C code to interact with Lua. It comprises functions to read and write Lua global variables, to call Lua functions, to run pieces of Lua code, to register C functions so that they can later be called by Lua code, and so on. (Throughout this text, the term "function" actually means "function or macro". The API implements several facilities as macros.)

The C API follows the *modus operandi* of C, which is quite different from the *modus operandi* of Lua. When programming in C, we must care about type checking (and type errors), error recovery, memory-allocation errors, and several other sources of complexity. Most functions in the API do not check the correctness of their arguments; it is your responsibility to make sure that the arguments are valid before calling a function. If you make mistakes, you can get a "segmentation fault" error or something similar, instead of a well-behaved error message. Moreover, the API emphasizes flexibility and simplicity, sometimes at the cost of ease of use. Common tasks may involve several API calls. This may be boring, but it gives you full control over all details.

As the title says, the goal of this chapter is to give an overview of what is involved when you use Lua from C. Do not bother understanding all the details of what is going on now. Later we will fill in the details. Nevertheless, do not forget that you can find more details about specific functions in the Lua reference manual. Moreover, you can find several examples of the use of the API in the Lua distribution itself. The Lua stand-alone interpreter (lua.c) provides examples of application code, while the standard libraries (lmathlib.c, lstrlib.c, etc.) provide examples of library code.

From now on, we are wearing a C programmers' hat. When I talk about "you", I mean you when programming in C, or you impersonated by the C code you write.

A major component in the communication between Lua and C is an omnipresent virtual *stack*. Almost all API calls operate on values on this stack. All data exchange from Lua to C and from C to Lua occurs through this stack. Moreover, you can use the stack to keep intermediate results too. The stack helps to solve two impedance mismatches between Lua and C: the first is caused by Lua being garbage collected, whereas C requires explicit deallocation; the second results from the shock between dynamic typing in Lua versus the static typing of C. We will discuss the stack in more detail in Section 24.2.

24.1   A First Example

We will start this overview with a simple example of an application program: a stand-alone Lua interpreter. We can write a primitive stand-alone interpreter as in Listing 24.1. The header file lua.h defines the basic functions provided by Lua. It includes functions to create a new Lua environment, to invoke Lua functions (such as lua_pcall), to read and write global variables in the Lua environment, to register new functions to be called by Lua, and so on. Everything defined in lua.h has a lua_ prefix.

The header file lauxlib.h defines the functions provided by the *auxiliary library* (auxlib). All its definitions start with luaL_ (e.g., luaL_loadbuffer). The auxiliary library uses the basic API provided by lua.h to provide a higher abstraction level; all Lua standard libraries use the auxlib. The basic API

Listing 24.1. A simple stand-alone Lua interpreter:

```c
#include <stdio.h>
#include "lua.h"
#include "lauxlib.h"
#include "lualib.h"

int main (void) {
  char buff[256];
  int error;
  lua_State *L = luaL_newstate();            /* opens Lua */
  luaL_openlibs(L);           /* opens the standard libraries */

  while (fgets(buff, sizeof(buff), stdin) != NULL) {
    error = luaL_loadbuffer(L, buff, strlen(buff), "line") ||
            lua_pcall(L, 0, 0, 0);
    if (error) {
      fprintf(stderr, "%s", lua_tostring(L, -1));
      lua_pop(L, 1);  /* pop error message from the stack */
    }
  }

  lua_close(L);
  return 0;
}
```

strives for economy and orthogonality, whereas auxlib strives for practicality for common tasks. Of course, it is very easy for your program to create other abstractions that it needs, too. Keep in mind that the auxlib has no access to the internals of Lua. It does its entire job through the official basic API.

The Lua library defines no global variables at all. It keeps all its state in the dynamic structure lua_State, and a pointer to this structure is passed as an argument to all functions inside Lua. This implementation makes Lua reentrant and ready to be used in multithreaded code.

The luaL_newstate function creates a new environment (or *state*). When luaL_newstate creates a fresh environment, this environment contains no pre-defined functions, not even print. To keep Lua small, all standard libraries are provided as separate packages, so that you do not have to use them if you do not need to. The header file lualib.h defines functions to open the libraries. The function luaL_openlibs opens all standard libraries.

After creating a state and populating it with the standard libraries, it is time to interpret the user input. For each line the user enters, the program first calls luaL_loadbuffer to compile the code. If there are no errors, the call returns zero and pushes the resulting chunk on the stack. (Remember that we will discuss this "magic" stack in detail in the next section.) Then the program calls lua_pcall, which pops the chunk from the stack and runs it in protected mode. Like luaL_loadbuffer, lua_pcall returns zero if there are no errors. In case of error, both functions push an error message on the stack; we get this message with lua_tostring and, after printing it, we remove it from the stack with lua_pop.

Notice that, in case of error, this program simply prints the error message to the standard error stream. Real error handling can be quite complex in C, and how to do it depends on the nature of your application. The Lua core never writes anything directly to any output stream; it signals errors by returning error codes and error messages. Each application can handle these messages in a way most appropriate for its needs. To simplify our discussions, we will assume for now a simple error handler like the following one, which prints an error message, closes the Lua state, and exits from the whole application:

```
#include <stdarg.h>
#include <stdio.h>
#include <stdlib.h>

void error (lua_State *L, const char *fmt, ...) {
  va_list argp;
  va_start(argp, fmt);
  vfprintf(stderr, fmt, argp);
  va_end(argp);
  lua_close(L);
  exit(EXIT_FAILURE);
}
```

Later we will discuss more about error handling in the application code.

Because you can compile Lua both as C and as C++ code, lua.h does not include this typical adjustment code that is present in several other C libraries:

```
#ifdef __cplusplus
extern "C" {
#endif
    ...
#ifdef __cplusplus
}
#endif
```

If you have compiled Lua as C code (the most common case) and are using it in C++, you can include lua.hpp instead of lua.h. It is defined as follows:

```
extern "C" {
#include "lua.h"
}
```

24.2 The Stack

We face two problems when trying to exchange values between Lua and C: the mismatch between a dynamic and a static type system and the mismatch between automatic and manual memory management.

In Lua, when we write a[k] =v, both k and v can have several different types; even a may have different types, due to metatables. If we want to offer this operation in C, however, any given settable function must have a fixed type. We would need dozens of different functions for this single operation (one function for each combination of types for the three arguments).

We could solve this problem by declaring some kind of union type in C, let us call it lua_Value, that could represent all Lua values. Then, we could declare settable as

```
void lua_settable (lua_Value a, lua_Value k, lua_Value v);
```

This solution has two drawbacks. First, it can be difficult to map such a complex type to other languages; Lua has been designed to interface easily not only with C/C++, but also with Java, Fortran, C#, and the like. Second, Lua does garbage collection: if we keep a Lua table in a C variable, the Lua engine has no way to know about this use; it may (wrongly) assume that this table is garbage and collect it.

Therefore, the Lua API does not define anything like a lua_Value type. Instead, it uses an abstract stack to exchange values between Lua and C. Each slot in this stack can hold any Lua value. Whenever you want to ask for a value from Lua (such as the value of a global variable), you call Lua, which pushes the required value on the stack. Whenever you want to pass a value to Lua, you first push the value on the stack, and then you call Lua (which will pop the value). We still need a different function to push each C type on the stack and a different function to get each value from the stack, but we avoid the combinatorial explosion. Moreover, because this stack is managed by Lua, the garbage collector knows which values C is using.

Nearly all functions in the API use the stack. As we saw in our first example, luaL_loadbuffer leaves its result on the stack (either the compiled chunk or an error message); lua_pcall gets the function to be called from the stack and leaves any occasional error message there too.

Lua manipulates this stack in a strict LIFO discipline (Last In, First Out). When you call Lua, it changes only the top part of the stack. Your C code has more freedom; specifically, it can inspect any element inside the stack and even insert and delete elements in any arbitrary position.

Pushing elements

The API has one push function for each C type that can be represented in Lua: lua_pushnil for the constant **nil**, lua_pushnumber for doubles, lua_pushinteger for integers, lua_pushboolean for booleans (integers, in C), lua_pushlstring for arbitrary strings (char* plus a length), and lua_pushstring for zero-terminated strings:

```
void lua_pushnil     (lua_State *L);
void lua_pushboolean (lua_State *L, int bool);
void lua_pushnumber  (lua_State *L, lua_Number n);
void lua_pushinteger (lua_State *L, lua_Integer n);
void lua_pushlstring (lua_State *L, const char *s, size_t len);
void lua_pushstring  (lua_State *L, const char *s);
```

There are also functions to push C functions and userdata values on the stack; we will discuss them later.

The type lua_Number is the numeric type in Lua. It is a double by default, but some installations may change it to a float or even a long integer, to accommodate Lua to restricted machines. The type lua_Integer is a signal integral type large enough to store the size of large strings. Usually, it is defined as the ptrdiff_t type.

Strings in Lua are not zero-terminated; they can contain arbitrary binary data. In consequence, they must rely on an explicit length. The basic function to push a string onto the stack is lua_pushlstring, which requires an explicit length as an argument. For zero-terminated strings, you can use also lua_pushstring, which uses strlen to supply the string length. Lua never keeps pointers to external strings (or to any other external object except C functions, which are always static). For any string that it has to keep, Lua either makes an internal copy or reuses one. Therefore, you can free or modify your buffer as soon as these functions return.

Whenever you push an element onto the stack, it is your responsibility to ensure that the stack has space for it. Remember, you are a C programmer now; Lua will not spoil you. When Lua starts and any time that Lua calls C, the stack has at least 20 free slots (this constant is defined as LUA_MINSTACK in lua.h). This space is more than enough for most common uses, so usually we do not even think about it. However, some tasks may need more stack space (e.g., calling a function with too many arguments). In such cases, you may want to call lua_checkstack, which checks whether the stack has enough space for your needs:

```
int lua_checkstack (lua_State *L, int sz);
```

Querying elements

To refer to elements in the stack, the API uses *indices*. The first element pushed on the stack has index 1, the next one has index 2, and so on until the top. We can also access elements using the top of the stack as our reference, using negative indices. In this case, –1 refers to the element at the top (that is, the last element pushed), –2 to the previous element, and so on. For instance, the call lua_tostring(L, -1) returns the value at the top of the stack as a string. As we will see, there are several occasions when it is natural to index the stack from the bottom (that is, with positive indices), and several other occasions when the natural way is to use negative indices.

To check whether an element has a specific type, the API offers a family of functions lua_is*, where the * can be any Lua type. So, there are lua_isnumber, lua_isstring, lua_istable, and the like. All these functions have the same prototype:

```
int lua_is* (lua_State *L, int index);
```

Actually, lua_isnumber does not check whether the value has that specific type, but whether the value can be converted to that type; lua_isstring is similar. For instance, any number satisfies lua_isstring.

There is also a function lua_type, which returns the type of an element in the stack. Each type is represented by a constant defined in the header file lua.h: LUA_TNIL, LUA_TBOOLEAN, LUA_TNUMBER, LUA_TSTRING, LUA_TTABLE, LUA_TTHREAD, LUA_TUSERDATA, and LUA_TFUNCTION. This function is mainly used in conjunction with a switch statement. It is also useful when we need to check for strings and numbers without coercions.

To get a value from the stack, there are the lua_to* functions:

```
int         lua_toboolean (lua_State *L, int index);
lua_Number  lua_tonumber  (lua_State *L, int index);
lua_Integer lua_tointeger (lua_State *L, int index);
const char *lua_tolstring (lua_State *L, int index, size_t *len);
size_t      lua_objlen    (lua_State *L, int index);
```

It is OK to call them even when the given element does not have the correct type. In this case, lua_toboolean, lua_tonumber, lua_tointeger, and lua_objlen return zero; the other functions return NULL. The zero is not useful, but ANSI C provides us with no invalid numeric value that we could use to signal errors. For the other functions, however, we frequently do not need to use the corresponding lua_is* function: we just call lua_to* and then test whether the result is not NULL.

The lua_tolstring function returns a pointer to an internal copy of the string and stores the string's length in the position given by len. You cannot change this internal copy (there is a const there to remind you). Lua ensures that this pointer is valid as long as the corresponding string value is in the stack. When a C function called by Lua returns, Lua clears its stack; therefore, as a rule, you should never store pointers to Lua strings outside the function that got them.

Any string that lua_tolstring returns always has an extra zero at its end, but it may have other zeros inside it. The size returned through the third argument, len, is the real string's length. In particular, assuming that the value at the top of the stack is a string, the following assertions are always valid:

```
size_t l;
const char *s = lua_tolstring(L, -1, &l);   /* any Lua string */
assert(s[l] == '\0');
assert(strlen(s) <= l);
```

You can call `lua_tolstring` with `NULL` as its third argument if you do not need the length. Better yet, you can use the macro `lua_tostring`, which simply calls `lua_tolstring` with a `NULL` third argument.

The `lua_objlen` function returns the "length" of an object. For strings and tables, this value is the result of the length operator '#'. This function can also be used to get the size of a full userdata. (We will discuss userdata in Section 28.1.)

To illustrate the use of these functions, Listing 24.2 presents a useful helper function that dumps the entire content of the stack.   This function traverses the stack from bottom to top, printing each element according to its type. It prints strings between quotes; for numbers it uses a '%g' format; for other values (tables, functions, etc.), it prints only their types (`lua_typename` converts a type code to a type name).

Other stack operations

Besides the previous functions, which interchange values between C and the stack, the API offers also the following operations for generic stack manipulation:

```
int  lua_gettop   (lua_State *L);
void lua_settop   (lua_State *L, int index);
void lua_pushvalue (lua_State *L, int index);
void lua_remove   (lua_State *L, int index);
void lua_insert   (lua_State *L, int index);
void lua_replace  (lua_State *L, int index);
```

The `lua_gettop` function returns the number of elements in the stack, which is also the index of the top element. `lua_settop` sets the top (that is, the number of elements in the stack) to a specific value. If the previous top was higher than the new one, the top values are discarded. Otherwise, the function pushes **nil**s on the stack to get the given size. As a particular case, `lua_settop(L, 0)` empties the stack. You can also use negative indices with `lua_settop`. Using this facility, the API offers the following macro, which pops n elements from the stack:

```
#define lua_pop(L,n)  lua_settop(L, -(n) - 1)
```

The `lua_pushvalue` function pushes on the stack a copy of the element at the given index; `lua_remove` removes the element at the given index, shifting down all elements on top of this position to fill in the gap; `lua_insert` moves the top element into the given position, shifting up all elements on top of this position to open space; finally, `lua_replace` pops a value from the top and sets it as the value of the given index, without moving anything. Notice that the following operations have no effect on the stack:

```
lua_settop(L, -1);  /* set top to its current value */
lua_insert(L, -1);  /* move top element to the top */
```

Listing 24.2. Dumping the stack:

```
static void stackDump (lua_State *L) {
  int i;
  int top = lua_gettop(L);
  for (i = 1; i <= top; i++) {  /* repeat for each level */
    int t = lua_type(L, i);
    switch (t) {
      case LUA_TSTRING: {  /* strings */
        printf("'%s'", lua_tostring(L, i));
        break;
      }
      case LUA_TBOOLEAN: {  /* booleans */
        printf(lua_toboolean(L, i) ? "true" : "false");
        break;
      }
      case LUA_TNUMBER: {  /* numbers */
        printf("%g", lua_tonumber(L, i));
        break;
      }
      default: {  /* other values */
        printf("%s", lua_typename(L, t));
        break;
      }
    }
    printf("  ");  /* put a separator */
  }
  printf("\n");  /* end the listing */
}
```

The program in Listing 24.3 uses stackDump (defined in Listing 24.2) to illustrate these stack operations.

24.3   Error Handling with the C API

Unlike C++ or Java, the C language does not offer an exception handling mechanism. To ameliorate this difficulty, Lua uses the setjmp facility from C, which results in a mechanism similar to exception handling.

All structures in Lua are dynamic: they grow as needed, and eventually shrink again when possible. This means that the possibility of a memory-allocation failure is pervasive in Lua. Almost any operation may face this eventuality. Instead of using error codes for each operation in its API, Lua uses exceptions to signal these errors. This means that almost all API functions may

Listing 24.3. An example of stack manipulation:

```
#include <stdio.h>
#include "lua.h"
#include "lauxlib.h"

static void stackDump (lua_State *L) {
  <as in Listing 24.2>
}

int main (void) {
  lua_State *L = luaL_newstate();

  lua_pushboolean(L, 1);
  lua_pushnumber(L, 10);
  lua_pushnil(L);
  lua_pushstring(L, "hello");

  stackDump(L);
                  /* true  10  nil  'hello' */

  lua_pushvalue(L, -4); stackDump(L);
                  /* true  10  nil  'hello'  true */

  lua_replace(L, 3); stackDump(L);
                  /* true  10  true  'hello' */

  lua_settop(L, 6); stackDump(L);
                  /* true  10  true  'hello'  nil  nil */

  lua_remove(L, -3); stackDump(L);
                  /* true  10  true  nil  nil */

  lua_settop(L, -5); stackDump(L);
                  /* true */

  lua_close(L);
  return 0;
}
```

throw an error (that is, call `longjmp`) instead of returning.

When we write library code (that is, C functions to be called from Lua), the use of long jumps is almost as convenient as a real exception-handling facility, because Lua catches any occasional error. When we write application code (that is, C code that calls Lua), however, we must provide a way to catch those errors.

Error handling in application code

Typically, your application code runs *unprotected*. Because its code is not called by Lua, Lua cannot set an appropriate context to catch errors (that is, it cannot call `setjmp`). In such environments, when Lua faces an error like "not enough memory", there is not much that it can do. It calls a panic function and, if that function returns, exits the application. You can set your own panic function with the `lua_atpanic` function.

Not all API functions throw exceptions. Functions `luaL_newstate`, `lua_load`, `lua_pcall`, and `lua_close` are all safe. Moreover, most other functions can throw an exception only in case of memory-allocation failure: for instance, `luaL_loadfile` fails if there is not enough memory for a copy of the file name. Several programs have nothing to do when they run out of memory, so they may ignore these exceptions. For those programs, if Lua runs out of memory, it is OK to panic.

If you do not want your application to exit, even in case of a memory-allocation failure, you have two options. The first is to set a panic function that does not return to Lua, for instance using a `longjmp` to your own `setjmp`. The second is to run your code in *protected mode*.

Most applications (including the stand-alone interpreter) run Lua code by calling `lua_pcall`; therefore, typically your Lua code will run in protected mode. Even in case of memory-allocation failure, `lua_pcall` returns an error code, leaving the interpreter in a consistent state. If you also want to protect all your C code that interacts with Lua, then you can use `lua_cpcall`. This function is similar to `lua_pcall`, but it takes as argument the C function to be called, so there is no danger of a memory-allocation failure while pushing the given function into the stack.

Error handling in library code

Lua is a *safe* language. This means that, no matter what you write, no matter how wrong it is, you can always understand the behavior of a program in terms of Lua itself. Moreover, errors are detected and explained in terms of Lua, too. You can contrast that with C, where the behavior of many wrong programs can be explained only in terms of the underling hardware, and where error positions are given as a program counter.

Whenever you add new C functions to Lua, you can break its safety. For instance, a function like `poke`, which stores an arbitrary byte at an arbitrary memory address, can cause all sorts of memory corruption. You must strive to ensure that your add-ons are safe to Lua and provide good error handling.

As we discussed earlier, each C program has its own way to handle errors. When you write library functions for Lua, however, there is a standard way to handle errors. Whenever a C function detects an error, it simply calls `lua_error` (or better yet `luaL_error`, which formats the error message and then calls `lua_error`). The `lua_error` function clears whatever needs to be cleared in Lua and jumps back to the `lua_pcall` that originated that execution, passing along the error message.

25

Extending Your Application

An important use of Lua is as a *configuration* language. In this chapter, we will illustrate how we can use Lua to configure a program, starting with a simple example and evolving it to perform more complex tasks.

25.1 The Basics

As our first task, let us imagine a simple configuration scenario: your C program has a window and you want the user to be able to specify the initial window size. Clearly, for such simple tasks, there are several options simpler than using Lua, such as environment variables or files with name-value pairs. But even using a simple text file, you have to parse it somehow; so, you decide to use a Lua configuration file (that is, a plain text file that happens to be a Lua program). In its simplest form, this file can contain something like the next lines:

```
-- define window size
width = 200
height = 300
```

Now, you must use the Lua API to direct Lua to parse this file, and then to get the values of the global variables `width` and `height`. Function `load`, in Listing 25.1, does the job. It assumes that you have already created a Lua state, following what we saw in the previous chapter. It calls `luaL_loadfile` to load the chunk from file `filename`, and then calls `lua_pcall` to run the compiled chunk. In case of errors (e.g., a syntax error in your configuration file), these functions push the error message onto the stack and return a non-zero error code. Our program then uses `lua_tostring` with index –1 to get the message from the top of the stack. (We defined the `error` function in Section 24.1.)

Listing 25.1. Getting user information from a configuration file:

```
void load (lua_State *L, const char *fname, int *w, int *h) {
  if (luaL_loadfile(L, fname) || lua_pcall(L, 0, 0, 0))
    error(L, "cannot run config. file: %s", lua_tostring(L, -1));
  lua_getglobal(L, "width");
  lua_getglobal(L, "height");
  if (!lua_isnumber(L, -2))
    error(L, "'width' should be a number\n");
  if (!lua_isnumber(L, -1))
    error(L, "'height' should be a number\n");
  *w = lua_tointeger(L, -2);
  *h = lua_tointeger(L, -1);
}
```

After running the chunk, the program needs to get the values of the global variables. For that, it calls twice `lua_getglobal`, whose single parameter (besides the omnipresent `lua_State`) is the variable name. Each call pushes the corresponding global value onto the stack, so that the width will be at index –2 and the height at index –1 (at the top). (Because the stack was previously empty, you could also index from the bottom, using the index 1 for the first value and 2 for the second. By indexing from the top, however, your code works even if the stack is not empty.) Next, our example uses `lua_isnumber` to check whether each value is numeric. It then calls `lua_tointeger` to convert such values to integer, and assigns them to their respective positions.

Is it worth using Lua for that task? As I said before, for such simple tasks, a simple file with only two numbers in it would be easier to use than Lua. Even so, the use of Lua brings some advantages. First, Lua handles all syntax details (and errors) for you; your configuration file can even have comments! Second, the user is already able to do more complex configurations with it. For instance, the script may prompt the user for some information, or it can query an environment variable to choose a proper size:

```
-- configuration file
if getenv("DISPLAY") == ":0.0" then
  width = 300; height = 300
else
  width = 200; height = 200
end
```

Even in such simple configuration scenarios, it is hard to anticipate what users will want; but as long as the script defines the two variables, your C application works without changes.

A final reason for using Lua is that now it is easy to add new configuration facilities to your program; this easiness creates an attitude that results in programs that are more flexible.

25.2 Table Manipulation

Let us adopt that attitude: now, we want to configure a background color for
the window, too. We will assume that the final color specification is composed
of three numbers, where each number is a color component in RGB. Usually, in
C, these numbers are integers in some range like $[0, 255]$. In Lua, because all
numbers are real, we can use the more natural range $[0, 1]$.

A naive approach here is to ask the user to set each component in a different
global variable:

```
-- configuration file
width = 200
height = 300
background_red = 0.30
background_green = 0.10
background_blue = 0
```

This approach has two drawbacks: it is too verbose (real programs may need
dozens of different colors, for window background, window foreground, menu
background, etc.); and there is no way to predefine common colors, so that, later,
the user can simply write something like background=WHITE. To avoid these
drawbacks, we will use a table to represent a color:

```
background = {r=0.30, g=0.10, b=0}
```

The use of tables gives more structure to the script; now it is easy for the user
(or for the application) to predefine colors for later use in the configuration file:

```
BLUE = {r=0, g=0, b=1}
<other color definitions>

background = BLUE
```

To get these values in C, we can do as follows:

```
lua_getglobal(L, "background");
if (!lua_istable(L, -1))
  error(L, "'background' is not a table");

red = getfield(L, "r");
green = getfield(L, "g");
blue = getfield(L, "b");
```

We first get the value of the global variable background and ensure that it is
a table. Next, we use getfield to get each color component. However, this
function is not part of the API; we must define it. Again, we face the problem
of polymorphism: there are potentially many versions of getfield functions,
varying the key type, value type, error handling, etc. The Lua API offers one
function, lua_gettable, that works for all types. It takes the position of the
table in the stack, pops the key from the stack, and pushes the corresponding

Listing 25.2. A particular `getfield` implementation:

```
#define MAX_COLOR        255

/* assume that table is on the stack top */
int getfield (lua_State *L, const char *key) {
  int result;
  lua_pushstring(L, key);
  lua_gettable(L, -2);  /* get background[key] */
  if (!lua_isnumber(L, -1))
    error(L, "invalid component in background color");
  result = (int)lua_tonumber(L, -1) * MAX_COLOR;
  lua_pop(L, 1);  /* remove number */
  return result;
}
```

value. Our private `getfield`, defined in Listing 25.2, assumes that the table is at the top of the stack; so, after pushing the key with `lua_pushstring`, the table will be at index –2. Before returning, `getfield` pops the retrieved value from the stack, leaving the stack at the same level that it was before the call.

Because indexing a table with a string key is so common, Lua 5.1 offers a specialized version of `lua_gettable` for this case: `lua_getfield`. Using this function, we can rewrite the two lines

```
lua_pushstring(L, key);
lua_gettable(L, -2);  /* get background[key] */
```

as

```
lua_getfield(L, -1, key);
```

(As we do not push the string onto the stack, the table index is still –1 when we call `lua_getfield`.)

We will extend our example a little further and introduce color names for the user. The user can still use color tables, but she can also use predefined names for the more common colors. To implement this feature, we need a color table in our C application:

```
struct ColorTable {
  char *name;
  unsigned char red, green, blue;
} colortable[] = {
  {"WHITE",   MAX_COLOR, MAX_COLOR, MAX_COLOR},
  {"RED",     MAX_COLOR,  0,    0},
  {"GREEN",    0, MAX_COLOR,    0},
  {"BLUE",     0,   0, MAX_COLOR},
  <other colors>
  {NULL,       0, 0, 0}  /* sentinel */
};
```

Our implementation will create global variables with the color names and initialize these variables using color tables. The result is the same as if the user had the following lines in her script:

```
WHITE = {r=1, g=1, b=1}
RED   = {r=1, g=0, b=0}
<other colors>
```

To set the table fields, we define an auxiliary function, setfield; it pushes the index and the field value on the stack, and then calls lua_settable:

```
/* assume that table is at the top */
void setfield (lua_State *L, const char *index, int value) {
  lua_pushstring(L, index);
  lua_pushnumber(L, (double)value/MAX_COLOR);
  lua_settable(L, -3);
}
```

Like other API functions, lua_settable works for many different types, so it gets all its operands from the stack. It takes the table index as an argument and pops the key and the value. The setfield function assumes that before the call the table is at the top of the stack (index –1); after pushing the index and the value, the table will be at index –3.

Lua 5.1 also offers a specialized version of lua_settable for string keys, called lua_setfield. Using this new function, we can rewrite our previous definition for setfield as follows:

```
void setfield (lua_State *L, const char *index, int value) {
  lua_pushnumber(L, (double)value/MAX_COLOR);
  lua_setfield(L, -2, index);
}
```

The next function, setcolor, defines a single color. It creates a table, sets the appropriate fields, and assigns this table to the corresponding global variable:

```
void setcolor (lua_State *L, struct ColorTable *ct) {
  lua_newtable(L);                    /* creates a table */
  setfield(L, "r", ct->red);          /* table.r = ct->r */
  setfield(L, "g", ct->green);        /* table.g = ct->g */
  setfield(L, "b", ct->blue);         /* table.b = ct->b */
  lua_setglobal(L, ct->name);         /* 'name' = table */
}
```

The lua_newtable function creates an empty table and pushes it on the stack; the setfield calls set the table fields; finally, lua_setglobal pops the table and sets it as the value of the global with the given name.

With these previous functions, the following loop will register all colors for the configuration script:

```
int i = 0;
while (colortable[i].name != NULL)
  setcolor(L, &colortable[i++]);
```

Listing 25.3. Colors as strings or tables:

```
lua_getglobal(L, "background");
if (lua_isstring(L, -1)) {    /* value is a string? */
  const char *name = lua_tostring(L, -1);  /* get string */
  int i;    /* search the color table */
  for (i = 0; colortable[i].name != NULL; i++) {
    if (strcmp(colorname, colortable[i].name) == 0)
      break;
  }
  if (colortable[i].name == NULL)   /* string not found? */
    error(L, "invalid color name (%s)", colorname);
  else {  /* use colortable[i] */
    red = colortable[i].red;
    green = colortable[i].green;
    blue = colortable[i].blue;
  }
} else if (lua_istable(L, -1)) {
  red = getfield(L, "r");
  green = getfield(L, "g");
  blue = getfield(L, "b");
} else
    error(L, "invalid value for 'background'");
```

Remember that the application must execute this loop before running the script.

There is another option for implementing named colors, as shown in Listing 25.3. Instead of global variables, the user can denote color names with strings, writing her settings as background="BLUE". Therefore, background can be either a table or a string. With this implementation, the application does not need to do anything before running the user's script. Instead, it needs more work to get a color. When it gets the value of the variable background, it must test whether the value has type string, and then look up the string in the color table.

What is the best option? In C programs, the use of strings to denote options is not a good practice, because the compiler cannot detect misspellings. In Lua, however, global variables do not need declarations, so Lua does not signal any error when a user misspells a color name. If the user writes WITE instead of WHITE, the background variable receives **nil** (the value of WITE, a variable not initialized), and this is all that the application knows: that background is **nil**. There is no other information about what was wrong. With strings, on the other hand, the value of background would be the misspelled string; so, the application can add this information to the error message. The application can also compare strings regardless of case, so that a user can write "white", "WHITE", or even "White". Moreover, if the user script is small and there are many colors, it may be odd to register hundreds of colors (and to create hundreds of tables and global variables) only for the user to choose a few. With strings, you avoid this overhead.

25.3 Calling Lua Functions

A great strength of Lua is that a configuration file can define functions to be called by the application. For instance, you can write an application to plot the graph of a function and use Lua to define the function to be plotted.

The API protocol to call a function is simple: first, you push the function to be called; second, you push the arguments to the call; then you use `lua_pcall` to do the actual call; finally, you pop the results from the stack.

As an example, let us assume that your configuration file has a function like this:

```
function f (x, y)
  return (x^2 * math.sin(y))/(1 - x)
end
```

You want to evaluate, in C, $z=f(x, y)$ for given x and y. Assuming that you have already opened the Lua library and run the configuration file, you can encapsulate this call in the following C function:

```
/* call a function 'f' defined in Lua */
double f (double x, double y) {
  double z;

  /* push functions and arguments */
  lua_getglobal(L, "f");  /* function to be called */
  lua_pushnumber(L, x);   /* push 1st argument */
  lua_pushnumber(L, y);   /* push 2nd argument */

  /* do the call (2 arguments, 1 result) */
  if (lua_pcall(L, 2, 1, 0) != 0)
    error(L, "error running function 'f': %s",
            lua_tostring(L, -1));

  /* retrieve result */
  if (!lua_isnumber(L, -1))
    error(L, "function 'f' must return a number");
  z = lua_tonumber(L, -1);
  lua_pop(L, 1);  /* pop returned value */
  return z;
}
```

You call `lua_pcall` with the number of arguments you are passing and the number of results you want. The fourth argument indicates an error-handling function; we will discuss it in a moment. As in a Lua assignment, `lua_pcall` adjusts the actual number of results to what you have asked for, pushing **nil**s or discarding extra values as needed. Before pushing the results, lua_pcall removes from the stack the function and its arguments. If a function returns multiple results, the first result is pushed first; for instance, if there are three results, the first one will be at index –3 and the last at index –1.

If there is any error while lua_pcall is running, lua_pcall returns a value different from zero; moreover, it pushes the error message on the stack (but still pops the function and its arguments). Before pushing the message, however, lua_pcall calls the error handler function, if there is one. To specify an error handler function, we use the last argument of lua_pcall. A zero means no error handler function; that is, the final error message is the original message. Otherwise, this argument should be the index in the stack where the error handler function is located. In such cases, the handler must be pushed in the stack somewhere below the function to be called and its arguments.

For normal errors, lua_pcall returns the error code LUA_ERRRUN. Two special kinds of errors deserve different codes, because they never run the error handler. The first kind is a memory allocation error. For such errors, lua_pcall always returns LUA_ERRMEM. The second kind is an error while Lua is running the error handler itself. In this case it is of little use to call the error handler again, so lua_pcall returns immediately with a code LUA_ERRERR.

25.4   A Generic Call Function

As a more advanced example, we will build a wrapper for calling Lua functions, using the vararg facility in C. Our wrapper function, let us call it call_va, takes the name of the function to be called, a string describing the types of the arguments and results, then the list of arguments, and finally a list of pointers to variables to store the results; it handles all the details of the API. With this function, we could write our previous example simply as

```
call_va("f", "dd>d", x, y, &z);
```

where the string "dd>d" means "two arguments of type double, one result of type double". This descriptor can use the letters 'd' for double, 'i' for integer, and 's' for strings; a '>' separates arguments from the results. If the function has no results, the '>' is optional.

Listing 25.4 shows the implementation of function call_va. Despite its generality, this function follows the same steps of our first example: it pushes the function, pushes the arguments (Listing 25.5), does the call, and gets the results (Listing 25.6). Most of its code is straightforward, but there are some subtleties. First, it does not need to check whether func is a function; lua_pcall will trigger any error. Second, because it pushes an arbitrary number of arguments, it must check the stack space. Third, because the function may return strings, call_va cannot pop the results from the stack. It is up to the caller to pop them, after it finishes using occasional string results (or after copying them to other buffers).

Listing 25.4. A generic call function:

```
#include <stdarg.h>

void call_va (const char *func, const char *sig, ...) {
  va_list vl;
  int narg, nres;  /* number of arguments and results */

  va_start(vl, sig);
  lua_getglobal(L, func);  /* push function */

  <push arguments (Listing 25.5)>

  nres = strlen(sig);  /* number of expected results */

  /* do the call */
  if (lua_pcall(L, narg, nres, 0) != 0)  /* do the call */
    error(L, "error calling '%s': %s", func,
                                 lua_tostring(L, -1));

  <retrieve results (Listing 25.6)>

  va_end(vl);
}
```

Listing 25.5. Generic call function: pushing arguments:

```
for (narg = 0; *sig; narg++) {  /* repeat for each argument */

  /* check stack space */
  luaL_checkstack(L, 1, "too many arguments");

  switch (*sig++) {

    case 'd':  /* double argument */
      lua_pushnumber(L, va_arg(vl, double));
      break;

    case 'i':  /* int argument */
      lua_pushinteger(L, va_arg(vl, int));
      break;

    case 's':  /* string argument */
      lua_pushstring(L, va_arg(vl, char *));
      break;

    case '>':  /* end of arguments */
      goto endargs;

    default:
      error(L, "invalid option (%c)", *(sig - 1));
  }

}
endargs:
```

Listing 25.6. Generic call function: retrieving results:

```
nres = -nres;  /* stack index of first result */
while (*sig) {  /* repeat for each result */
  switch (*sig++) {

    case 'd':  /* double result */
      if (!lua_isnumber(L, nres))
        error(L, "wrong result type");
      *va_arg(vl, double *) = lua_tonumber(L, nres);
      break;

    case 'i':  /* int result */
      if (!lua_isnumber(L, nres))
        error(L, "wrong result type");
      *va_arg(vl, int *) = lua_tointeger(L, nres);
      break;

    case 's':  /* string result */
      if (!lua_isstring(L, nres))
        error(L, "wrong result type");
      *va_arg(vl, const char **) = lua_tostring(L, nres);
      break;

    default:
      error(L, "invalid option (%c)", *(sig - 1));
  }
  nres++;
}
```

26

Calling C from Lua

One of the basic means for extending Lua is for the application to *register* new C functions into Lua.

When we say that Lua can call C functions, this does not mean that Lua can call any C function.[18] As we saw in the previous chapter, when C calls a Lua function, it must follow a simple protocol to pass the arguments and to get the results. Similarly, for a C function to be called from Lua, it must follow a protocol to get its arguments and to return its results. Moreover, for a C function to be called from Lua, we must register it, that is, we must give its address to Lua in an appropriate way.

When Lua calls a C function, it uses the same kind of stack that C uses to call Lua. The C function gets its arguments from the stack and pushes the results on the stack. To distinguish the results from other values on the stack, the function returns (in C) the number of results it is leaving on the stack.

An important concept here is that the stack is not a global structure; each function has its own private local stack. When Lua calls a C function, the first argument will always be at index 1 of this local stack. Even when a C function calls Lua code that calls the same (or another) C function again, each of these invocations sees only its own private stack, with its first argument at index 1.

26.1 C Functions

As a first example, let us see how to implement a simplified version of a function that returns the sine of a given number:

---

[18]There are packages that allow Lua to call any C function, but they are neither portable nor safe.

```
static int l_sin (lua_State *L) {
  double d = lua_tonumber(L, 1);  /* get argument */
  lua_pushnumber(L, sin(d));  /* push result */
  return 1;  /* number of results */
}
```

Any function registered with Lua must have this same prototype, defined as `lua_CFunction` in `lua.h`:

```
typedef int (*lua_CFunction) (lua_State *L);
```

From the point of view of C, a C function gets as its single argument the Lua state and returns an integer with the number of values it is returning in the stack. Therefore, the function does not need to clear the stack before pushing its results. After it returns, Lua automatically removes whatever is in the stack below the results.

Before we can use this function from Lua, we must register it. We do this little magic with `lua_pushcfunction`: it gets a pointer to a C function and creates a value of type "`function`" that represents this function inside Lua. Once registered, a C function behaves like any other function inside Lua.

A quick-and-dirty way to test `l_sin` is to put its code directly into the file `lua.c` and add the following lines right after the call to `luaL_openlibs`:

```
lua_pushcfunction(L, l_sin);
lua_setglobal(L, "mysin");
```

The first line pushes a value of type function. The second line assigns it to the global variable `mysin`. After these modifications, you rebuild your Lua executable; then you can use the new function `mysin` in your Lua programs. (In the next section, we will discuss better ways to link new C functions with Lua.)

For a more professional sine function, we must check the type of its argument. Here, the auxiliary library helps us. The `luaL_checknumber` function checks whether a given argument is a number: in case of error, it throws an informative error message; otherwise, it returns the number. The modification to our function is minimal:

```
static int l_sin (lua_State *L) {
  double d = luaL_checknumber(L, 1);
  lua_pushnumber(L, sin(d));
  return 1;  /* number of results */
}
```

With the above definition, if you call `mysin('a')`, you get the message

```
bad argument #1 to 'mysin' (number expected, got string)
```

Notice how `luaL_checknumber` automatically fills the message with the argument number (#1), the function name ("mysin"), the expected parameter type (number), and the actual parameter type (string).

Listing 26.1. A function to read a directory:

```
#include <dirent.h>
#include <errno.h>

static int l_dir (lua_State *L) {
  DIR *dir;
  struct dirent *entry;
  int i;
  const char *path = luaL_checkstring(L, 1);

  /* open directory */
  dir = opendir(path);
  if (dir == NULL) {  /* error opening the directory? */
    lua_pushnil(L);  /* return nil */
    lua_pushstring(L, strerror(errno));  /* and error message */
    return 2;  /* number of results */
  }

  /* create result table */
  lua_newtable(L);
  i = 1;
  while ((entry = readdir(dir)) != NULL) {
    lua_pushnumber(L, i++);  /* push key */
    lua_pushstring(L, entry->d_name);  /* push value */
    lua_settable(L, -3);
  }

  closedir(dir);
  return 1;  /* table is already on top */
}
```

As a more complex example, let us write a function that returns the contents of a given directory. Lua does not provide this function in its standard libraries, because ANSI C does not have functions for this job. Here, we will assume that we have a POSIX compliant system. Our function (called dir in Lua, l_dir in C) gets as argument a string with the directory path and returns an array with the directory entries. For instance, a call dir("/home/lua") may return the table {".", "..", "src", "bin", "lib"}. In case of error, the function returns **nil** plus a string with the error message. The complete code for this function is in Listing 26.1. Note the use of the luaL_checkstring function, from the auxiliary library, which is the equivalent of luaL_checknumber for strings.

(In extreme conditions, this implementation of l_dir may cause a small memory leak. Three of the Lua functions that it calls can fail due to insufficient memory: lua_newtable, lua_pushstring, and lua_settable. If any of these functions fails, it will raise an error and interrupt l_dir, which therefore will not call `closedir`. As we discussed earlier, on many programs this is not a big problem: if the program runs out of memory, the best it can do is to shut down anyway. Nevertheless, in Chapter 29 we will see an alternative implementation for a directory function that avoids this problem.)

26.2   C Modules

A Lua module is a chunk that defines several Lua functions and stores them in appropriate places, typically as entries in a table. A C module for Lua mimics this behavior. Besides the definition of its C functions, it must also define a special function that corresponds to the main chunk of a Lua library. This function should register all C functions of the module and store them in appropriate places. Like a Lua main chunk, it should also initialize anything else that needs initialization in the module.

Lua perceives C functions through this registration process. Once a C function is represented and stored in Lua, Lua calls it through a direct reference to its address (which is what we give to Lua when we register a function). In other words, Lua does not depend on a function name, package location, or visibility rules to call a function, once it is registered. Typically, a C module has one single public (extern) function, which is the function that opens the library. All other functions may be private, declared as `static` in C.

When you extend Lua with C functions, it is a good idea to design your code as a C module, even when you want to register only one C function: sooner or later (usually sooner) you will need other functions. As usual, the auxiliary library offers a helper function for this job. The `luaL_register` function takes a list of C functions with their respective names and registers all of them inside a table with the library name. As an example, suppose we want to create a library with the `l_dir` function that we defined earlier. First, we must define the library functions:

```
static int l_dir (lua_State *L) {
   <as before>
}
```

Next, we declare an array with all functions in the module with their respective names. This array has elements of type `luaL_Reg`, which is a structure with two fields: a string and a function pointer:

```
static const struct luaL_Reg mylib [] = {
  {"dir", l_dir},
  {NULL, NULL}  /* sentinel */
};
```

In our example, there is only one function (`l_dir`) to declare. The last pair in the array is always `{NULL,NULL}`, to signal its end. Finally, we declare a main function, using `luaL_register`:

```
int luaopen_mylib (lua_State *L) {
  luaL_register(L, "mylib", mylib);
  return 1;
}
```

The call to `luaL_register` creates (or reuses) a table with the given name ("mylib"), and fills it with the pairs name–function specified by the array `mylib`. When it returns, `luaL_register` leaves on the stack the table wherein it opened the library. The `luaopen_mylib` function then returns 1 to return this value to Lua.

After finishing the library, we must link it to the interpreter. The most convenient way to do it is with the dynamic linking facility, if your Lua interpreter supports this facility. In this case, you must create a dynamic library with your code (`mylib.dll` in Windows, `mylib.so` in several other systems) and put it somewhere in the C path. After these steps, you can load your library directly from Lua, with `require`:

```
require "mylib"
```

This call links the dynamic library `mylib` with Lua, finds the `luaopen_mylib` function, registers it as a C function, and calls it, opening the module. (This behavior explains why `luaopen_mylib` must have the same prototype as any other C function.)

If your interpreter does not support dynamic linking, then you have to recompile Lua with your new library. Besides this recompilation, you need some way of telling the stand-alone interpreter that it should open this library when it opens a new state. A simple way to do this is to add `luaopen_mylib` into the list of standard libraries to be opened by `luaL_openlibs`, in file `linit.c`.

27

Techniques for Writing C Functions

Both the official API and the auxiliary library provide several mechanisms to help writing C functions. In this chapter, we cover the mechanisms for array manipulation, for string manipulation, and for storing Lua values in C.

27.1 Array Manipulation

"Array", in Lua, is just a name for a table used in a specific way. We can manipulate arrays using the same functions we use to manipulate tables, namely `lua_settable` and `lua_gettable`. However, the API provides special functions for array manipulation. One reason for these extra functions is performance: frequently we have an array-access operation inside the inner loop of an algorithm (e.g., sorting), so that any performance gain in this operation can have a big impact on the overall performance of the algorithm. Another reason is convenience: like string keys, integer keys are common enough to deserve some special treatment.

The API provides two functions for array manipulation:

```
void lua_rawgeti (lua_State *L, int index, int key);
void lua_rawseti (lua_State *L, int index, int key);
```

The description of `lua_rawgeti` and `lua_rawseti` may sound a little confusing, as it involves two indices: index refers to where the table is in the stack; key refers to where the element is in the table. The call `lua_rawgeti(L,t,key)` is

Listing 27.1. The map function in C:

```
int l_map (lua_State *L) {
  int i, n;

  /* 1st argument must be a table (t) */
  luaL_checktype(L, 1, LUA_TTABLE);

  /* 2nd argument must be a function (f) */
  luaL_checktype(L, 2, LUA_TFUNCTION);

  n = lua_objlen(L, 1);   /* get size of table */

  for (i = 1; i <= n; i++) {
    lua_pushvalue(L, 2);    /* push f */
    lua_rawgeti(L, 1, i);   /* push t[i] */
    lua_call(L, 1, 1);      /* call f(t[i]) */
    lua_rawseti(L, 1, i);   /* t[i] = result */
  }

  return 0;   /* no results */
}
```

equivalent to the following sequence when t is positive (otherwise, you must compensate for the new item in the stack):

```
lua_pushnumber(L, key);
lua_rawget(L, t);
```

The call lua_rawseti(L,t,key) (again for t positive) is equivalent to this sequence:

```
lua_pushnumber(L, key);
lua_insert(L, -2);   /* put 'key' below previous value */
lua_rawset(L, t);
```

Note that both functions use raw operations. They are faster and, anyway, tables used as arrays seldom use metamethods.

As a concrete example of the use of these functions, Listing 27.1 implements the map function: it applies a given function to all elements of an array, replacing each element by the result of the call. This example also introduces two new functions. The luaL_checktype function (from lauxlib.h) ensures that a given argument has a given type; otherwise, it raises an error. The lua_call function does an unprotected call. It is similar to lua_pcall, but in case of error it propagates the error, instead of returning an error code. When you are writing the main code in an application, you should not use lua_call, because you want to catch any errors. When you are writing functions, however, it is usually a good idea to use lua_call; if there is an error, just leave it to someone that cares about it.

Listing 27.2. Splitting a string:

```
static int l_split (lua_State *L) {
  const char *s = luaL_checkstring(L, 1);
  const char *sep = luaL_checkstring(L, 2);
  const char *e;
  int i = 1;

  lua_newtable(L);  /* result */

  /* repeat for each separator */
  while ((e = strchr(s, *sep)) != NULL) {
    lua_pushlstring(L, s, e-s);  /* push substring */
    lua_rawseti(L, -2, i++);
    s = e + 1;  /* skip separator */
  }

  /* push last substring */
  lua_pushstring(L, s);
  lua_rawseti(L, -2, i);

  return 1;  /* return the table */
}
```

27.2 String Manipulation

When a C function receives a string argument from Lua, there are only two rules that it must observe: not to pop the string from the stack while accessing it, and never to modify the string.

Things get more demanding when a C function needs to create a string to return to Lua. Now, it is up to the C code to take care of buffer allocation/deallocation, buffer overflow, and the like. Nevertheless, the Lua API provides some functions to help with these tasks.

The standard API provides support for two of the most basic string operations: substring extraction and string concatenation. To extract a substring, remember that the basic operation lua_pushlstring gets the string length as an extra argument. Therefore, if you want to pass to Lua a substring of a string s ranging from position i to j (inclusive), all you have to do is this:

```
lua_pushlstring(L, s + i, j - i + 1);
```

As an example, suppose you want a function that splits a string according to a given separator (a single character) and returns a table with the substrings. For instance, the call split("hi,ho,there",",") should return the table {"hi", "ho", "there"}. Listing 27.2 presents a simple implementation for this function. It needs no extra buffers and puts no constraints on the size of the strings it can handle.

To concatenate strings, Lua provides a specific function in its API, called `lua_concat`. It is similar to the `..` operator in Lua: it converts numbers to strings and triggers metamethods when necessary. Moreover, it can concatenate more than two strings at once. The call `lua_concat(L, n)` will concatenate (and pop) the n values at the top of the stack, pushing the result on the top.

Another helpful function is `lua_pushfstring`:

```
const char *lua_pushfstring (lua_State *L, const char *fmt, ...);
```

It is somewhat similar to the C function `sprintf`, in that it creates a string according to a format string and some extra arguments. Unlike `sprintf`, however, you do not need to provide a buffer. Lua dynamically creates the string for you, as large as it needs to be. There are no worries about buffer overflow and the like. The function pushes the resulting string on the stack and returns a pointer to it. Currently, this function accepts only the directives %% (for the character '%'), %s (for strings), %d (for integers), %f (for Lua numbers, that is, doubles), and %c (accepts an integer and formats it as a character). It does not accept any options like width or precision.

Both `lua_concat` and `lua_pushfstring` are useful when we want to concatenate only a few strings. However, if we need to concatenate many strings (or characters) together, a one-by-one approach can be quite inefficient, as we saw in Section 11.6. Instead, we can use the buffer facilities provided by the auxiliary library. Auxlib implements these buffers in two levels. The first level is similar to buffers in I/O operations: it collects small strings (or individual characters) in a local buffer and passes them to Lua (with `lua_pushlstring`) when the buffer fills up. The second level uses `lua_concat` and a variant of the stack algorithm that we saw in Section 11.6 to concatenate the results of multiple buffer flushes.

To describe the buffer facilities from auxlib in more detail, let us see a simple example of its use. The next code shows the implementation of the `string.upper` function, right from the source file `lstrlib.c`:

```
static int str_upper (lua_State *L) {
  size_t l;
  size_t i;
  luaL_Buffer b;
  const char *s = luaL_checklstr(L, 1, &l);
  luaL_buffinit(L, &b);
  for (i = 0; i < l; i++)
    luaL_addchar(&b, toupper((unsigned char)(s[i])));
  luaL_pushresult(&b);
  return 1;
}
```

The first step for using a buffer from auxlib is to declare a variable with type `luaL_Buffer`, and then to initialize it with a call to `luaL_buffinit`. After the initialization, the buffer keeps a copy of the state L, so we do not need to pass it when calling other functions that manipulate the buffer. The macro luaL_addchar puts a single character into the buffer. Auxlib also offers functions to put into the buffer strings with an explicit length (luaL_addlstring) and zero-terminated strings (luaL_addstring). Finally, luaL_pushresult flushes the buffer and leaves the final string at the top of the stack. The prototypes of these functions are as follows:

```
void luaL_buffinit   (lua_State *L, luaL_Buffer *B);
void luaL_addchar    (luaL_Buffer *B, char c);
void luaL_addlstring (luaL_Buffer *B, const char *s, size_t l);
void luaL_addstring  (luaL_Buffer *B, const char *s);
void luaL_pushresult (luaL_Buffer *B);
```

Using these functions, we do not have to worry about buffer allocation, overflows, and other such details. Moreover, as we saw, the concatenation algorithm is quite efficient. The str_upper function handles huge strings (more than 1 Mbyte) without any problem.

When you use the auxlib buffer, you have to worry about one detail. As you put things into the buffer, it keeps some intermediate results in the Lua stack. Therefore, you cannot assume that the stack top will remain where it was before you started using the buffer. Moreover, although you can use the stack for other tasks while using a buffer (even to build another buffer), the push/pop count for these uses must be balanced every time you access the buffer. There is one obvious situation where this restriction is too severe, namely when you want to put into the buffer a string returned from Lua. In such cases, you cannot pop the string before adding it to the buffer, because you should never use a string from Lua after popping it from the stack; but also you cannot add the string to the buffer before popping it, because then the stack would be in the wrong level.

Because this is a frequent situation, auxlib provides a special function to add the value at the top of the stack into the buffer:

```
void luaL_addvalue (luaL_Buffer *B);
```

Of course, it is an error to call this function if the value on the top is not a string or a number.

27.3 Storing State in C Functions

Frequently, C functions need to keep some non-local data, that is, data that outlive their invocation. In C, we typically use global or static variables for this need. When you are programming library functions for Lua, however, global and static variables are not a good approach. First, you cannot store a generic Lua value in a C variable. Second, a library that uses such variables cannot be used in multiple Lua states.

A Lua function has three basic places to store non-local data: global variables, function environments, and non-local variables. The C API also offers three basic places to store non-local data: the registry, environments, and up-values.

The *registry* is a global table that can be accessed only by C code. Typically, you use it to store data to be shared among several modules. If you need to store data private to a module, you should use environments. Like a Lua function, each C function has its own environment table. Frequently all functions in a module share the same environment table, so that they can share data. Finally, a C function may also have upvalues, which are Lua values associated to that particular function.

The registry

The registry is always located at a *pseudo-index*, whose value is defined by LUA_REGISTRYINDEX. A pseudo-index is like an index into the stack, except that its associated value is not in the stack. Most functions in the Lua API that accept indices as arguments also accept pseudo-indices — the exceptions being those functions that manipulate the stack itself, such as lua_remove and lua_insert. For instance, to get a value stored with key "Key" in the registry, you can use the following call:

```
lua_getfield(L, LUA_REGISTRYINDEX, "Key");
```

The registry is a regular Lua table. As such, you can index it with any Lua value but **nil**. However, because all C modules share the same registry, you must choose with care what values you use as keys, to avoid collisions. String keys are particularly useful when you want to allow other independent libraries to access your data, because all they need to know is the key name. For such keys, there is no bulletproof method of choosing names, but there are some good practices, such as avoiding common names and prefixing your names with the library name or something like it. Prefixes like lua or lualib are not good choices. Another option is to use a *universal unique identifier* (uuid), as most systems now have programs to generate such identifiers (e.g., uuidgen in Linux). An uuid is a 128-bit number (written in hexadecimal to form an alphanumeric string) that is generated by a combination of the host MAC address, a time stamp, and a random component, so that it is assuredly different from any other uuid.

You should never use numbers as keys in the registry, because such keys are reserved for the *reference system*. This system is composed by a couple of functions in the auxiliary library that allow you to store values in a table without worrying about how to create unique names. The call

```
int r = luaL_ref(L, LUA_REGISTRYINDEX);
```

pops a value from the stack, stores it into the registry with a fresh integer key, and returns this key. We call this key a *reference*.

As the name implies, we use references mainly when we need to store a reference to a Lua value inside a C structure. As we have seen, we should never store pointers to Lua strings outside the C function that retrieved them. Moreover, Lua does not even offer pointers to other objects, such as tables or functions. So, we cannot refer to Lua objects through pointers. Instead, when we need such pointers, we create a reference and store it in C.

To push the value associated with a reference r onto the stack, we simply write

```
lua_rawgeti(L, LUA_REGISTRYINDEX, r);
```

Finally, to release both the value and the reference, we call

```
luaL_unref(L, LUA_REGISTRYINDEX, r);
```

After this call, a new call to luaL_ref may return again this reference.

The reference system treats **nil** as a special case. Whenever we call luaL_ref for a nil value, it does not create a new reference, but instead returns the constant reference LUA_REFNIL. The call

```
luaL_unref(L, LUA_REGISTRYINDEX, LUA_REFNIL);
```

has no effect, whereas

```
lua_rawgeti(L, LUA_REGISTRYINDEX, LUA_REFNIL);
```

pushes a **nil**, as expected.

The reference system also defines the constant LUA_NOREF, which is an integer different from any valid reference. It is useful to mark references as invalid. As with LUA_REFNIL, any attempt to retrieve LUA_NOREF returns **nil**, and any attempt to release it has no effect.

Another bulletproof method to create keys into the registry is to use as key the address of a static variable in your code: the C link editor ensures that this key is unique among all libraries. To use this option, you need the function lua_pushlightuserdata, which pushes on the Lua stack a value representing a C pointer. The following code shows how to store and retrieve a string from the registry using this method:

```
/* variable with an unique address */
static const char Key = 'k';

/* store a string */
lua_pushlightuserdata(L, (void *)&Key);  /* push address */
lua_pushstring(L, myStr);  /* push value */
lua_settable(L, LUA_REGISTRYINDEX);  /* registry[&Key] = myStr */

/* retrieve a string */
lua_pushlightuserdata(L, (void *)&Key);  /* push address */
lua_gettable(L, LUA_REGISTRYINDEX);  /* retrieve value */
myStr = lua_tostring(L, -1);  /* convert to string */
```

We will discuss light userdata in more detail in Section 28.5.

Environments for C functions

Since Lua 5.1, each C function that we register in Lua has its own environment table. A function can access its environment in the same way it accesses the registry, with a pseudo-index. For the environment, the pseudo index is `LUA_ENVIRONINDEX`.

Typically, we use these environments in the same way that we use environments for Lua modules. We create a new table for the module and make all its functions share this table. The way to set such shared environments in C is also similar to the way we set these environments in Lua: we simply change the environment of the main chunk, so that all functions it creates automatically inherit the new environment. In C, the code to set such an environment looks like this:

```
int luaopen_foo (lua_State *L) {
  lua_newtable(L);
  lua_replace(L, LUA_ENVIRONINDEX);
  luaL_register(L, <libname>, <funclist>);
  ...
}
```

The open function `luaopen_foo` creates a new table to be the shared environment and uses `lua_replace` to set this table as its own environment. Then, when it calls `luaL_register`, all new functions created there will inherit this current environment.

You should always favor the environment over the register, unless you need to share data with other modules. In particular, you can use the reference system using the environment table, to create references visible only to the module.

Upvalues

While the registry offers global variables and environments offer module variables, the *upvalue* mechanism implements an equivalent of C static variables that are visible only inside a particular function. Every time you create a new C function in Lua, you can associate with it any number of upvalues; each upvalue can hold a single Lua value. Later, when the function is called, it has free access to any of its upvalues, using pseudo-indices.

We call this association of a C function with its upvalues a *closure*. A C closure is a C approximation to a Lua closure. One interesting fact about closures is that you can create different closures using the same function code, but with different upvalues.

To see a simple example, let us create a `newCounter` function in C.[19] This function is a factory: it returns a new counter function each time it is called. Although all counters share the same C code, each one keeps its own independent counter. The factory function is like this:

---

[19]We already defined this same function in Lua, in Section 6.1.

```
static int counter (lua_State *L);  /* forward declaration */

int newCounter (lua_State *L) {
  lua_pushinteger(L, 0);
  lua_pushcclosure(L, &counter, 1);
  return 1;
}
```

The key function here is lua_pushcclosure, which creates a new closure. Its
second argument is the base function (counter, in the example) and the third
is the number of upvalues (1, in the example). Before creating a new closure,
we must push on the stack the initial values for its upvalues. In our example,
we push the number 0 as the initial value for the single upvalue. As expected,
lua_pushcclosure leaves the new closure on the stack, so the closure is ready to
be returned as the result of newCounter.

Now, let us see the definition of counter:

```
static int counter (lua_State *L) {
  int val = lua_tointeger(L, lua_upvalueindex(1));
  lua_pushinteger(L, ++val);  /* new value */
  lua_pushvalue(L, -1);  /* duplicate it */
  lua_replace(L, lua_upvalueindex(1));  /* update upvalue */
  return 1;  /* return new value */
}
```

Here, the key function is lua_upvalueindex (which is actually a macro), which
produces the pseudo-index of an upvalue. Again, this pseudo-index is like
any stack index, except that it does not live in the stack. The expression
lua_upvalueindex(1) refers to the index of the first upvalue of the function.
So, the call to lua_tointeger retrieves the current value of the first (and only)
upvalue as a number. Then, function counter pushes the new value ++val,
makes a copy of it, and uses one of the copies to replace the upvalue's value.
Finally, it returns the other copy as its return value.

As a more advanced example, we will implement tuples using upvalues. A
tuple is a kind of constant record with anonymous fields; you can retrieve a
specific field with a numerical index, or you can retrieve all fields at once. In
our implementation, we represent tuples as functions that store their values in
their upvalues. When called with a numerical argument, the function returns
that specific field. When called without arguments, it returns all its fields. The
following code illustrates the use of tuples:

```
x = tuple.new(10, "hi", {}, 3)
print(x(1))     --> 10
print(x(2))     --> hi
print(x())      --> 10  hi  table: 0x8087878  3
```

In C, we represent all tuples by the same function t_tuple, presented in
Listing 27.3. Because we can call a tuple with or without a numeric argument,

t_tuple uses luaL_optint to get its optional argument. The luaL_optint function is similar to luaL_checkint, but it does not complain if the argument is absent; instead, it returns a given default value (0, in the example).

When we index a non-existent upvalue, the result is a pseudo-value whose type is LUA_TNONE. (When we access a stack index above the current top, we also get a pseudo-value with this type LUA_TNONE.) So, our t_tuple function uses lua_isnone to test whether it has a given upvalue. However, we should never call lua_upvalueindex with a negative index, so we must check for this condition when the user provides the index. The luaL_argcheck function checks a given condition, raising an error if necessary.

The function to create tuples, t_new (also in Listing 27.3), is trivial: because its arguments are already in the stack, it just has to call lua_pushcclosure to create a closure of t_tuple with these arguments as upvalues. Finally, array tuplelib and function luaopen_tuple (also in Listing 27.3) are the standard code to create a library tuple with that single function new.

Listing 27.3. An implementation of tuples:

```
int t_tuple (lua_State *L) {
  int op = luaL_optint(L, 1, 0);
  if (op == 0) {  /* no arguments? */
    int i;
    /* push each valid upvalue onto the stack */
    for (i = 1; !lua_isnone(L, lua_upvalueindex(i)); i++)
      lua_pushvalue(L, lua_upvalueindex(i));
    return i - 1;  /* number of values in the stack */
  }
  else {  /* get field 'op' */
    luaL_argcheck(L, 0 < op, 1, "index out of range");
    if (lua_isnone(L, lua_upvalueindex(op)))
      return 0;  /* no such field */
    lua_pushvalue(L, lua_upvalueindex(op));
    return 1;
  }
}

int t_new (lua_State *L) {
  lua_pushcclosure(L, t_tuple, lua_gettop(L));
  return 1;
}

static const struct luaL_Reg tuplelib [] = {
  {"new", t_new},
  {NULL, NULL}
};

int luaopen_tuple (lua_State *L) {
  luaL_register(L, "tuple", tuplelib);
  return 1;
}
```

28

User-Defined Types in C

In the previous chapter, we saw how to extend Lua with new functions written in C. Now, we will see how to extend Lua with new types written in C. We will start with a small example, which will be extended through the chapter with metamethods and other goodies.

Our example is a quite simple type: boolean arrays. The main motivation for this example is that it does not involve complex algorithms, so we can concentrate on API issues. Nevertheless, the example is useful by itself. Of course we can use tables to implement arrays of booleans in Lua. But a C implementation, where we store each entry in one single bit, uses less than 3% of the memory used by a table.

Our implementation will need the following definitions:

```
#include <limits.h>

#define BITS_PER_WORD (CHAR_BIT*sizeof(unsigned int))
#define I_WORD(i)     ((unsigned int)(i) / BITS_PER_WORD)
#define I_BIT(i)      (1 << ((unsigned int)(i) % BITS_PER_WORD))
```

BITS_PER_WORD is the number of bits in an unsigned integer. The macro I_WORD computes the word where is stored the bit corresponding to a given index, and I_BIT computes a mask to access the correct bit inside this word.

We will represent our arrays with the following structure:

```
typedef struct NumArray {
  int size;
  unsigned int values[1];  /* variable part */
} NumArray;
```

We declare the array `values` with size 1 only as a placeholder, because C 89 does not allow an array with size 0; we will define the actual size when we allocate the array. The next expression gives this size for an array with n elements:

```
sizeof(NumArray) + I_WORD(n - 1)*sizeof(unsigned int)
```

(We do not need to add one to `I_WORD` because the original structure already includes space for one element.)

28.1 Userdata

Our first concern is how to represent the `NumArray` structure in Lua. Lua provides a basic type specifically for this: *userdata*. A userdatum offers a raw memory area, with no predefined operations in Lua, which we can use to store anything.

The `lua_newuserdata` function allocates a block of memory with the given size, pushes the corresponding userdatum on the stack, and returns the block address:

```
void *lua_newuserdata (lua_State *L, size_t size);
```

If for some reason you need to allocate memory by other means, it is very easy to create a userdatum with the size of a pointer and to store there a pointer to the real memory block. We will see examples of this technique in the next chapter.

Using `lua_newuserdata`, the function that creates new boolean arrays is as follows:

```
static int newarray (lua_State *L) {
  int i, n;
  size_t nbytes;
  NumArray *a;

  n = luaL_checkint(L, 1);
  luaL_argcheck(L, n >= 1, 1, "invalid size");
  nbytes = sizeof(NumArray) + I_WORD(n - 1)*sizeof(unsigned int);
  a = (NumArray *)lua_newuserdata(L, nbytes);

  a->size = n;
  for (i=0; i <= I_WORD(n-1); i++)
    a->values[i] = 0;  /* initialize array */

  return 1;  /* new userdatum is already on the stack */
}
```

(The `luaL_checkint` macro is only a type cast over `luaL_checkinteger`.) Once `newarray` is registered in Lua, you will be able to create new arrays with a statement like `a=array.new(1000)`.

To store an entry, we will use a call like `array.set(array,index,value)`. Later we will see how to use metatables to support the more conventional syntax `array[index]=value`. For both notations, the underlying function is the same. It assumes that indices start at 1, as is usual in Lua:

```
static int setarray (lua_State *L) {
  NumArray *a = (NumArray *)lua_touserdata(L, 1);
  int index = luaL_checkint(L, 2) - 1;
  luaL_checkany(L, 3);

  luaL_argcheck(L, a != NULL, 1, "'array' expected");

  luaL_argcheck(L, 0 <= index && index < a->size, 2,
                  "index out of range");

  if (lua_toboolean(L, 3))
    a->values[I_WORD(index)] |= I_BIT(index);   /* set bit */
  else
    a->values[I_WORD(index)] &= ~I_BIT(index);   /* reset bit */
  return 0;
}
```

Because Lua accepts any value for a boolean, we use luaL_checkany for the third
parameter: it ensures only that there is a value (any value) for this parameter.
If we call setarray with bad arguments, we get elucidative error messages:

```
array.set(0, 11, 0)
  --> stdin:1: bad argument #1 to 'set' ('array' expected)
array.set(a, 0)
  --> stdin:1: bad argument #3 to 'set' (value expected)
```

The next function retrieves an entry:

```
static int getarray (lua_State *L) {
  NumArray *a = (NumArray *)lua_touserdata(L, 1);
  int index = luaL_checkint(L, 2) - 1;

  luaL_argcheck(L, a != NULL, 1, "'array' expected");

  luaL_argcheck(L, 0 <= index && index < a->size, 2,
                  "index out of range");

  lua_pushboolean(L, a->values[I_WORD(index)] & I_BIT(index));
  return 1;
}
```

We define another function to retrieve the size of an array:

```
static int getsize (lua_State *L) {
  NumArray *a = (NumArray *)lua_touserdata(L, 1);
  luaL_argcheck(L, a != NULL, 1, "'array' expected");
  lua_pushinteger(L, a->size);
  return 1;
}
```

Finally, we need some extra code to initialize our library:

```
static const struct luaL_Reg arraylib [] = {
  {"new", newarray},
  {"set", setarray},
  {"get", getarray},
  {"size", getsize},
  {NULL, NULL}
};

int luaopen_array (lua_State *L) {
  luaL_register(L, "array", arraylib);
  return 1;
}
```

Again, we use luaL_register, from the auxiliary library. It creates a table
with the given name ("array", in our example) and fills it with the pairs name–
function specified by the array arraylib.

After opening the library, we are ready to use our new type in Lua:

```
a = array.new(1000)
print(a)                  --> userdata: 0x8064d48
print(array.size(a))    --> 1000
for i=1,1000 do
  array.set(a, i, i%5 == 0)
end
print(array.get(a, 10))  --> true
```

28.2 Metatables

Our current implementation has a major security hole. Suppose the user writes
something like array.set(io.stdin,1,false). The value in io.stdin is a userdatum with a pointer to a stream (FILE*). Because it is a userdatum, array.set
will gladly accept it as a valid argument; the probable result will be a memory
corruption (with luck you can get an index-out-of-range error instead). Such behavior is unacceptable for any Lua library. No matter how you use a C library,
it should not corrupt C data or produce a core dump from Lua.

The usual method to distinguish one type of userdata from other userdata is
to create a unique metatable for that type. Every time we create a userdata, we
mark it with the corresponding metatable; and every time we get a userdata, we
check whether it has the right metatable. Because Lua code cannot change the
metatable of a userdatum, it cannot fake our code.

We also need a place to store this new metatable, so that we can access it to
create new userdata and to check whether a given userdatum has the correct
type. As we saw earlier, there are three options for storing the metatable: in the
registry, in the environment, or as an upvalue for the functions in the library. It
is customary, in Lua, to register any new C type into the registry, using a *type
name* as the index and the metatable as the value. As with any other registry

index, we must choose a type name with care, to avoid clashes. In our example, we will use the name "LuaBook.array" for its new type.

As usual, the auxiliary library offers some functions to help us here. The new auxiliary functions we will use are these:

```
int   luaL_newmetatable (lua_State *L, const char *tname);
void  luaL_getmetatable (lua_State *L, const char *tname);
void *luaL_checkudata   (lua_State *L, int index,
                                       const char *tname);
```

The `luaL_newmetatable` function creates a new table (to be used as a metatable), leaves the new table in the top of the stack, and associates the table to the given name in the registry. The `luaL_getmetatable` function retrieves the metatable associated with `tname` from the registry. Finally, `luaL_checkudata` checks whether the object at the given stack position is a userdatum with a metatable that matches the given name. It raises an error if the object does not have the correct metatable or if it is not a userdata; otherwise, it returns the userdata address.

Now we can start our implementation. The first step it to change the function that opens the library. The new version must create the metatable for arrays:

```
int luaopen_array (lua_State *L) {
  luaL_newmetatable(L, "LuaBook.array");
  luaL_register(L, "array", arraylib);
  return 1;
}
```

The next step is to change `newarray` so that it sets this metatable in all arrays that it creates:

```
static int newarray (lua_State *L) {

  <as before>

  luaL_getmetatable(L, "LuaBook.array");
  lua_setmetatable(L, -2);

  return 1;  /* new userdatum is already on the stack */
}
```

The `lua_setmetatable` function pops a table from the stack and sets it as the metatable of the object at the given index. In our case, this object is the new userdatum.

Finally, `setarray`, `getarray`, and `getsize` have to check whether they got a valid array as their first argument. To simplify their tasks we define the following macro:

```
#define checkarray(L) \
        (NumArray *)luaL_checkudata(L, 1, "LuaBook.array")
```

Using this macro, the new definition for `getsize` is straightforward:

```
static int getsize (lua_State *L) {
  NumArray *a = checkarray(L);
  lua_pushinteger(L, a->size);
  return 1;
}
```

Because setarray and getarray also share code to check the index as their second argument, we factor out their common parts in the following function:

```
static unsigned int *getindex (lua_State *L,
                                 unsigned int *mask) {
  NumArray *a = checkarray(L);
  int index = luaL_checkint(L, 2) - 1;

  luaL_argcheck(L, 0 <= index && index < a->size, 2,
                   "index out of range");

  /* return element address */
  *mask = I_BIT(index);
  return &a->values[I_WORD(index)];
}
```

After the definition of getelem, setarray and getarray are straightforward:

```
static int setarray (lua_State *L) {
  unsigned int mask;
  unsigned int *entry = getindex(L, &mask);
  luaL_checkany(L, 3);
  if (lua_toboolean(L, 3))
    *entry |= mask;
  else
    *entry &= ~mask;

  return 0;
}

static int getarray (lua_State *L) {
  unsigned int mask;
  unsigned int *entry = getindex(L, &mask);
  lua_pushboolean(L, *entry & mask);
  return 1;
}
```

Now, if you try something like array.get(io.stdin, 10), you will get a proper error message:

```
error: bad argument #1 to 'getarray' ('array' expected)
```

28.3   Object-Oriented Access

Our next step is to transform our new type into an object, so that we can operate on its instances using the usual object-oriented syntax, like this:

```
a = array.new(1000)
print(a:size())     --> 1000
a:set(10, true)
print(a:get(10))    --> true
```

Remember that a:size() is equivalent to a.size(a). Therefore, we have to arrange for the expression a.size to return our getsize function. The key mechanism here is the __index metamethod. For tables, this metamethod is called whenever Lua cannot find a value for a given key. For userdata, it is called in every access, because userdata have no keys at all.

Assume that we run the following code:

```
local metaarray = getmetatable(array.new(1))
metaarray.__index = metaarray
metaarray.set = array.set
metaarray.get = array.get
metaarray.size = array.size
```

In the first line, we create an array only to get its metatable, which we assign to metaarray. (We cannot set the metatable of a userdata from Lua, but we can get its metatable without restrictions.) Then we set metaarray.__index to metaarray. When we evaluate a.size, Lua cannot find the key "size" in object a, because the object is a userdatum. Therefore, Lua tries to get this value from the field __index of the metatable of a, which happens to be metaarray itself. But metaarray.size is array.size, so a.size(a) results in array.size(a), as we wanted.

Of course, we can write the same thing in C. We can do even better: now that arrays are objects, with their own operations, we do not need to have these operations in the table array anymore. The only function that our library still has to export is new, to create new arrays. All other operations come only as methods. The C code can register them directly as such.

The operations getsize, getarray, and setarray do not change from our previous approach. What will change is how we register them. That is, we have to change the function that opens the library. First, we need two separate function lists, one for regular functions and one for methods:

```
static const struct luaL_Reg arraylib_f [] = {
  {"new", newarray},
  {NULL, NULL}
};
```

```
static const struct luaL_Reg arraylib_m [] = {
  {"set", setarray},
  {"get", getarray},
  {"size", getsize},
  {NULL, NULL}
};
```

The new version of the open function `luaopen_array` has to create the metatable, assign it to its own `__index` field, register all methods there, and create and fill the array table:

```
int luaopen_array (lua_State *L) {
  luaL_newmetatable(L, "LuaBook.array");

  /* metatable.__index = metatable */
  lua_pushvalue(L, -1);   /* duplicates the metatable */
  lua_setfield(L, -2, "__index");

  luaL_register(L, NULL, arraylib_m);

  luaL_register(L, "array", arraylib_f);
  return 1;
}
```

Here we use another feature from `luaL_register`. In the first call, when we pass NULL as the library name, `luaL_register` does not create any table to pack the functions; instead, it assumes that the package table is at the top of the stack. In this example, the package table is the metatable itself, which is where `luaL_register` will put the methods. The next call to `luaL_register` works regularly: it creates a new table with the given name (`array`) and registers the given functions there (only `new`, in this case).

As a final touch, we will add a `__tostring` method to our new type, so that `print(a)` prints `array` plus the size of the array inside parentheses; something like `array(1000)`. The function itself is here:

```
int array2string (lua_State *L) {
  NumArray *a = checkarray(L);
  lua_pushfstring(L, "array(%d)", a->size);
  return 1;
}
```

The `lua_pushfstring` call formats the string and leaves it on the stack top. We also have to add `array2string` to the list `arraylib_m`, to include it in the metatable of array objects:

```
static const struct luaL_Reg arraylib_m [] = {
  {"__tostring", array2string},
  <other methods>
};
```

28.4 Array Access

An alternative to the object-oriented notation is to use a regular array notation to access our arrays. Instead of writing a:get(i), we could simply write a[i]. For our example, this is easy to do, because our functions setarray and getarray already receive their arguments in the order that they are given to the corresponding metamethods. A quick solution is to define these metamethods right into our Lua code:

```
local metaarray = getmetatable(array.new(1))
metaarray.__index = array.get
metaarray.__newindex = array.set
metaarray.__len = array.size
```

(We must run this code on the original implementation for arrays, without the modifications for object-oriented access.) That is all we need to use the standard syntax:

```
a = array.new(1000)
a[10] = true          -- setarray
print(a[10])          -- getarray    --> true
print(#a)             -- getsize     --> 1000
```

If we prefer, we can register these metamethods in our C code. For this, we change again our initialization function:

```
static const struct luaL_Reg arraylib_f [] = {
  {"new", newarray},
  {NULL, NULL}
};

static const struct luaL_Reg arraylib_m [] = {
  {"__newindex", setarray},
  {"__index", getarray},
  {"__len", getsize},
  {"__tostring", array2string},
  {NULL, NULL}
};

int luaopen_array (lua_State *L) {
  luaL_newmetatable(L, "LuaBook.array");
  luaL_register(L, NULL, arraylib_m);
  luaL_register(L, "array", arraylib_f);
  return 1;
}
```

In this new version, we have only one public function, new. All other functions are available only as metamethods for specific operations.

28.5   Light Userdata

The kind of userdata that we have been using until now is called *full userdata*.
Lua offers another kind of userdata, called *light userdata*.

A light userdatum is a value that represents a C pointer (that is, a void*
value). Because it is a value, we do not create them (in the same way that
we do not create numbers). To put a light userdatum into the stack, we call
lua_pushlightuserdata:

```
void lua_pushlightuserdata (lua_State *L, void *p);
```

Despite their common name, light userdata and full userdata are quite different things. Light userdata are not buffers, but single pointers. They have
no metatables. Like numbers, light userdata do not need to be managed by the
garbage collector, and are not.

Sometimes we use light userdata as a cheap alternative to full userdata. This
is not a typical use, however. First, with light userdata you have to manage
memory by yourself, because they are not subject to garbage collection. Second,
despite the name, full userdata are inexpensive, too. They add little overhead
compared to a malloc for the given memory size.

The real use of light userdata comes from equality. As a full userdata is an
object, it is only equal to itself. A light userdata, on the other hand, represents
a C pointer value. As such, it is equal to any userdata that represents the same
pointer. Therefore, we can use light userdata to find C objects inside Lua.

As a typical scenario, suppose we are implementing a binding between Lua
and a Window system. In this binding, we use full userdata to represent
windows. Each userdatum may contain the whole window structure or only
a pointer to a window created by the system. When there is an event inside a
window (e.g., a mouse click), the system calls a specific callback, identifying the
window by its address. To pass the callback to Lua, we must find the userdata
that represents the given window. To find this userdata, we can keep a table
where the indices are light userdata with the window addresses and the values
are the full userdata that represent the windows in Lua. Once we have a window
address, we push it into the API stack as a light userdata and use this userdata
as an index into that table. (Probably that table should have weak values.
Otherwise, those full userdata would never be collected.)

29

Managing Resources

In our implementation of boolean arrays in the previous chapter, we did not need to worry about managing resources. Those arrays need only memory. Each userdatum representing an array has its own memory, which is managed by Lua. When an array becomes garbage (that is, inaccessible by the program), Lua eventually collects it and frees its memory.

Life is not always that easy. Sometimes, an object needs other resources besides raw memory, such as file descriptors, window handles, and the like. (Often these resources are just memory too, but managed by some other part of the system.) In such cases, when the object becomes garbage and is collected, somehow these other resources must be released too. Several object-oriented languages provide a specific mechanism (called *finalizer*) for this need. Lua provides finalizers in the form of the __gc metamethod. This metamethod works only for userdata values. When a userdatum is about to be collected and its metatable has a __gc field, Lua calls the value of this field (which should be a function), passing as an argument the userdatum itself. This function can then release any resource associated with this userdatum.

To illustrate the use of this metamethod and of the API as a whole, in this chapter we will develop two bindings from Lua to external facilities. The first example is another implementation for a function to traverse a directory. The second (and more substantial) example is a binding to *Expat*, an open source XML parser.

29.1   A Directory Iterator

Previously, we implemented a dir function that returned a table with all files from a given directory. Our new implementation will return an iterator that returns a new entry each time it is called. With this new implementation, we will be able to traverse a directory with a loop like this:

```
for fname in dir(".") do  print(fname)  end
```

To iterate over a directory, in C, we need a DIR structure. Instances of DIR are created by opendir and must be explicitly released with a call to closedir. Our previous implementation of dir kept its DIR instance as a local variable and closed this instance after retrieving the last file name. Our new implementation cannot keep this DIR instance in a local variable, because it must query this value over several calls. Moreover, it cannot close the directory only after retrieving the last name; if the program breaks the loop, the iterator will never retrieve this last name. Therefore, to make sure that the DIR instance is always released, we store its address in a userdatum and use the __gc metamethod of this userdatum to release the directory structure.

Despite its central role in our implementation, this userdatum representing a directory does not need to be visible from Lua. The dir function returns an iterator function; this is what Lua sees. The directory may be an upvalue of the iterator function. As such, the iterator function has direct access to this structure, but Lua code has not (and does not need to).

In all, we need three C functions. First, we need the dir function, a factory that Lua calls to create iterators; it must open a DIR structure and put it as an upvalue of the iterator function. Second, we need the iterator function. Third, we need the __gc metamethod that closes a DIR structure. As usual, we also need an extra function to make initial arrangements, such as to create a metatable for directories and to initialize this metatable.

Let us start our code with the dir function, shown in Listing 29.1. A subtle point in this function is that it must create the userdatum before opening the directory. If it first opens the directory, and then the call to lua_newuserdata raises an error, it loses the DIR structure. With the correct order, the DIR structure, once created, is immediately associated with the userdatum; whatever happens after that, the __gc metamethod will eventually release the structure.

The next function is dir_iter (in Listing 29.2), the iterator itself. Its code is straightforward. It gets the DIR-structure address from its upvalue and calls readdir to read the next entry.

Function dir_gc (also in Listing 29.2) is the __gc metamethod. This metamethod closes a directory, but it must take one precaution: because we create the userdatum before opening the directory, this userdatum will be collected whatever the result of opendir. If opendir fails, there will be nothing to close.

The last function in Listing 29.2, luaopen_dir, is the function that opens this one-function library.

This whole example has an interesting subtlety. At first, it may seem that dir_gc should check whether its argument is a directory. Otherwise, a malicious user could call it with another kind of userdata (a file, for instance), with disastrous consequences. However, there is no way for a Lua program to access this function: it is stored only in the metatable of directories, and Lua programs never access these directories.

Listing 29.1. The `dir` factory function:

```c
#include <dirent.h>
#include <errno.h>

/* forward declaration for the iterator function */
static int dir_iter (lua_State *L);

static int l_dir (lua_State *L) {
  const char *path = luaL_checkstring(L, 1);

  /* create a userdatum to store a DIR address */
  DIR **d = (DIR **)lua_newuserdata(L, sizeof(DIR *));

  /* set its metatable */
  luaL_getmetatable(L, "LuaBook.dir");
  lua_setmetatable(L, -2);

  /* try to open the given directory */
  *d = opendir(path);
  if (*d == NULL)  /* error opening the directory? */
    luaL_error(L, "cannot open %s: %s", path, strerror(errno));

  /* creates and returns the iterator function;
     its sole upvalue, the directory userdatum,
     is already on the stack top */
  lua_pushcclosure(L, dir_iter, 1);
  return 1;
}
```

29.2 An XML Parser

Now we will look at a simplified implementation of lxp, a binding between Lua and Expat version 1.2. Expat is an open source XML 1.0 parser written in C. It implements SAX, the *Simple API for XML*. SAX is an event-based API. This means that a SAX parser reads an XML document and, as it goes, reports to the application what it finds, through callbacks. For instance, if we instruct Expat to parse a string like "<tag cap="5">hi</tag>", it will generate three events: a *start-element* event, when it reads the substring "<tag cap="5">"; a *text* event (also called a *character data* event), when it reads "hi"; and an *end-element* event, when it reads "</tag>". Each of these events calls an appropriate *callback handler* in the application.

Here we will not cover the entire Expat library. We will concentrate only on those parts that illustrate new techniques for interacting with Lua. Although Expat handles more than a dozen different events, we will consider only the three events that we saw in the previous example (start elements, end elements,

Listing 29.2. Other functions for the `dir` library:

```c
static int dir_iter (lua_State *L) {
  DIR *d = *(DIR **)lua_touserdata(L, lua_upvalueindex(1));
  struct dirent *entry;
  if ((entry = readdir(d)) != NULL) {
    lua_pushstring(L, entry->d_name);
    return 1;
  }
  else return 0;  /* no more values to return */
}

static int dir_gc (lua_State *L) {
  DIR *d = *(DIR **)lua_touserdata(L, 1);
  if (d) closedir(d);
  return 0;
}

int luaopen_dir (lua_State *L) {
  luaL_newmetatable(L, "LuaBook.dir");

  /* set its __gc field */
  lua_pushstring(L, "__gc");
  lua_pushcfunction(L, dir_gc);
  lua_settable(L, -3);

  /* register the 'dir' function */
  lua_pushcfunction(L, l_dir);
  lua_setglobal(L, "dir");

  return 0;
}
```

and text).[20]

The part of the Expat API that we need for this example is small. First, we need functions to create and destroy an Expat parser:

```c
XML_Parser XML_ParserCreate (const char *encoding);
void XML_ParserFree (XML_Parser p);
```

The argument `encoding` is optional; we will use NULL in our binding.

After we have a parser, we must register its callback handlers:

```c
XML_SetElementHandler(XML_Parser p,
                      XML_StartElementHandler start,
                      XML_EndElementHandler end);
```

---

[20]The package LuaExpat, from the Kepler project, offers a quite complete interface to Expat.

```
XML_SetCharacterDataHandler(XML_Parser p,
                            XML_CharacterDataHandler hndl);
```

The first function registers handlers for start and end elements. The second function registers handlers for text (*character data*, in XML parlance).

All callback handlers receive some user data as their first parameter. The start-element handler receives also the tag name and its attributes:

```
typedef void (*XML_StartElementHandler)(void *uData,
                                        const char *name,
                                        const char **atts);
```

The attributes come as a NULL-terminated array of strings, where each pair of consecutive strings holds an attribute name and its value. The end-element handler has only one extra parameter, the tag name:

```
typedef void (*XML_EndElementHandler)(void *uData,
                                      const char *name);
```

Finally, a text handler receives only the text as an extra parameter. This text string is not null-terminated; instead, it has an explicit length:

```
typedef void (*XML_CharacterDataHandler)(void *uData,
                                         const char *s,
                                         int len);
```

To feed text to Expat, we use the following function:

```
int XML_Parse (XML_Parser p, const char *s, int len, int isLast);
```

Expat receives the document to be parsed in pieces, through successive calls to XML_Parse. The last argument to XML_Parse, isLast, informs Expat whether that piece is the last one of a document. Notice that each piece of text does not need to be zero terminated; instead, we supply an explicit length. The XML_Parse function returns zero if it detects a parse error. (Expat also provides functions to retrieve error information, but we will ignore them here, for the sake of simplicity.)

The last function we need from Expat allows us to set the user data that will be passed to the handlers:

```
void XML_SetUserData (XML_Parser p, void *uData);
```

Now let us have a look at how we can use this library in Lua. A first approach is a direct approach: simply export all those functions to Lua. A better approach is to adapt the functionality to Lua. For instance, because Lua is untyped, we do not need different functions to set each kind of callback. Better yet, we can avoid the callback registering functions altogether. Instead, when we create a parser, we give a callback table that contains all callback handlers, each with an appropriate key. For instance, if we want to print a layout of a document, we could use the following callback table:

```
local count = 0
```

```
callbacks = {
  StartElement = function (parser, tagname)
    io.write("+ ", string.rep("  ", count), tagname, "\n")
    count = count + 1
  end,

  EndElement = function (parser, tagname)
    count = count - 1
    io.write("- ", string.rep("  ", count), tagname, "\n")
  end,
}
```

Fed with the input "<to> <yes/> </to>", these handlers would print this:

```
+ to
+   yes
-   yes
- to
```

With this API, we do not need functions to manipulate callbacks. We manipulate them directly in the callback table. Thus, the whole API needs only three functions: one to create parsers, one to parse a piece of text, and one to close a parser. Actually, we will implement the last two functions as methods of parser objects. A typical use of the API could be like this:

```
p = lxp.new(callbacks)      -- create new parser

for l in io.lines() do      -- iterate over input lines
  assert(p:parse(l))              -- parse the line
  assert(p:parse("\n"))           -- add a newline
end

assert(p:parse())           -- finish document
p:close()
```

Now let us turn our attention to the implementation. The first decision is how to represent a parser in Lua. It is quite natural to use a userdatum, but what do we need to put inside it? At least, we must keep the actual Expat parser and the callback table. We cannot store a Lua table inside a userdatum (or inside any C structure). In Lua 5.0, we should use a reference to the table. In Lua 5.1, we can set the table as the userdata's environment. We must store also a Lua state into a parser object, because these parser objects is all that an Expat callback receives, and the callbacks need to call Lua. Therefore, the definition for a parser object is as follows:

```
#include <stdlib.h>
#include "xmlparse.h"
#include "lua.h"
#include "lauxlib.h"
```

```
typedef struct lxp_userdata {
  lua_State *L;
  XML_Parser *parser;              /* associated expat parser */
} lxp_userdata;
```

The next step is the function that creates parser objects, lxp_make_parser. Listing 29.3 shows its code. This function has four main steps:

- Its first step follows a common pattern: it first creates a userdatum; then it pre-initializes the userdatum with consistent values; and finally sets its metatable. The reason for the pre-initialization is subtle: if there is any error during the initialization, we must make sure that the finalizer (the __gc metamethod) will find the userdata in a consistent state.

- In step 2, the function creates an Expat parser, stores it in the userdatum, and checks for errors.

- Step 3 ensures that the first argument to the function is actually a table (the callback table), and sets it as the environment for the new userdatum.

- The last step initializes the Expat parser. It sets the userdatum as the object to be passed to callback functions and it sets the callback functions. Notice that these callback functions are the same for all parsers; after all, it is impossible to dynamically create new functions in C. Instead, those fixed C functions will use the callback table to decide which Lua functions they should call each time.

The next step is the parse method lxp_parse (Listing 29.4), which parses a piece of XML data. It gets two arguments: the parser object (the *self* of the method) and an optional piece of XML data. When called without any data, it informs Expat that the document has no more parts.

When lxp_parse calls XML_Parse, the latter function will call the handlers for each relevant element that it finds in the given piece of document. Therefore, lxp_parse first prepares an environment for these handlers. There is one more detail in the call to XML_Parse: remember that the last argument to this function tells Expat whether the given piece of text is the last one. When we call parse without an argument s will be NULL, so this last argument will be true.

Now let us turn our attention to the callback functions f_StartElement, f_EndElement, and f_CharData. All these three functions have a similar structure: each checks whether the callback table defines a Lua handler for its specific event and, if so, prepares the arguments and then calls this Lua handler.

Let us first see the f_CharData handler, in Listing 29.5. Its code is quite simple. This handler (and the others too) receives a lxp_userdata structure as its first argument, due to our call to XML_SetUserData when we create the parser. After retrieving the Lua state, the handler can access the environment set by lxp_parse: the callback table at stack index 3 and the parser itself at stack index 1. Then it calls its corresponding handler in Lua (when present), with two arguments: the parser and the character data (a string).

Listing 29.3. Function to create parser objects:

```
/* forward declarations for callback functions */
static void f_StartElement (void *ud,
                            const char *name,
                            const char **atts);
static void f_CharData (void *ud, const char *s, int len);
static void f_EndElement (void *ud, const char *name);

static int lxp_make_parser (lua_State *L) {
  XML_Parser p;
  lxp_userdata *xpu;

  /* (1) create a parser object */
  xpu = (lxp_userdata *)lua_newuserdata(L,
                                  sizeof(lxp_userdata));

  /* pre-initialize it, in case of error */
  xpu->parser = NULL;

  /* set its metatable */
  luaL_getmetatable(L, "Expat");
  lua_setmetatable(L, -2);

  /* (2) create the Expat parser */
  p = xpu->parser = XML_ParserCreate(NULL);
  if (!p)
    luaL_error(L, "XML_ParserCreate failed");

  /* (3) check and store the callback table */
  luaL_checktype(L, 1, LUA_TTABLE);
  lua_pushvalue(L, 1);  /* put table on the stack top */
  lua_setfenv(L, -2);   /* set it as environment for udata */

  /* (4) configure Expat parser */
  XML_SetUserData(p, xpu);
  XML_SetElementHandler(p, f_StartElement, f_EndElement);
  XML_SetCharacterDataHandler(p, f_CharData);
  return 1;
}
```

Listing 29.4. Function to parse an XML fragment:

```
static int lxp_parse (lua_State *L) {
  int status;
  size_t len;
  const char *s;
  lxp_userdata *xpu;

  /* get and check first argument (should be a parser) */
  xpu = (lxp_userdata *)luaL_checkudata(L, 1, "Expat");

  /* get second argument (a string) */
  s = luaL_optlstring(L, 2, NULL, &len);

  /* prepare environment for handlers: */
  /* put callback table at stack index 3 */
  lua_settop(L, 2);
  lua_getfenv(L, 1);
  xpu->L = L;  /* set Lua state */

  /* call Expat to parse string */
  status = XML_Parse(xpu->parser, s, (int)len, s == NULL);

  /* return error code */
  lua_pushboolean(L, status);
  return 1;
}
```

Listing 29.5. Handler for character data:

```
static void f_CharData (void *ud, const char *s, int len) {
  lxp_userdata *xpu = (lxp_userdata *)ud;
  lua_State *L = xpu->L;

  /* get handler */
  lua_getfield(L, 3, "CharacterData");
  if (lua_isnil(L, -1)) {  /* no handler? */
    lua_pop(L, 1);
    return;
  }

  lua_pushvalue(L, 1);  /* push the parser ('self') */
  lua_pushlstring(L, s, len);  /* push Char data */
  lua_call(L, 2, 0);  /* call the handler */
}
```

Listing 29.6. Handler for end elements:

```
static void f_EndElement (void *ud, const char *name) {
  lxp_userdata *xpu = (lxp_userdata *)ud;
  lua_State *L = xpu->L;

  lua_getfield(L, 3, "EndElement");
  if (lua_isnil(L, -1)) {   /* no handler? */
    lua_pop(L, 1);
    return;
  }

  lua_pushvalue(L, 1);   /* push the parser ('self') */
  lua_pushstring(L, name);   /* push tag name */
  lua_call(L, 2, 0);   /* call the handler */
}
```

The f_EndElement handler is quite similar to f_CharData; see Listing 29.6. It also calls its corresponding Lua handler with two arguments—the parser and the tag name (again a string, but now null-terminated).

Listing 29.7 shows the last handler, f_StartElement. It calls Lua with three arguments: the parser, the tag name, and a list of attributes. This handler is a little more complex than the others, because it needs to translate the tag's list of attributes into Lua. It uses a quite natural translation, building a table that associates attribute names to their values. For instance, a start tag like

```
<to method="post" priority="high">
```

generates the following table of attributes:

```
{method = "post", priority = "high"}
```

The last method for parsers is close, in Listing 29.8. When we close a parser, we have to free its resources, namely the Expat structure. Remember that, due to occasional errors during its creation, a parser may not have this resource. Notice how we keep the parser in a consistent state as we close it, so there is no problem if we try to close it again or when the garbage collector finalizes it. Actually, we will use exactly this function as the finalizer. This ensures that every parser eventually frees its resources, even if the programmer does not close it.

Listing 29.9 is the final step: it opens the library, putting all previous parts together. We use here the same scheme that we used in the object-oriented boolean-array example from Section 28.3: we create a metatable, put all methods inside it, and make its __index field point to itself. For that, we need a list with the parser methods (lxp_meths). We also need a list with the functions of this library (lxp_funcs). As is common with object-oriented libraries, this

Listing 29.7. Handler for start elements:

```
static void f_StartElement (void *ud,
                            const char *name,
                            const char **atts) {
  lxp_userdata *xpu = (lxp_userdata *)ud;
  lua_State *L = xpu->L;

  lua_getfield(L, 3, "StartElement");
  if (lua_isnil(L, -1)) {  /* no handler? */
    lua_pop(L, 1);
    return;
  }

  lua_pushvalue(L, 1);  /* push the parser ('self') */
  lua_pushstring(L, name);  /* push tag name */

  /* create and fill the attribute table */
  lua_newtable(L);
  for (; *atts; atts += 2) {
    lua_pushstring(L, *(atts + 1));
    lua_setfield(L, -2, *atts);  /* table[*atts] = *(atts+1) */
  }

  lua_call(L, 3, 0);  /* call the handler */
}
```

Listing 29.8. Method to close a parser:

```
static int lxp_close (lua_State *L) {
  lxp_userdata *xpu =
                (lxp_userdata *)luaL_checkudata(L, 1, "Expat");
  /* free Expat parser (if there is one) */
  if (xpu->parser)
    XML_ParserFree(xpu->parser);
  xpu->parser = NULL;
  return 0;
}
```

Listing 29.9. Initialization code for the `lxp` library:

```
static const struct luaL_Reg lxp_meths[] = {
  {"parse", lxp_parse},
  {"close", lxp_close},
  {"__gc", lxp_close},
  {NULL, NULL}
};

static const struct luaL_Reg lxp_funcs[] = {
  {"new", lxp_make_parser},
  {NULL, NULL}
};

int luaopen_lxp (lua_State *L) {
  /* create metatable */
  luaL_newmetatable(L, "Expat");

  /* metatable.__index = metatable */
  lua_pushvalue(L, -1);
  lua_setfield(L, -2, "__index");

  /* register methods */
  luaL_register(L, NULL, lxp_meths);

  /* register functions (only lxp.new) */
  luaL_register(L, "lxp", lxp_funcs);
  return 1;
}
```

list has a single function, which creates new parsers. Finally, the open function `luaopen_lxp` must create the metatable, make it point to itself (through `__index`), and register methods and functions.

30

Threads and States

Lua does not support true multithreading, that is, preemptive threads sharing memory. There are two reasons for this lack of support: the first reason is that ANSI C does not offer it, and so there is no portable way to implement this mechanism in Lua. The second and stronger reason is that we do not think multithreading is a good idea for Lua.

Multithreading was developed for low-level programming. Synchronization mechanisms like semaphores and monitors were proposed in the context of operating systems (and seasoned programmers), not application programs. It is very hard to find and correct bugs related to multithreading, and some of these bugs can lead to security breaches. Moreover, multithreading may lead to performance penalties related to the need of synchronization in some critical parts of a program, such as the memory allocator.

The problems with multithreading arise from the combination of preemptive threads and shared memory, so we can avoid them either using non-preemptive threads or not sharing memory. Lua offers support for both. *Lua threads* (a.k.a. coroutines) are collaborative, and therefore avoid the problems created by unpredictable thread switching. *Lua states* share no memory, and therefore form a good base for concurrency in Lua. We will cover both options in this chapter.

30.1   Multiple Threads

A *thread* is the essence of a coroutine in Lua. We can think of a coroutine as a thread plus a nice interface, or we can think of a thread as a coroutine with a lower-level API.

From the C API perspective, you may find it useful to think of a thread as a stack — which is what a thread actually is, from an implementation point of view. Each stack keeps information about the pending calls of a thread and the parameters and local variables of each call. In other words, a stack has all the information that a thread needs to continue running. So, multiple threads mean multiple independent stacks.

When we call most functions from the Lua-C API, that function operates on a specific stack. For instance, `lua_pushnumber` must push the number on a specific stack; `lua_pcall` needs a call stack. How does Lua know which stack to use? What do we do to push a number on a different stack? The secret is that the type `lua_State`, the first argument to these functions, represents not only a Lua state, but also a thread within that state.

Whenever you create a Lua state, Lua automatically creates a new thread within this state, which is called the *main thread*. The main thread is never collected. It is released together with the state, when you close the state with `lua_close`.

You can create other threads in a state calling `lua_newthread`:

```
lua_State *lua_newthread (lua_State *L);
```

This function returns a `lua_State` pointer representing the new thread, and also pushes the new thread on the stack, as a value of type "thread". For instance, after the statement

```
L1 = lua_newthread(L);
```

we have two threads, L1 and L, both referring internally to the same Lua state. Each thread has its own stack. The new thread L1 starts with an empty stack; the old thread L has the new thread on the top of its stack:

```
printf("%d\n", lua_gettop(L1));          --> 0
printf("%s\n", luaL_typename(L, -1));    --> thread
```

Except for the main thread, threads are subject to garbage collection, like any other Lua object. When you create a new thread, the value pushed on the stack ensures that the thread is not garbage. You should never use a thread that is not properly anchored in the state. (The main thread is internally anchored, so you do not have to worry about it.) Any call to the Lua API may collect a non-anchored thread, even a call using this thread. For instance, consider the following fragment:

```
lua_State *L1 = lua_newthread (L);
lua_pop(L, 1);          /* L1 now is garbage for Lua */
lua_pushstring(L1, "hello");
```

The call to `lua_pushstring` may trigger the garbage collector and collect L1 (crashing the application), despite the fact that L1 is in use. To avoid this, always keep a reference to the threads you are using (e.g., in the stack of an anchored thread or in the registry).

Once we have a new thread, we can use it like the main thread. We can push on and pop elements from its stack, we can use it to call functions, and the like. For instance, the following code does the call f(5) in the new thread and then moves the result to the old thread:

```
lua_getglobal(L1, "f");    /* assume a global function 'f' */
lua_pushinteger(L1, 5);
lua_call(L1, 1, 1);
lua_xmove(L1, L, 1);
```

The lua_xmove function moves Lua values between two stacks. A call like lua_xmove(F, T, n) pops n elements from the stack F and pushes them on T.

For these uses, however, we do not need a new thread; we could just use the main thread as well. The main point of using multiple threads is to implement coroutines, so that we can suspend their execution to be resumed later. For that, we need the lua_resume function:

```
int lua_resume (lua_State *L, int narg);
```

To start running a coroutine, we use lua_resume as we use lua_pcall: we push the function to be called, push its arguments, and call lua_resume passing in narg the number of arguments. The behavior is also much like lua_pcall, with three differences. First, lua_resume does not have a parameter for the number of wanted results; it always returns all results from the called function. Second, it does not have a parameter for an error handler; an error does not unwind the stack, so you can inspect the stack after the error. Third, if the running function yields, lua_resume returns a special code LUA_YIELD and leaves the thread in a state that can be resumed later.

When lua_resume returns LUA_YIELD, the visible part of the thread's stack contains only the values passed to yield. A call to lua_gettop will return the number of yielded values. To move these values to another thread, we can use lua_xmove.

To resume a suspended thread, we call lua_resume again. In such calls, Lua assumes that all values in the stack are to be returned by the call to yield. As a peculiar case, if you do not touch the thread's stack between a return from lua_resume and the next resume, yield will return exactly the values it yielded.

Typically, we start a coroutine with a Lua function as its body. This Lua function may call other Lua functions, and any of these functions may eventually yield, finishing the call to lua_resume. For instance, assume the following definitions:

```
function foo (x)  coroutine.yield(10, x)  end

function foo1 (x)  foo(x + 1); return 3  end
```

Now, we run this C code:

```
lua_State *L1 = lua_newthread(L);
lua_getglobal(L1, "foo1");
lua_pushinteger(L1, 20);
lua_resume(L1, 1);
```

The call to lua_resume will return LUA_YIELD, to signal that the thread yielded. At this point, the L1 stack has the values given to yield:

```
printf("%d\n", lua_gettop(L1));                --> 2
printf("%d\n", lua_tointeger(L1, 1));          --> 10
printf("%d\n", lua_tointeger(L1, 2));          --> 21
```

When we resume the thread again, it continues from where it stopped (the call to yield). From there, foo returns to foo1, which in turn returns to lua_resume:

```
lua_resume(L1, 0);
printf("%d\n", lua_gettop(L1));                --> 1
printf("%d\n", lua_tointeger(L1, 1));          --> 3
```

This second call to lua_resume will return 0, which means a normal return.

A coroutine may also call C functions. So, a natural question when programming in C is this: is it possible to yield from a C function?

Standard Lua cannot yield across C function calls.[21] This restriction implies that a C function cannot suspend itself. The only way for a C function to yield is when returning, so that it actually does not suspend itself, but its caller — which should be a Lua function. To suspend its caller, a C function must call lua_yield in the following way:

```
return lua_yield(L, nres);
```

Here, nres is the number of values at the top of the stack to be returned by the corresponding resume. When the thread resumes again, the caller will receive the values given to resume.

We can circumvent the limitation that C functions cannot yield by calling them inside a loop in Lua. In this way, after the function yields and the thread resumes, the loop calls the function again. As an example, assume we want to code a function that reads some data, yielding while the data is not available. We may write the function in C like this:

```
int prim_read (lua_State *L) {
  if (nothing_to_read())
    return lua_yield(L, 0);
  lua_pushstring(L, read_some_data());
  return 1;
}
```

If the function has some data to read, it reads and returns this data. Otherwise it yields. When the thread resumes, however, it does not return to prim_read, but to the caller.

Now, assume the caller calls prim_read in a loop like this:

---

[21]There are some interesting patches to Lua that allow this. However, they must use non-portable code, including small parts in assembly.

```
function read ()
  local line
  repeat
    line = prim_read()
  until line
  return line
end
```

When `prim_read` yields, the thread is suspended. When it resumes, it continues from the return point of `prim_read`, which is the assignment to `line`. The actual value assigned will be the value given to `resume`. Assuming that no value was given, `line` gets **nil** and the loop continues, calling `prim_read` again. The whole process repeats itself, until some data is read or `resume` passes a non-nil value.

30.2   Lua States

Each call to `luaL_newstate` (or to `lua_newstate`, as we will see in Chapter 31) creates a new Lua state. Different Lua states are completely independent of each other. They share no data at all. This means that no matter what happens inside a Lua state, it cannot corrupt another Lua state. It also means that Lua states cannot communicate directly; we have to use some intervening C code. For instance, given two states L1 and L2, the following command pushes in L2 the string at the top of the stack in L1:

```
lua_pushstring(L2, lua_tostring(L1, -1));
```

Because data must pass through C, Lua states can exchange only types that are representable in C, like strings and numbers.

In systems that offer multithreading, an interesting way to use them with Lua is to create an independent Lua state for each thread. This architecture results in threads similar to Unix processes, where we have concurrency without shared memory. In this section we will develop a prototype implementation for multithreading following this approach. I will use POSIX threads (pthreads) for this implementation. It should not be difficult to port the code to other thread systems, as it uses only basic facilities.

The system we are going to develop is very simple. Its main purpose is to show the use of multiple Lua states in a multithreading context. After you have it up and running, you can add more advanced features on top of it. We will call our library `lproc`. It offers only four functions:

`lproc.start(chunk)` starts a new process to run the given chunk (a string). A Lua *process* is implemented as a C *thread* plus its associated Lua state.

`lproc.send(channel, val1, val2, ...)` sends all given values (which should be strings) to the given channel (identified by its name, also a string).

`lproc.receive(channel)` receives the values sent to the given channel.

`lproc.exit()` finishes a process. Only the main process needs this function. If this process ends without calling `lproc.exit`, the whole program terminates, without waiting for the end of the other processes.

Channels are simply strings used to match senders and receivers. A send operation may send any number of string values, which are returned by the matching receive operation. All communication is synchronous: a process sending a message to a channel blocks until there is a process receiving from this channel, while a process receiving from a channel blocks until there is a process sending to it.

Like the system's interface, the implementation is also simple. It uses two circular double-linked lists, one for processes waiting to send a message and another for processes waiting to receive a message. It uses one single mutex to control the access to these lists. Each process has an associated condition variable. When a process wants to send a message to a channel, it traverses the receiving list looking for a process waiting for that channel. If it finds one, it removes the process from the waiting list, moves the message's values from itself to the found process, and signals the other process. Otherwise, it inserts itself into the sending list and waits on its condition variable. To receive a message it does a symmetrical operation.

A main element in the implementation is the structure that represents a process:

```
struct Proc {
  lua_State *L;
  pthread_t thread;
  pthread_cond_t cond;
  const char *channel;
  struct Proc *previous, *next;
} Proc;
```

The first two fields represent the Lua state used by the process and the C thread that runs the process. The other fields are used only when the process has to wait for a matching send/receive. The third field, `cond`, is the condition variable that the thread uses to block itself; the fourth field stores the channel that the process is waiting; and the last two fields, `previous` and `next`, are used to link the process in a waiting list.

The two waiting lists and the associated mutex are declared as follows:

```
static Proc *waitsend = NULL;
static Proc *waitreceive = NULL;

static pthread_mutex_t kernel_access = PTHREAD_MUTEX_INITIALIZER;
```

Each process needs a `Proc` structure, and it needs access to its structure whenever its script calls `send` or `receive`. The only parameter that these functions receive is the process' Lua state; so, each process should store its `Proc` structure inside its Lua state, for instance as a full userdata in the registry. In

Listing 30.1. Function to search for a process waiting for a channel:

```
static Proc *searchmatch (const char *channel, Proc **list) {
  Proc *node = *list;
  if (node == NULL) return NULL;  /* empty list? */
  do {
    if (strcmp(channel, node->channel) == 0) {  /* match? */
      /* remove node from the list */
      if (*list == node)  /* is this node the first element? */
        *list = (node->next == node) ? NULL : node->next;
      node->previous->next = node->next;
      node->next->previous = node->previous;
      return node;
    }
    node = node->next;
  } while (node != *list);
  return NULL;  /* no match */
}
```

our implementation, each state keeps its corresponding Proc structure in the
registry, associated with the key "_SELF". The getself function retrieves the
Proc structure associated with a given state:

```
static Proc *getself (lua_State *L) {
  Proc *p;
  lua_getfield(L, LUA_REGISTRYINDEX, "_SELF");
  p = (Proc *)lua_touserdata(L, -1);
  lua_pop(L, 1);
  return p;
}
```

The next function, movevalues, moves values from a sender process to a
receiver process:

```
static void movevalues (lua_State *send, lua_State *rec) {
  int n = lua_gettop(send);
  int i;
  for (i = 2; i <= n; i++)  /* move values to receiver */
    lua_pushstring(rec, lua_tostring(send, i));
}
```

It moves to the receiver all values in the sender stack but the first, which is the
channel.

Listing 30.1 defines searchmatch, which traverses a waiting list looking for
a process waiting for a given channel. If it finds one, the function removes the
process from the list and returns it; otherwise the function returns NULL.

Listing 30.2. Function to add a process to a waiting list:

```
static void waitonlist (lua_State *L, const char *channel,
                                      Proc **list) {
  Proc *p = getself(L);

  /* link itself at the end of the list */
  if (*list == NULL) {  /* empty list? */
    *list = p;
    p->previous = p->next = p;
  }
  else {
    p->previous = (*list)->previous;
    p->next = *list;
    p->previous->next = p->next->previous = p;
  }

  p->channel = channel;

  do {  /* waits on its condition variable */
    pthread_cond_wait(&p->cond, &kernel_access);
  } while (p->channel);
}
```

The last auxiliary function, defined in Listing 30.2, is called when a process cannot find a match. In this case, the process links itself at the end of the appropriate waiting list and waits until another process matches with it and wakes it up: (The loop around pthread_cond_wait protects from spurious wakeups allowed in POSIX threads.) When a process wakes up another, it sets the other process' field channel to NULL. So, if p->channel is not NULL, it means that nobody matched process p, so it has to keep waiting.

With these auxiliary functions in place, we can write send and receive (Listing 30.3). The send function starts checking for the channel. Then it locks the mutex and searches for a matching receiver. If it finds one, it moves its values to this receiver, marks the receiver as ready, and wakes it up. Otherwise, it puts itself on wait. When it finishes the operation, it unlocks the mutex and returns with no values to Lua. The receive function is similar, but it has to return all received values.

Now let us see how to create new processes. A new process needs a new thread, and a new thread needs a body. We will define this body later; here is its prototype, dictated by POSIX threads:

```
static void *ll_thread (void *arg);
```

To create and run a new process, the system must create a new Lua state, start a new thread, compile the given chunk, call the chunk, and finally free its

Listing 30.3. Functions to send and receive a message:

```
static int ll_send (lua_State *L) {
  Proc *p;
  const char *channel = luaL_checkstring(L, 1);

  pthread_mutex_lock(&kernel_access);

  p = searchmatch(channel, &waitreceive);

  if (p) {  /* found a matching receiver? */
    movevalues(L, p->L);  /* move values to receiver */
    p->channel = NULL;  /* mark receiver as not waiting */
    pthread_cond_signal(&p->cond);  /* wake it up */
  }
  else
    waitonlist(L, channel, &waitsend);

  pthread_mutex_unlock(&kernel_access);
  return 0;
}

static int ll_receive (lua_State *L) {
  Proc *p;
  const char *channel = luaL_checkstring(L, 1);
  lua_settop(L, 1);

  pthread_mutex_lock(&kernel_access);

  p = searchmatch(channel, &waitsend);

  if (p) {  /* found a matching sender? */
    movevalues(p->L, L);  /* get values from sender */
    p->channel = NULL;  /* mark sender as not waiting */
    pthread_cond_signal(&p->cond);  /* wake it up */
  }
  else
    waitonlist(L, channel, &waitreceive);

  pthread_mutex_unlock(&kernel_access);

  /* return all stack values but channel */
  return lua_gettop(L) - 1;
}
```

Listing 30.4. Function to create new processes:

```
static int ll_start (lua_State *L) {
  pthread_t thread;
  const char *chunk = luaL_checkstring(L, 1);
  lua_State *L1 = luaL_newstate();

  if (L1 == NULL)
    luaL_error(L, "unable to create new state");

  if (luaL_loadstring(L1, chunk) != 0)
    luaL_error(L, "error starting thread: %s",
                  lua_tostring(L1, -1));

  if (pthread_create(&thread, NULL, ll_thread, L1) != 0)
    luaL_error(L, "unable to create new thread");

  pthread_detach(thread);
  return 0;
}
```

resources. The original thread does the first three tasks, and the new thread does the rest. (To simplify error handling, the system only starts the new thread after it has successfully compiled the given chunk.)

A new process is created by `ll_start` (Listing 30.4). This function creates a new Lua state L1 and compiles in it the given chunk. In case of error, it signals the error to the original state L. Then it creates a new thread (`pthread_create`) with body `ll_thread`, passing the new state L1 as the argument to the body. The call to `pthread_detach` tells the system that we will not want any final answer from this thread.

The body of each new thread is the `ll_thread` function (Listing 30.5). It receives its corresponding Lua state from `ll_start`, with only the pre-compiled main chunk on the stack. The new thread opens the standard Lua libraries, opens the `lproc` library, and then calls its main chunk. Finally, it destroys its condition variable (which was created by `luaopen_lproc`) and closes its Lua state.

The last function from the module, `exit`, is quite simple:

```
static int ll_exit (lua_State *L) {
  pthread_exit(NULL);
  return 0;
}
```

Remember that only the main process needs to call this function when it finishes, to avoid the immediate end of the whole program.

Listing 30.5. Body for new threads:

```
static void *ll_thread (void *arg) {
  lua_State *L = (lua_State *)arg;
  luaL_openlibs(L);  /* open standard libraries */
  lua_cpcall(L, luaopen_lproc, NULL);  /* open lproc library */
  if (lua_pcall(L, 0, 0, 0) != 0)  /* call main chunk */
    fprintf(stderr, "thread error: %s", lua_tostring(L, -1));
  pthread_cond_destroy(&getself(L)->cond);
  lua_close(L);
  return NULL;
}
```

Our last step is to define the open function for the lproc module. The open function luaopen_lproc (Listing 30.6) must register the module functions, as usual, but it also has to create and initialize the Proc structure of the running process.

As I said earlier, this implementation of processes in Lua is a very simple one. There are endless improvements you can make. Here I will briefly discuss some of them.

A first obvious improvement is to change the linear search for a matching channel. A nice alternative is to use a hash table to find a channel and to use independent waiting lists for each channel.

Another improvement relates to the efficiency of process creation. The creation of new Lua states is a light operation. However, the opening of all standard libraries takes more than ten times the time to open a new state. Most processes probably will not need all standard libraries; actually, most will need only one or two libraries. We can avoid the cost of opening a library by using the pre-registration of libraries we discussed in Section 15.1. With this approach, instead of calling the luaopen_* function for each standard library, we just put this function into the package.preload table. If the process calls require "lib", then—and only then—require will call the associated function to open the library. The following function does this registration:

```
static void registerlib (lua_State *L, const char *name,
                                        lua_CFunction f) {
  lua_getglobal(L, "package");
  lua_getfield(L, -1, "preload");  /* get 'package.preload' */
  lua_pushcfunction(L, f);
  lua_setfield(L, -2, name);  /* package.preload[name] = f */
  lua_pop(L, 2);  /* pop 'package' and 'preload' tables */
}
```

It is always a good idea to open the basic library. You also need the package library; otherwise you will not have require available to open other libraries.

Listing 30.6. Open function for the `lproc` module:

```
static const struct luaL_reg ll_funcs[] = {
  {"start", ll_start},
  {"send", ll_send},
  {"receive", ll_receive},
  {"exit", ll_exit},
  {NULL, NULL}
};

int luaopen_lproc (lua_State *L) {
  /* create own control block */
  Proc *self = (Proc *)lua_newuserdata(L, sizeof(Proc));
  lua_setfield(L, LUA_REGISTRYINDEX, "_SELF");
  self->L = L;
  self->thread = pthread_self();
  self->channel = NULL;
  pthread_cond_init(&self->cond, NULL);
  luaL_register(L, "lproc", ll_funcs);  /* open library */
  return 1;
}
```

All other libraries can be optional. So, instead of calling `luaL_openlibs`, we can call the following `openlibs` function when opening new states:

```
static void openlibs (lua_State *L) {
  lua_cpcall(L, luaopen_base, NULL);    /* open basic library */
  lua_cpcall(L, luaopen_package, NULL); /* open package lib. */
  registerlib(L, "io", luaopen_io);
  registerlib(L, "os", luaopen_os);
  registerlib(L, "table", luaopen_table);
  registerlib(L, "string", luaopen_string);
  registerlib(L, "math", luaopen_math);
  registerlib(L, "debug", luaopen_debug);
}
```

Whenever a process needs one of these libraries, it requires the library explicitly, and `require` will call the corresponding `luaopen_*` function.

Other improvements involve the communication primitives. For instance, it would be useful to provide limits on how long `lproc.send` and `lproc.receive` should wait for a match. As a particular case, a zero limit would make these functions non-blocking. With POSIX threads, we could implement this facility using `pthread_cond_timedwait`.

31

Memory Management

Except for a few arrays that the recursive-descendent parser allocates on the C stack, Lua allocates all its data structures dynamically. All these structures grow when needed, and eventually shrink or disappear.

Lua keeps a tight control over its memory use. When we close a Lua state, Lua explicitly frees all its memory. Moreover, all objects in Lua are subject to garbage collection: not only tables and strings, but also functions, threads, and modules (as they are actually tables). If you load a huge Lua module and later delete all references to it, Lua will eventually recover all memory used by this module.

The way Lua manages memory is convenient for most applications. Some special applications, however, may require adaptations, for instance to run in memory-constrained environments or to reduce garbage-collection pauses to a minimum. Lua allows these adaptations in two levels. In the low level, we can set the allocation function used by Lua. In a higher level, we can set some parameters that control its garbage collector, or we can even get direct control over the collector. In this chapter we will cover these facilities.

31.1 The Allocation Function

The Lua 5.1 core does not assume anything about how to allocate memory. It calls neither `malloc` nor `realloc` to allocate memory. Instead, it does all its memory allocation and deallocation through one single *allocation function*, which the user must provide when she creates a Lua state.

The function `luaL_newstate`, which we have been using to create states, is an auxiliary function that creates a Lua state with a default allocation function. This default allocation function uses the standard `malloc–realloc–free` functions from the C standard library, which are (or should be) good enough for regular applications. However, it is quite easy to get full control over Lua allocation, by creating your state with the primitive lua_newstate:

```
lua_State *lua_newstate (lua_Alloc f, void *ud);
```

This function receives two arguments: an allocation function and a user data. A state created in this way does all its memory allocation and deallocation by calling f. (Even the structure lua_State itself is allocated by f.)

The type lua_Alloc of the allocation function is defined as follows:

```
typedef void * (*lua_Alloc) (void *ud,
                             void *ptr,
                             size_t osize,
                             size_t nsize);
```

The first parameter is always the user data we provided to lua_newstate; the second parameter is the address of the block being reallocated or deallocated; the third parameter is the original block size; and the last parameter is the requested block size.

Lua ensures that, if ptr is not NULL, then it was previously allocated with size osize. Lua identifies NULL with blocks of size zero: if ptr is NULL, then (and only then) osize is zero. Lua does not ensure that osize is different from nsize, even when both are zero; in these cases the allocation function may simply return ptr (which will be NULL when both are zero).

Lua expects that the allocation function also identifies NULL with blocks of size zero. When nsize is zero, the allocation function must free the block pointed to by ptr and return NULL, which corresponds to a block of the required size (zero). When osize is zero (and therefore ptr is NULL), the function must allocate and return a block with the given size; if it cannot allocate the given block, it must return NULL. (If both osize and nsize are zero, both previous descriptions apply: the net result is that the allocation function does nothing and returns NULL.) Finally, when both osize and nsize are not zero, the allocation function should reallocate the block, like realloc, and return the new address (which may or may not be the same as the original). Again, in case of error, it must return NULL. Lua assumes that the allocation function never fails when the new size is smaller than or equal to the old one. (Lua shrinks some structures during garbage collection, and it is unable to recover from errors there.)

The standard allocation function used by luaL_newstate has the following definition (extracted directly from file lauxlib.c):

```
void *l_alloc (void *ud, void *ptr, size_t osize, size_t nsize) {
  if (nsize == 0) {
    free(ptr);
    return NULL;
  }
  else
    return realloc(ptr, nsize);
}
```

It assumes that free(NULL) does nothing and that realloc(NULL, size) is equivalent to malloc(size). The ANSI C standard assures both behaviors.

You can get the memory allocator of a Lua state by calling lua_getallocf:

```
lua_Alloc lua_getallocf (lua_State *L, void **ud);
```

If ud is not NULL, the function sets *ud with the value of the user data for this allocator. You can change the memory allocator of a Lua state by calling lua_setallocf:

```
void lua_setallocf (lua_State *L, lua_Alloc f, void *ud);
```

Keep in mind that any new allocator should be responsible for freeing blocks that were allocated by the previous one. More often than not, the new function is a wrapper around the old one, for instance to trace allocations or to synchronize accesses to the heap.

Internally, Lua does not cache free memory blocks for reuse. It assumes that the allocation function does this. Good allocators do. Lua also does not attempt to minimize fragmentation. Again, studies show that fragmentation is more the result of poor allocation strategies than of program behavior.

It is difficult to beat a well-implemented allocator, but sometimes you may try. For instance, Lua gives you the old size of any block it frees or reallocates; you do not get this size from the conventional free. Therefore, a specialized allocator does not need to keep information about the block size, reducing the memory overhead for each block.

Another situation where you can improve memory allocation is in multi-threading systems. Such systems typically demand synchronization for their memory-allocation functions, as they use a global resource (memory). However, the access to a Lua state must be synchronized too — or, better yet, restricted to one thread, as in our implementation of lproc in Chapter 30. So, if each Lua state allocates memory from a private pool, the allocator can avoid the costs of extra synchronization.

31.2   The Garbage Collector

Since its first version until version 5.0, Lua always used a simple mark-and-sweep garbage collector. This collector is sometimes called a "stop-the-world" collector. This means that, from time to time, Lua stops interpreting the main program to perform a whole garbage-collection cycle. Each cycle comprises four phases: *mark*, *cleaning*, *sweep*, and *finalization*.

Lua starts the mark phase marking as alive its *root set*, the objects that Lua has direct access to: the registry and the main thread. Any object stored in a live object is reachable by the program, and therefore is marked as alive too. The mark phase ends when all reachable objects are marked as alive.

Before starting the sweep phase, Lua performs the cleaning phase, which is related to finalizers and weak tables. First, it traverses all userdata looking for non-marked userdata with a __gc metamethod; those userdata are marked as alive and put in a separate list, to be used in the finalization phase. Second, Lua traverses its weak tables and removes from them all entries wherein either the key or the value is not marked.

The sweep phase traverses all Lua objects. (To allow this traversal, Lua keeps all objects it creates in a linked list.) If an object is not marked as alive, Lua collects it. Otherwise, Lua clears its mark, in preparation for the next cycle.

The last phase, finalization, calls the finalizers of the userdata that were separated in the cleaning phase. This is done after the other phases to simplify error handling. A wrong finalizer may throw an error, but the garbage collector cannot stop during other phases of a collection, at the risk of leaving Lua in an inconsistent state. If it stops during this last phase, however, there is no problem: the next cycle will call the finalizers of the userdata that were left in the list.

With version 5.1 Lua got an *incremental collector*. This new incremental collector performs the same steps as the old one, but it does not need to stop the world while it runs. Instead, it runs interleaved with the interpreter. Every time the interpreter allocates some fixed amount of memory, the collector runs a small step. This means that, while the collector works, the interpreter may change an object's reachability. To ensure the correctness of the collector, some operations in the interpreter have *barriers* that detect dangerous changes and correct the marks of the objects involved.

Atomic operations

To avoid too much complexity, the incremental collector performs some operations atomically; that is, it cannot stop while performing those operations. In other words, Lua still "stops the world" during an atomic operation. If an atomic operation takes too long to complete, it may interfere with the timing of your program. The main atomic operations are table traversal and the cleaning phase.

The atomicity of table traversal means that the collector never stops while traversing a table. This can be a problem only if your program has a really huge table. If you have this kind of problem, you should break the table in smaller parts. (That may be a good idea even if you do not have problems with the garbage collector.) A typical reorganization is to break the table hierarchically, grouping related entries into subtables. Notice that what matters is the number of entries in the table, not the size of each entry.

The atomicity of the cleaning phase implies that the collector collects all userdata to be finalized and clears all weak tables in one step. This can be a problem if your program has huge quantities of userdata or huge numbers of entries in weak tables (either in a few large weak tables or in countless weak tables).

Both problems do not seem to arise in practice, but we need more experience with the new collector to be sure.

Garbage-collector's API

Lua offers an API that allows us to exert some control over the garbage collector. From C we use `lua_gc`:

```
int lua_gc (lua_State *L, int what, int data);
```

From Lua we use the `collectgarbage` function:

```
collectgarbage(what [, data])
```

Both offer the same functionality. The `what` argument (an enumeration value in C, a string in Lua) specifies what to do. The options are:

LUA_GCSTOP ("stop"): stops the collector until another call to `collectgarbage` (or to `lua_gc`) with the option "restart", "collect", or "step".

LUA_GCRESTART ("restart"): restarts the collector.

LUA_GCCOLLECT ("collect"): performs a complete garbage-collection cycle, so that all unreachable objects are collected and finalized. This is the default option for `collectgarbage`.

LUA_GCSTEP ("step"): performs some garbage-collection work. The amount of work is given by the value of `data` in a non-specified way (larger values mean more work).

LUA_GCCOUNT ("count"): returns the number of kilobytes of memory currently in use by Lua. The count includes dead objects that were not collected yet.

LUA_GCCOUNTB (*not available*): returns the fraction of the number of kilobytes of memory currently in use by Lua. In C, the total number of bytes can be computed by the next expression (assuming that it fits in an `int`):

```
lua_gc(L, LUA_GCCOUNT, 0)*1024 + lua_gc(L, LUA_GCCOUNTB, 0)
```

In Lua, the result of `collectgarbage("count")` is a floating-point number, and the total number of bytes can be computed as follows:

```
collectgarbage("count") * 1024
```

So, `collectgarbage` has no equivalent to this option.

LUA_GCSETPAUSE ("setpause"): sets the collector's pause parameter. The value is given by `data` in percentage points: when `data` is 100 the parameter is set to 1 (100%).

LUA_GCSETSTEPMUL ("setstepmul"): sets the collector's `stepmul` parameter. The value is given by `data` also in percentage points.

The two parameters `pause` and `stepmul` allow some control over the collector's character. Both are still experimental, as we still do not have a clear picture of how they affect the overall performance of a program.

The `pause` parameter controls how long the collector waits between finishing a collection and starting a new one. Lua uses an adaptive algorithm to start a collection: given that Lua is using `m` Kbytes when a collection ends, it waits until it is using `m*pause` Kbytes to start a new collection. So, a pause of 100% starts a new collection as soon as the previous one ends. A pause of 200% waits for memory usage to double before starting the collector; this is the default value. You can set a lower pause if you want to trade more CPU time for lower memory usage. Typically, you should keep this value between 100% and 300%.

The `stepmul` parameter controls how much work the collector does for each kilobyte of memory allocated. The higher this value the less incremental is the collector. A huge value like 100 000 000% makes the collector work like a non-incremental collector. The default value is 200%. Values lower than 100% make the collector so slow that it may never finish a collection.

The other options of `lua_gc` give you more explicit control over the collector. Games are typical clients for this kind of control. For instance, if you do not want any garbage-collection work during some periods, you can stop it with a call `collectgarbage("stop")` and then restart it with `collectgarbage("restart")`. In systems where you have periodic idle phases, you can keep the collector stopped and call `collectgarbage("step", n)` during the idle time. To set how much work to do at each idle period, you can either choose experimentally an appropriate value for `n` or calls `collectgarbage` in a loop, with `n` set to zero (meaning small steps), until the period expires.

Index

Printed in the United States
209441BV00003B/22/A